'el lenguaje de los tecnócratas del conocimiento'

Thinking Barcelona

Contemporary Hispanic and Lusophone Cultures

This series aims to provide a forum for new research on modern and contemporary hispanic and lusophone cultures and writing. The volumes published in Contemporary Hispanic and Lusophone Cultures reflect a wide variety of critical practices and theoretical approaches, in harmony with the intellectual, cultural and social developments that have taken place over the past few decades. All manifestations of contemporary hispanic and lusophone culture and expression are considered, including literature, cinema, popular culture, theory. The volumes in the series will participate in the wider debate on key aspects of contemporary culture.

Thinking Barcelona

Ideologies of a Global City

EDGAR ILLAS

LIVERPOOL UNIVERSITY PRESS

First published 2012 by
Liverpool University Press
4 Cambridge Street
Liverpool
L69 7ZU

British Library Cataloguing-in-Publication data
A British Library CIP record is available

ISBN 978-184631-832-0 cased

Typeset in Borges by
Koinonia, Manchester
Printed and bound by
CPI Group (UK) Ltd, Croydon CR0 4YY

For Maria

Contents

Acknowledgements

I wish to thank my advisor Teresa M. Vilarós for her immense enthusiasm and valuable guidance. I am also very grateful to my professors Stephanie Sieburth, Fredric Jameson, Alberto Moreiras, Roberto Dainotto, and Helen Solterer. Without their inspiration and great advice, this book would have never been possible.

Thanks to the departments of Spanish and Portuguese and West European Studies at Indiana University, and the department of Romance Studies, the Center for European Studies, and the Graduate School at Duke University for their generous support.

I am grateful to Oriol Bohigas, Quim Monzó, Xavier Rubert de Ventós, Llàtzer Moix, Joan Roca i Albert and Francesc Muñoz for their availability and illuminating conversations. Thanks to the Centre Documental de la Comunicació, and to Berta Cerezuela at the Centre d'Estudis Olímpics i de l'Esport, Universitat Autònoma de Barcelona.

Many thanks to friends and colleagues Javier Krauel, Elena Delgado, Joan Ramon Resina, Mario Santana, Elisa Martí-López, Patrick Dove, Tabea Linhard, Samuel Steinberg, Pere Gómez, Quim Masoliver, and Talia Weltman; their comments and encouragement have been extremely helpful. Special thanks to Anthony Cond for his fine editorial guidance.

Parts of Chapters One and Three were previously published in *The Colorado Review of Hispanic Studies* and *Transtext(e)s Transcultures. Journal of Global Cultural Studies*; thanks to their editors for permission to reprint.

Finally, I cannot express my gratitude enough to my parents Margarida and Lluís, my sister Neus, my grandmother Elisabet, my cousin Elisabet (thanks for the reports on Monzó!), my aunt Maria Assumpció, and my uncle Jordi. Most of all, my infinite thanks to my beloved wife Maria.

Introduction
The Euphoric Politics of Postmodern Barcelona

Woody Allen's 2008 film *Vicky Cristina Barcelona* depicts Barcelona as a charming and cosmopolitan city. Foreigners find its fusion of European sophistication and Mediterranean lifestyle irresistible. The city is so appealing that it seems to have engendered the series of sexual encounters, romantic scenes, and artistic impulses experienced by the characters. It is true that, given the empty aestheticism and lack of social significance of his recent films, Allen could have set the movie in, say, Bagdad, and still manage to portray a group of affluent individuals only worried about their sexual dissatisfaction and their cultural taste. However, Barcelona seemed to serve especially well as a delightful and nonconflictive setting.

The enchanting powers of Barcelona that attract Scarlett Johansson and Rebecca Hall, together with millions of visitors every year, are the result of a specific historical process. During the 1980s, and in preparation for the 1992 Olympic Games, Barcelona's city hall launched an extensive transformation of the city at all levels. Under the leadership of socialist mayor Pasqual Maragall, the municipal government undertook a process of "city-building" that profoundly altered the social, urbanistic, economic, cultural, and political spheres of the city. The transformation of Barcelona did not consist in a mere renewal of its waterfront, the gentrification of an old neighborhood, or the promotion of its cultural assets, even though these elements were also a central part of it. The transformation consisted rather in the articulation of a municipal political project that aimed to have an effect on each social sphere of the city while implementing a comprehensive urban renovation.

This transformation was motivated by the emergence of a new economy based on tourism, real estate investment, and the culture industry. When in the 1970s and 1980s most Western industrial cities began to see manufacturing relocated in Third World countries, and the globalization of production started to be a reality, Barcelona adjusted to this new situation rather quickly and became specialized in the industries of tourism, real estate and culture. While Barcelona's economy remained quite diversified, these three industries, which grew in close correlation to each other, took on a dominant role in the transformation of the city.

The unusual speed of the city's adaptation to a new economy can be attributed to two factors. First, the city already possessed a good amount of "raw materials" for these industries, mainly in the form of a great architectural heritage: the medieval buildings, the Gothic neighborhood and the *modernista* architecture were easily available for promotion as unique and spectacular marvels. Second, the 1992 Olympic Games facilitated this adjustment process for two subsequent reasons: on the one hand, they provided a perfect occasion to convince national and foreign companies to invest in the renovation of the city and, on the other hand, they allowed the city hall to establish an internal political consensus. The basic premise (or promise) of this consensus was that the transformation would not only bring economic development, but also fulfill the public needs of the people. Barcelona's municipal project attempted to reconcile private interests and long-term public demands (especially regarding the provision of services in the more peripheral areas), and it was this particular effort that became one of the most celebrated features of "the Barcelona model" of urban transformation. Given the fact that this internal consensus was enhanced by the widespread euphoria that the concession of the Games generated among the citizens of Barcelona, we can describe the municipal politics that accompanied the economic restructuring as a type of "euphoric politics." Olympic Barcelona offered a triumphant economic and political process of "city-building" and a happy model of what Tim Hall and Phil Hubbard call the contemporary "entrepreneurial city."

In order to understand the municipal politics of Barcelona during the 1980s, we must not only examine the set of policies, plans, and decrees ordained under the rule of mayor Maragall and his party, the Partit dels Socialistes de Catalunya (PSC). This set of policies, designed to instigate an intense process of urban reform, were also part of a larger set of ideological operations. This book studies this latter aspect: the ideological constructs that accompanied the conversion of Barcelona into a global city; or, if we do not want to use this term, we may say that a set of specific and dominant ideologies shaped the way Barcelona connected with the new global order.[1] At the same time, however, these dynamics also operated the other way round: the Barcelona model also contributed to define the ideologies of the urban within globalization. Similarly, the 1992 Games worked as a symbol of a re-emerging Catalan nation and a post-Francoist Spain, but they were also among the first global mega-events (to use Maurice Roche's term) which staged and celebrated the so-called "end of history" of post-Cold War globalization.

In trying to account for the variety of ideological premises that constituted the municipal politics of Olympic Barcelona, we must avoid two frequent procedures. On the one hand, we must not understand this historical situation as purely contingent and incomparable. This approach could provide a useful and detailed account of the situation, but its interpretive horizon would be a culturalist one. In this case, we would ultimately have to assume that the transformation of Barcelona took place the way it did because of a particular combination of historical elements, and our monograph could only adduce idiosyncratic cultural factors to explain it.

On the other hand, this specific set of ideologies and the historical situation that they helped to construct should not be interpreted either as a mere historical "stage" in the evolution of Barcelona, Catalonia, and Spain. This Hegelian perspective would presuppose an identity or a spirit of the city that unfolds teleologically through stages. But, if this idealist perspective would reduce historical complexity to a simple unity, its materialist counterpart would make the same misstep: the elucidation of the ideologies of Olympic Barcelona according to a clear-cut economic reason would be mere mechanism and the economy would function here as another reductive simple unity. In this sense, Marx would merely represent an inversion of Hegel and a replacement of the Spiritual Idea for the Economy.

Let me briefly develop this theoretical but also methodological point. As Althusser taught us, Marxism's theoretical revolution did not consist in a mere inversion of Hegelian dialectics. If Hegel conceived history as the unfolding of the Absolute Spirit, Marx did not simply invert the terms and considered the material base of history the true origin of the spiritual superstructure. Instead, Marx's decisive intervention consisted in dismantling the logical procedures that reduced historical complexity to transhistorical and metaphysical unities. Even if Marxism attempts to explain history through the analysis of social totalities, the unity of these wholes is not a spiritual and transcendental principle whose "expression" is the whole itself; on the contrary, as Althusser writes in *Reading Capital*:

> [the unity] is constituted by a certain type of complexity, the unity of a structured whole containing what can be called levels or instances which are distinct and "relatively autonomous," and co-exist within this complex structural unity, articulated with one another according to specific determinations, fixed in the last instance by the level or instance of the economy. (97)

For Marxism, the last instance of the economy asserts itself as a structural causality over the social whole. This causality, though, does not come from an identifiable unity that is expressed or actualized in historical situations; rather, it is the very complex structuring of the whole itself. This causality is the base whose effectivity is its very superstructure, that is, it is the intrinsic mode of production of the various and determinate social formations. For this reason, Althusser defines historical situations as "conjunctures," which are not simply determined by the economic instance but overdetermined through the very structuring of their different superstructural instances or levels. However, in order to understand this structuring and see which elements are dominant in it – what Althusser calls "structure in dominance" – we need the precondition of the economic instance:

> this "determination in the last instance" is an absolute precondition for the neces-sity and intelligibility of the displacements of the structures in the hierarchy of effectivity, or of the displacement of "dominance" between the structured levels of the whole;... only this "determination in the last instance" makes it possible to escape the arbitrary relativism of observable displacements by giving these displacements the necessity of a function. (99)

Thus, the economy is not an absent cause exerting its effects on historical situa-tions (as economic mechanicism or mechanicist intepretations of Marxism would claim); rather, it is a cause immanent in its effects – "*the whole existence of the structure consists of its effects*" (189).

A further complication arises here. If the structure and its effects could be immediately perceived and recognized, one would not need Marxism or any other theoretical inquiry to analyze them: structural essences would corre-spond to social phenomena in a clear and unequivocal way. But, as Althusser states, "the lonely hour of the 'last instance' never comes" (*For Marx* 113). That is to say, the economic instance never asserts itself as a recognizable element. If we assumed that it can be recognized, then we would be falling back into the idealist trap: we would be turning the economic form into a simple unity to which social complexity can be reduced. But the last instance never appears as such because it is part of the very structure of its effects. In other words, the difference between essence and phenomena, between interior and appearance, is not a difference between the (economic) structure and its (superstructural) effects. On the contrary, it is a fold within the structure itself; it is the way in which the structure constitutes itself in its very overdetermination and it is simultaneously the way in which the structure conceals itself. The economic instance asserts itself by precisely concealing – or realizing, dissolving, exerting – its determining force within the structure.

In consequence, when it comes to studying historical conjunctures, the materialist dialectic does not replicate the Hegelian logic of supersession (*Aufhebung*); rather, it emerges as a dialectic of overdetermination. Its theoret-ical focus is on "the *accumulation of effective determinations* (deriving from the superstructures and from special national and international circumstances) *on the determination in the last instance by the economic*" (*For Marx* 113). The dialec-tics of overdetermination accept the irreducibility of contingency, produced by the specific national circumstances of each historical situation; but they also assume that the mode of production exerts a structural force on the particular configuration of these situations. While systematic philosophy inscribes each concrete contingency into a teleological unity (Hegel's Absolute Spirit), the mode of production, or the economic last instance, never functions as a unity: its determination is the very structuring of its (superstructural) effects.

The materialist dialectic is not simply an approach or a methodology that we can now apply to the study of Olympic Barcelona. Rather, it imposes itself as a necessary theoretical practice if we want to account for the variety of (urban, economic, political, social, architectural, cultural) elements of the transformation of the city. In this sense, the central reference to the economic "last instance" should enable us to find correlations between these different and "relatively autonomous" spheres. These correlations, in turn, can help us shed light on the set of ideologies that became dominant, or at least that struggled to become dominant, in this particular conjuncture.

The theories of postmodernity are indispensable to begin to understand the overdetermined relation of these ideologies to the new global economy; in fact, postmodernity or postmodernism are terms that refer to the ideological superstructure of globalization itself. As David Harvey famously argues, the first key characteristic of the postmodern order are the strategies of differentiation that spaces must implement in order to attract the investments of global capital. The high mobility of finance capital and the global reach of investments compel cities, regions, and states to work on making themselves attractive to these investments (*Condition* 295). Hence, the transformation of Barcelona must be interpreted in accordance with these structural forces: the municipal government aimed to prepare the city to host the Olympic Games and to make it appealing in the long run to the new highly mobile capital.

But it was Fredric Jameson who first described postmodernism as an essentially superstructural ideology: as the cultural logic of global capital.[2] In a post-Fordist economy based on the constant supply of multiple, consumer-oriented choices and goods, products must work on differentiating themselves from each other by displaying special qualities and unique traits. Production in this context consists not only in the actual manufacturing of goods, but also in the simultaneous fabrication of the differentiating traits that will permit these goods to be identifiable in the marketplace. This production of differentiating traits is the cultural logic of postmodernism. If culture can be broadly defined as the production of signs of identity, then the consumer economy of late capitalism follows a cultural logic in the sense that products must contain visible features that identify them (or differentiate them) in order to compete among each other. Thus, the techniques of marketing and advertisement become an essential part of the production process, as they configure the distinctive qualities of products.

The key consequence of this situation is that the economic and the cultural spheres collapse into each other as they become structurally dedifferentiated. While the production process adopts a cultural logic, culture in the narrow sense of the word – literature, arts, music, cinema, architecture – is subsumed under this economic logic by becoming fully implicated in the production of special qualities of cities, countries, companies, and institutions of all sorts. Culture is no longer separate from the market, and late capitalism unfolds as a period of full commodification of all spheres of society. Given that the production of identity is incorporated into the economic logic, cultural products, knowledges, lifestyles, symbols, beliefs, signs, or buildings become matter – or often immaterial matter – with exchange value: they become commodities.

In this postmodern condition, Barcelona's municipal program was part of the strategies of spatial differentiation in which cities must engage to attract capital investments. More specifically, this renovation program can be interpreted in concrete economic terms as a perfect case of the so-called "productive expenditures" that public powers implement in order to stimulate capitalist growth. As Harvey explains, these expenditures constitute a financial technique employed by states to intensify the circulation of capital:

> By improving the productive forces in society, the state can contribute, directly or indirectly, to surplus value production. The money invested in state debt does not automatically cease to circulate as capital simply because it enters into the framework of public finance. Interest-bearing capital can continue to circulate if the increase in surplus value production achieved through productive state investments generates the increasing tax revenues that form, in turn, the basis for the interest payments to those who invested in state debt in the first place. (*Limits* 278)

As a pioneering example of this type of public productive expenditures that have become prevalent in contemporary times, Harvey mentions Baron Haussmann's demolition and reconstruction of Paris in the nineteenth century (278). This indicates how, since their beginning, public expenditures of modern states have very often consisted in spatial interventions. Indeed, in Olympic Barcelona, as I describe in Chapters Three and Four, the architectural and urban transformation was the most central aspect of the city hall's politics. This centrality must of course be attributed to the economic activity that the spatial interventions would generate.

As I already mentioned, the municipal politics of Barcelona planned to reconcile economic development with the attempt to fulfill public demands. These were long-standing demands that had emerged as a result of the previous autocratic practices of Francisco Franco's dictatorship (1939–75). Especially during the 1960s, widespread real estate speculation and uncontrolled construction were possible thanks to the authoritarianism of the dictatorship and, specifically, of Franco's appointed mayor in Barcelona, José María Porcioles, whose mandate lasted from 1957 to 1973. This period left a good amount of urban maladies (undersupplied districts, extreme densities, social fractures), which, together with the economic crisis produced by the initial outsourcing of manufactures of the 1970s, generated a high level of discontent. Within this context, the post-Francoist municipal government could proclaim that the transformation of Barcelona would bring not only economic progress, but also the process of democratization that the city needed after the dark years of the dictatorship.

This fusion of capitalist and democratic aims compels us to study these politics by means of a double articulation. On the one hand, this fusion seems to consist in the full subsumption of politics under the economic logic of late capitalism. This subsumption is disguised as a compromise between the economic and the political realms, but nonetheless results in the reduction of the political to a set of managerial or, rather, entrepreneurial procedures. Thus, our critique aims to decipher some of the ideological forms that made possible the staging of this compromise and the subsequent production of consensus. From this viewpoint, the euphoric politics of postmodern Barcelona emerge as a representative case of postpolitics – or of "consensual postdemocracy," to use Jacques Rancière's term (121) – designed to adjust Barcelona to the new service-oriented, global economy.

On the other hand, however, the fusion of capitalist and democratic aims was always problematic and never complete. One can detect in this project of urban transformation a series of political, ideological, cultural and architectural components that ultimately aimed to oppose, or at least contain, the purely economic logic of capitalism. The transformation's own conflicting aims gave way to a series of internal discordances, which were part of the transformation but at the same time opened paths to think beyond it. This will constitute the second direction of my critical approach: the examination of the discordances between declarations and facts, between projects and realizations, between aspirations and results in the official politics of postmodern Barcelona. These disagreements, in turn, might help us devise possibilities for future transformative urban projects.

The conjuncture of Olympic Barcelona has received a good amount of critical attention in Catalan, Spanish, and English. Even though most studies combine a variety of approaches, these can be roughly divided into three types. First, the transformation of contemporary Barcelona has been described as a unique and successful project that can represent a model for other cities.[3] Second, more critical accounts have examined the Barcelona model from urbanistic, sociological, anthropological, or journalistic disciplines. These accounts have especially focused on the negative and conflictive aspects of the urban renewal.[4]

Third, a few texts analyze the relationship between Olympic Barcelona and the new global order from a more theoretical standpoint. Joan Roca i Albert's ambitious *Recomposició capitalista i periferització social*, Mari Paz Balibrea's seminal articles "Urbanism, Culture and the Post-Industrial City: Challenging the 'Barcelona model'" and "Barcelona: del modelo a la marca," and Joan Ramon Resina's outstanding *Barcelona's Vocation of Modernity*, offer a more theoretical approach to the city which is naturally my approach too.[5] While I will return to most of these studies on Barcelona in the following chapters, let me now examine four of these previous important books on Olympic Barcelona. This examination should serve to explain the particular aspects of my contribution.

Roca i Albert's book is a comprehensive elucidation of the recomposition of Barcelona's social fabric during the Olympics. Roca i Albert analyzes the connection between the influx of transnational capital and the new multiple forms of social marginalization. He shows how this marginalization took place by means of a series of undetectable but calculated urban displacements. These changes were diligently concealed by the ideological discourses that the city hall could generate in relation to the Olympic project. For Roca i Albert, the Olympic Games served to conceal the transformation of Barcelona into a "ciutat-empresa" 'city-company' (600) and present it as the "culminació de la reconquesta de la ciutat pels ciutadans" 'culmination of the reconquest of the city by the citizens' (601).[6] The Olympic project provided the perfect occasion to disguise the social recomposition of Barcelona as an urban and architectural "reconstrucció" 'reconstruction' (618), which is how municipal architect Oriol Bohigas titled his 1985 urban program *Reconstrucció de Barcelona*.

Roca i Albert especially focuses on the production of consensus through the configuration of "identitats de barri" 'neighborhood identities' (571). The city hall drew new district maps, sponsored festive events, funded neighborhood associations, and offered various forms of participation in order to promote "la delimitació ecològicocultural d'espais diferenciats a les perifèries socials" 'the ecological and cultural delimitation of differentiated spaces in the social peripheries' (571). Roca i Albert explains how this production of neighborhood identities aimed to conceal the emergence of a new phenomenon, namely what he calls the "fifth world" of the neoproletariat. While the term "fourth world" refers to the poor and destitute riff-raff (the homeless, the itinerant, the unassisted sick), Roca i Albert uses the term "fifth world" to describe the new class of workers employed in the permanently temporary jobs of the post-Fordist marketplace. The members of this working class are not poor, but they function as a disposable, always replaceable contingent that can never aspire to improve their living conditions (592–6).

Roca i Albert considers that Barcelona's local administration promoted social marginalization through urban remodeling and assisted in a servile and complicitous way the demands of transnational capital. He proposes the creation of "fòrums tàctics de reflexió social" 'tactical forums for social reflection' (749), which can bring together popular and dissident groups that resist the municipal politics as well as the economic trends that are disarticulating Barcelona.

This is where my project moves in a somewhat different direction. While Roca i Albert's analysis of the connection between transnational capital and social marginalization in Barcelona remains invaluable, I believe that we can still extract a few useful and transformative guidelines from the municipal project and the architectural renewal of Barcelona. Even if these became subsumed under the logic of post-Fordist capitalism, perhaps we should not reject them as a whole. The work of the state must not necessarily be contested only through social movements and popular tactics. One can also contest it from within, that is, by reclaiming the transformative elements that might be contained within its apparatuses.

In fact, it is unclear whether we can still distinguish the inside from the outside of the state, and whether popular movements can disentangle themselves from the ideological ruses and mirages through which the state continues to reproduce itself. This is of course the fundamental unsolvable problem of the state founded on the will of the people: is the democratic state a structure that contains and channels the people's embryonic creation of political subjectivity (what Michael Hardt and Antonio Negri call constituent power), or is the constitution of the people as a political subject a result of the interpellation of the state? The greatest value of the first position is that it acknowledges and promotes the power of collectives to contest the system. But the second part of the puzzle reminds us of the inevitable logic of sovereignty, which compels all political actions to envision a new, alternative system of rule. Without the horizon of a new system of rule no political action can articulate itself as such. Whether this action is emancipatory, utopian, tactical or strategic, its emergence inherently brings forth the possibility of a new sovereignty, which both makes possible and cancels out the political import of such action. In other words, the horizon of constituent power is always necessarily that of constituted power (or, in classic Derridean terms, the conditions of possibility of the two are also their conditions of impossibility).[7]

An anecdotal but revealing example of these dialectics of democratic politics can be found in the version of Roca i Albert's tactical forums later deployed by Barcelona's city hall. In 2004, ten years after Roca i Albert wrote his proposal, the city hall organized a five-month-long festival, the Fòrum Universal de les Cultures, in which many social agents and experts from all around the world debated about the future of cities, capitalism, the Earth, endangered languages, global warming, or terrorism. One thing became clear in this Fòrum: that the state can deploy exact copies of all sorts of civil forums and social movements. In this case, the institutional production of popular and civil debate made it impossible to distinguish between real political struggle and its simulacrum, that is, between the discourses, affects, forces and struggles produced by the people and those generated by the state. Leaving aside its rather trivial magnitude, the Fòrum was an extreme, cynical version of the state appropriation of the people's political energies; or, even worse, it perfectly illustrated the impossibility of separating the space of the people from the space of the state.

The paradox of democracy inevitably traverses grassroots and anti-corporate globalization movements: the paradox that the more the people resist the state, the more they reinforce its source of legitimacy. In this sense, the tactical or strategic resistances of the present generate and inherently constitute the legitimacy of tomorrow's new authority. For this reason, resistance, a central premise of social movements, needs to be complemented with the plan to attain state power. Even when one fully rejects the constituted form of the state, or precisely in such case, the demand for a new jurisdiction and a new sovereignty is always inescapable.

My project aims to complement Roca i Albert's tactics of resistance by undertaking a parallel task: the task of expropriating Barcelona's local government of its own ideological premises. This critical task can reveal some of the transformative energies contained in Barcelona's municipal project. Even though this urban project represents a small portion of full-scale state politics, and its potential to devise new forms of radical politics might be quite limited, it nevertheless contains some directives worth retrieving. The task of analyzing, expropriating, and radicalizing these directives can shed light on alternative ways of conceiving the future city.

The reference to the 2004 Fòrum is a good occasion to indicate that we can roughly divide the transformation of Barcelona into two periods. First, from the late seventies to the mid-nineties the city hall undertook the transformation that not only prepared the city for the Olympics, but also aimed to serve the needs of the people. Second, beginning in the late nineties new municipal projects gradually adapted to the interests of multinational capital and disregarded large parts of the population. If the Olympic Games were the emblematic event of the first period, the Fòrum represented the corporate uses of the city of the second. As Mari Paz Balibrea has argued, the first period engendered the Barcelona model, whereas the second generated the "marca Barcelona," that is, the process of branding and selling the city in the global marketplace ("Del modelo a la marca"). While my project also refers to post-Olympic Barcelona (especially in Chapter Two, where I allude to some programmatic documents of the Fòrum), its main focus is the Barcelona model as it was conceived and deployed up to the Olympic event.

A second important book is Joan Ramon Resina's 2008 *Barcelona's Vocation of Modernity: Rise and Decline of an Urban Image*, which analyzes the evolution of the "modern image" (5) of the city from the mid-nineteenth century to the present day. Even if the book focuses only partially on Olympic Barcelona, its narrative attempts to contest the dominant configuration of contemporary Barcelona and the relationship that the city has established with its past. Resina argues that an "urban unconscious" (3) has emerged throughout modernity; this unconscious is an image that is not "something exclusively visual, but rather a representational configuration in the social imaginary" (5). This image confers the city with its underlying "character" (6), its "identity" (6), or, as the title says, its "vocation of modernity." Through the analyses of literary texts, historical events, architecture, or political figures, Resina traces the unfolding of this vocation in the nineteenth century and the first half of the twentieth century, when the process of modernization became inseparable from the project of Catalan nationalism.

The modernization of Barcelona involved its articulation as the capital of a nation without a state. Some of the main goals of political Catalanism as it emerged in the second half of the nineteenth century were the federalization of the Spanish state, the defense of Catalan civil law, the demand for protectionist measures for Catalonia's industry, and the strengthening of the public presence of Catalan language. This nationalist and also modernizing project, which gave rise to permanent clashes with the Spanish state, was directed by a prosperous Catalan bourgeoisie that had flourished thanks to the textile industry, and that strove to create a powerful civil society increasingly detached from the central state. Barcelona constituted the most visible materialization of this process of nation-building.

Resina's main concern is that, after the interruption of this process by the autocratic regimes of Primo de Rivera (1923–30) and Franco (1939–75), Barcelona's local rulers never embraced Catalanism again as a central driving force. Instead, one premise became dominant in post-Francoist Barcelona, namely that the city's "vocation" was to organize global mega-events. The city had attained historical splendor during the 1888 Universal Exhibition and the 1929 International Exhibition, and the 1992 Olympic Games, or, later, the 2004 Fòrum Universal de les Cultures, were new occasions to fulfill this vocation. But Resina argues that the Exhibitions were inscribed in a long project to articulate Barcelona as the capital of Catalonia. In the contemporary situation, on the contrary, the ruling elites and the PSC – governing the city hall since 1979 – made use of the Olympics and the Fòrum to configure a cosmopolitan and flamboyant global city. This entailed the erasure of Barcelona's "vocation of modernity" and the forgetting that, before Francoism, Catalanism had been a key agent of progress. For Resina, this is what the Spanish state, and not only Franco, had always wanted: to have a denationalized and politically nonconflictive city focused on its international but ultimately non-threatening projection.

While I acknowledge the critical usefulness of Resina's position, which shows us the extent to which the local rulers of Barcelona have used cosmopolitan doxa to depoliticize and touristify the contemporary city, my project interprets this new situation not only as the result of the ideological work of Barcelona's rulers but also as an effect of the postmodern conditions of production of the global city. Resina refuses the word "postmodern":

> The implications of the "post-" are particularly problematic in this case, because the present city does not activate all its historical resources but on the contrary seeks a rupture and a new beginning every so often, preferring short-lived illumination to the consciousness of what it experienced in the recent and not-so-recent past. (200)

But this is indeed a very accurate definition of the postmoden city: the city in which the past has been obliterated or turned into a short-lived representation as a result of two main phenomena: the speeding up of time, and the subsumption of space under the production of images, in what Harvey has defined as "time-space compression" (*Condition* 284). Given that this postmodern situation corresponds to a different stage of capitalism, we must explain the dominant ideologies of Olympic Barcelona not only in (diachronic) relation to the historical evolution of the city, but also in (synchronic) relation to this structure of postmodernity and globalization. From this viewpoint, Barcelona's modern Catalanism and Barcelona's postmodern cosmopolitanism may be ultimately considered equivalent dominant ideologies that correspond to two different stages of capitalism: the imperialist stage and the global stage (as I explain in Chapters One and Two).

By examining Xavier Rubert de Ventós' script for the ceremony of the Olympic flame in Empúries, and Oriol Bohigas' plan for the urban renewal of Barcelona, my project attempts to show how Catalanism was much more present and operative in Olympic Barcelona than Resina concedes. Or perhaps we could say that the force of Catalanism in Olympic Barcelona was not weaker than before, not so much because the new transformation of the city was overtly Catalanist, but because the construction of the Catalan nation had never been the first priority of Barcelona's ruling classes. The bourgeoisie certainly embraced nationalism, but in modern Barcelona their class interests always prevailed over the transformative project of Catalanism. Their articulation of this project was linked to a program to modernize Spain, play a hegemonic role in a federalized state, and defend their economic interests. In fact, given that Spain was a vital market for the Catalan industry, one of the reasons why the bourgeoisie invested in nationalism was precisely to counteract the more radical Catalan separatism. Thus, if Catalan nationalism has not achieved its alleged final goal,

Catalonia's independence, this must be attributed to the repressive and ideological apparatuses of the Spanish state and also to the economic interests of the Catalan ruling classes. Whatever we can gain from the collective energies of Catalan nationalism will only be obtained if, indeed, we embrace and radicalize Resina's stance and contest both the centralist ideologies of the state and the class ideologies of Barcelona's local rulers.

One third essential book is Donald McNeill's 1999 *Urban Change and the European Left: Tales from the New Barcelona*, which traces, in an operation that he defines as "muckraking" (177), the economic interests and ideological positions of some of the main actors in the city during the 1980s and early 1990s. McNeill describes from a sociological and even ethnographic point of view the programs of the protagonists of Olympic Barcelona, especially mayor Pasqual Maragall and the president of the Generalitat de Catalunya from 1980 to 2003, Jordi Pujol. He also examines the urban renewal as well as the connections between Barcelona's social movements during the 1970s and Manuel Castells' theories of the city and the grassroots.

McNeill also devotes a chapter to leftist writer Manuel Vázquez Montalbán and his journalistic and literary critique of postmodern Barcelona. In his chronicle *Barcelonas* and his novels *El laberinto griego* and *Sabotaje Olímpico*, Vázquez Montalbán has articulated an important critique of the city's transformation. But my project does not focus on him, not only because McNeill has already done so in a compelling way, but especially because of Vázquez Montalbán's particular positioning vis-à-vis the new Barcelona. His strategy consists in dissecting and satirizing the urban renewal from the position of, as McNeill puts it, a "socialist *flâneur*" (23). But, rather than the Baudelairian and Benjaminian *flâneur*, perhaps a more accurate figure to describe the writer's position is Michel de Certeau's walker in the city. Vázquez Montalbán, in journalistic formats or through his fictional alter ego Pepe Carvalho, questions Barcelona's municipal politics from the viewpoint of a lucid and disconcerted citizen who walks in the city and observes the effects of these politics on its urban and social fabric. In his critical portrait, the city hall's politics function as a panoptical power that is capturing and altering the city in order to reduce its heterogeneity to a simplified, predetermined image: the image that can sell Barcelona to global capital and tourism. To use Certeau's terms, Vázquez Montalbán or Carvalho are Daedalean figures that walk the labyrinth of the streets, versus the Icarian leaders who rule the city from their executive flight decks.[8]

As I already suggested in relation to Roca i Albert's tactical forums, my project follows a different direction. My suspicion is that the variable quality of Vázquez Montalbán's two Olympic novels, and the quick selling of *Barcelonas* as a guidebook for those socially aware tourists that like to visit the city while maintaining a critical distance, are perhaps symptoms of the fact that the Certeauian "walking-in-the-city" strategy is no longer as critically productive. In our contemporary context, this strategy seems to collapse into a mere alternative form of tourism: the "off-the-beaten-track" form, which, despite its critical eye, is also a specialized product of the all-pervasive tourist industry. The blurring of a series of distinctions between citizens and tourists, the real city and its image, and the diversity of the street and the diversity of the market, indicate that it may be time to adopt a different critical view of the city. Instead of relying on street tactics and the production of heterogeneity while adopting ethnographic or anthopological frameworks, an alternative effort is possible: the Promethean effort to understand the city as a totality, that is, as a space determined by structural forces that can only be effectively contested through the totalizing frame of (Marxist) political economy.

My aim is not to dismiss the necessary and creative forms of collective struggle of citizens, neighbors, immigrants, and other multiple groups. Rather, I want to point at some of the conceptual contradictions of the prevalent DeCerteuain path in urban studies. One of the books that particularly exemplifies these contradictions is Manuel Delgado's *La ciudad mentirosa: Fraude y miseria del "modelo Barcelona."* Delgado's critique is based on the conception of the city as the reality of the people over which the agents of power have imposed a false model or "lying city." Again, the problem with this division is that it does not account for the possibility that the very heterogeneity of the city is traversed by its double, that is, by the diversity that also sustains the market and the state. In this respect, a crucial problem emerges when groups of citizens carry out collective protests and activist practices with dubious contents, like in those occasions in which neighbors protest against immigrants, against the relocation of marginal collectives, or against undesirable facilities. Delgado examines in detail some of these cases in Barcelona, but he does not reach the logical conclusion: namely that the category of the people never guarantees the production of progressive politics.[9] Popular insubordination against "power" is a critical framework that results in an anthropological fetishization of the people. This framework not only overlooks the possibility that multitudes can be utterly reactionary and "power" effectively progressive, but it also forgets the dialectical interdependence between the two.

Furthermore, another contradiction emerges when the official renewal of the city is denounced as the imposition of a "lie" that erases the historical fabric. On the one hand, Delgado, following Deleuze and Guattari, defines the real city as what "acaece" 'occurs' versus the state, which "ante todo está" 'primarily is' (106). This is the city of the heterogeneous walkers whose paths are untraceable and enigmatic. On the other hand, however, when the "traces" of these citizens (that is, their neighborhoods, their lived spaces, their streets with their shops and their factories) are erased by new construction projects or are transformed into mere monuments, this process is denounced as "la continu-ación de una vieja obsesión de los poderosos por controlar lo que de crónica-mente incontrolable ocurre en las calles" 'the continuation of an old obsession of the powerful to control the chronically uncontrollable events occurring on the streets' (17). Thus, a contradiction emerges between the conception of the citizen as nomad and the condemnation of the destruction of the city. The nomad is not concerned about demolition, as for her construction and demoli-tion are continuous and essential. In fact, strictly speaking, for the nomad the city should not even be erected, as erection is a business of the state "that is" and not of the city "that occurs."[10]

The frame of political economy might help us disentangle some of these contradictions. Yet, this frame faces a further objection, namely that it reduces the diversity of social agencies to class politics. This is the reasoning that traverses most studies on Barcelona and on contemporary cities. McNeill, for instance, relates the political "tales" from Barcelona to the global context, but he refuses to adopt the theoretical scope of political economy. As he argues in his article "Writing the New Barcelona," this frame tends to reduce "the political to class politics" and leaves aside "struggles going on in the city over ethnicity, gender, sexuality, mobility or urban space" (250). McNeill aims to analyze the street as "the material, the palpable, the everyday" (252), where this variety of struggles take place. This approach belongs to a specific critical genre of urban studies that explores the reality of cities, their underworlds, their street-level dynamics, and also the hidden conspiracies devised by local powers to neutralize social antagonisms and displace unwanted collectives.[11]

The supposition that class politics reduce the multiplicity of social phenomena to the Procrustean bed of class struggle, is one of the most common misconceptions of Marxism. This misconception begins by presenting "class" as an identifiable attribute of subjects and collectives, and as another category among those of gender, race, sexuality, or nationality. Within these premises it seems logical that, if one of these particular categories (class) aims to explain the others, the multiple attributes of social subjects are reduced and their singularity is eliminated.

In a narrow sense, class is in fact a subjective category that defines the identity of individuals: in this case, it is determined by the amount of money that one owns, the clothes that one wears, or the social distinctions that one pursues. And, indeed, social class can have many sociological, political, histor-ical, or tactical definitions. But class as the underlying basis of class struggle has a qualitatively different meaning that results from three main interrelated oppositions: 1) the struggle for the abstraction of labor; 2) the internal antago-nism of the commodity value; and 3) the dialectics between the content and the form of the social within capitalism.

The fundamental antagonism of capitalist society is that between those who must sell their labor in exchange for money and those who purchase it and employ it to produce commodities. Class struggle is the permanent tension that this social exchange entails. Given the necessity to produce commodities greater in value than the sum of values used to produce them, capitalists must permanently find ways to lower the costs of labor, a process which workers logically oppose. This division between capitalists and workers, however, should not be understood, again, sociologically, as it does not refer to two different subject positions. The reality is that, especially in contemporary society, subjects are often workers and capitalists at the same time: factory employees have pension funds that are part of the financial investments of a bank, or corporate executives may be paying astronomical rental fees to their landowner. Today, the categories of the proletariat and the bourgeoisie are more diffuse than ever, and their power to represent actual collectives is uncertain. But this diffusion does not imply the obsolescence of class struggle; on the contrary, the development of capitalism involves the complexification of its social forms of presentation, so that the antagonism between capital and labor can be concealed and the emergence of class consciousness can be prevented.

This opposition corresponds to another struggle inherent in capitalism: the internal antagonism of the value of the commodity. Let us recall Marx's analysis: commodities can be exchanged because their use values are abstracted into exchange value: "the value of a commodity is independently expressed through its presentation [*Darstellung*] as 'exchange value'" (*Capital* 152). As a result of this duality, human labor is embodied in the commodity also as exchange value, or, specifically, as "*congealed labour-time*" (130). Labor is thus transformed into time, and this time of production is measured according to "socially average unit[s] of labour-power" (129). This average labor-time is the "normal" or "prevalent" (129) time that it takes to produce a given commodity, and it therefore determines the value of commodities, while also setting the standard for the competition to produce them at the lowest cost possible.

Since labor is a commodity that capitalists buy, its use value must also be transformed into exchange value. Quality is reduced to quantity: human subjects are objectified as workers; their social labor is quantified as labor-time and objectified in the value of the products of their labor. This is another primordial form of class struggle: the struggle for the appropriation of all types of productive forces (creative powers, subjective talents, physical strength, affective aptitudes) and their transformation into labor-power that can be purchased and whose use value is expressed, like the value of all commodities, as exchange value.

Today, as a result of the dominance of immaterial labor and biopolitical production, the limits of work and life have become more blurred than ever.

We experience what Christian Marazzi calls "the *crisis of measurability* of single work operations (of the work time necessary to produce goods)" (43). And yet, the commodification of labor power has not gone away; on the contrary, all aspects of social life have been put to work and subsumed under the logic of capital. The Marxist imperative to calculate work time and account for the transformation of labor into exchange value is indispensable to understand the ways in which capital extracts labor outside of salaried work. Marazzi speaks of "*blocks of social time*" (52) and Antonio Negri has talked about "a cartography" of value (92), two suggestive notions that redefine Marx's "socially average units of labor-power" and try to calculate the impossible measure of work time in a situation in which life and work have become one.

The antagonism between use value and exchange value, and the resultant transformation of labor into wage labor, institute class struggle as the inescapable structural dynamic of capitalism. And, if politics consists in the effort to negotiate positions, contend hegemonies, control bodies, or pursue collective emancipations, within capitalism they are engraved in this structure of class struggle. It is in this structural or formal sense that they are always necessarily "class politics."

If, instead, one considers class struggle to be primarily political conflict between agents, then Marxism becomes a foreclosure of the political. That is, Marxism becomes a formula to predetermine the content of politics and attribute them an economic derivation. But this involves a conceptual displacement from structure to phenomena, or from form to content, by which the economic is conceived as another sphere of the social and not as its very structure. This misconstruction of the problematic of Marxism has become predominant in our post-Althusserian theoretical scene, in which the political constitutes the primary ontological horizon.

This primacy of the political has had a positive effect, namely that political struggle is no longer reduced to the proletarian road to socialism but is open to all types of collective movements and aleatory events (related to gender, race, nation, etc). Yet, the structure of class struggle remains indispensable if we want to determine whether given social events or political practices are resisting the capitalist system, or whether they are secretly obeying its logic. Even though this structure never appears as a visible element of the social, its "structural causality" can be recomposed through the analysis of certain social phenomena, texts, and events.

In addition to vindicating the primacy of the mode of production over the ontology of the political, my project also engages in the deconstructive questioning of ontology itself. In fact, Marxism already takes this path in defining itself not as a transcendental philosophy but as a theoretical and historical confrontation with capitalism. But, by considering the mode of production as the fundamental condition of historical time and consciousness, Marxism makes a non-materialist assumption: that of considering human production as transcendental. "Production" and "labor" constitute the inferred metaphysical premises of a theoretical practice that uncovers all thought as historical and all idealisms as materially overdetermined. As Marx states, "Labour, then, as the creator of use values, as useful labour, is a condition of human existence which is independent of all forms of society; it is an eternal natural necessity which mediates the metabolism between man and nature, and therefore human life itself" (*Capital* 133).

The fact that Marxism does not get rid of the anchors of transcendence must not be a reason to abandon its directives for ideological critique and social transformation. To discard the question of capitalism in order to avoid instituting a metaphysics of production would be a perfect case of throwing the baby out with the bath water. But the dialogue with the deconstructive questioning of ontology continues to be necessary. The rebalancing of the critique of capitalism and the critique of metaphysics (and this is the central theoretical point that traverses my book) can help us contest the organizational forms of the system and at the same time think through its own systematicity. The effectiveness of the paradigm of the mode of production in confronting the rules of capitalism, and the ethical necessity to remain open to the possibility of radical alterity, make Marxism and deconstruction indispensable tools for the potential transformation of the world and our thinking of it. My study of the ideological constructs of postmodern Barcelona aims to be a modest space for the encounter of these two lines of thought.

My focus on Olympic Barcelona as a case study and also as a space of enunciation of more speculative questions has produced a hybrid text that is neither a pure monograph nor a strictly theoretical book. Other hybridities traverse the project. The project studies the immaterial production of the ideologies that structured postmodern Barcelona, but it also incorporates a variety of materials from the palpable "realities" analyzed by other scholars. This book aims to understand a particular city in a certain historical period, but it also reflects on the conditions of the urban in our contemporary times. It is a necessarily fragmentary project, as one can never describe the infinite multiplicity of a city; at the same time, however, it obeys the imperative of political economy and aims to understand the full significance of its materials by means of a comprehensive approach. The project wants to explain a historical conjuncture, but many of its theses are based on fictional narratives (as the literary manipulation of reality can reveal some ideologies that otherwise would remain invisible). More defeating dialectics: the more this project wants to establish connections between heterogeneous materials, the more patchy it seems to become; the more it aims to structure coherent theoretical narratives, the more it distances itself from its infinitely multiple object of study. This is a journey through erratic paths in search of grand speculative conjectures.

The book contains four chapters. Chapter One focuses on specters of the past that might have haunted the euphoric politics of Barcelona. The speeches at the Olympic opening ceremony by the president of the International Olympic Committee (IOC), Juan Antonio Samaranch, and by mayor Pasqual Maragall, staged a tactical reconciliation of these two formerly opposite figures. Samaranch's transition from being a Francoist governor to running the global IOC, and Maragall's evolution from his engagement in anti-Franco struggles to the management of the new liberal Left, are representative moves in the seemingly post-ideological context of 1992 Spain. At the international level, the Barcelona Games became one of the first global mega-events that staged the post-1989 reconciliation celebrated by Francis Fukuyama as the end of history. After decades of Games tainted by violence and boycotts, in 1992 the Olympic ideals seemed to finally materialize in a truly universal Games: a total of 172 national teams participated, including a post-apartheid South Africa, a communist Cuba, and various ex-USSR republics. Symptomatically, this (national and international) reconciliation was staged at the stadium in which, in 1936, a Popular Olympics that had been created against the Nazi Games were supposed to open. The outbreak of the Spanish Civil War cancelled those Olympics and, 56 years later, Maragall presented the 1992 Games as the final fulfillment of that aborted event. But, in this new context, the oppositional content of the 1936 Games had been erased, and their retrieval became a mere populist simulacrum and a perfect symbol of the post-ideological content of contemporary democracy. Along these lines, Maragall's main agenda was to build "the city of the people," in an effort to enhance a close bond between the local government and the citizens. These conciliatory politics must be interpreted in relation to Ernest Mandel's analysis of the way the state in late capitalism deploys ideological machinery in order to appear "closer to the people" and thus integrate the proletarian worker as a consumer or social partner.

In this chapter, I also examine Eduardo Mendoza's 1986 novel *La ciudad de los prodigios* and its portrait of the historical specters of the Universal Exhibition of 1888 and the International Exhibition of 1929. Mendoza's novel confronts Maragall's discourse with the fact that Barcelona's ruling classes would have never known any historical splendor without two key historical processes: the exploitation of the immigrant underclasses and the Faustian pact with the Spanish state – two spectral processes concealed by the euphoric narrative of "the city of the people." My exploration of these various specters aims to reinstate class struggle as a fundamental historical force. However, these ghosts were not simply unwelcome specters from the past; rather, they were simultaneously retrieved and repressed by the new narratives of the city. That is, the very simulacrum of the Olympic spectacle turned every social agent and historical character into a specter. This caused a repressive de-ideologization of the past, but it also opened up the possibility of dismantling these ideological narratives if one brings to light their inherent spectrality.

Chapter Two focuses on the city hall's calculated use of three notions that created a hegemonic definition of Barcelona. These notions were the Mediterranean, Europe, and the city – or what I call "urban cosmopolitanism." While Chapter One contextualizes Olympic Barcelona in the global moment of the end of history, and it therefore inscribes my object of study in a temporal frame, this chapter approaches Barcelona's euphoric politics from a more spatial perspective. Mayor Pasqual Maragall declared that his main goal was to transform Barcelona into the "Northern capital of the European South," and the Olympic Games provided an occasion to advertise the city as a mixture of European cosmopolitanism and Mediterranean rootedness. This ideological fabrication was visibly deployed at the Olympic ceremonies through various performances and at the reception of the Olympic flame in Empúries. While John Hargreaves has already examined the nationalist battles during the Games, this section provides the first close reading of the Empúries' script. This script was defined by his author, Xavier Rubert de Ventós, as "state work" for the Catalan nation.

By avoiding the geographies of nation-states, Barcelona's city hall aimed to reinforce cities as autonomous political entities. In 1992, Barcelona and Rio de Janeiro signed "The Rio–Barcelona 1992 Declaration," another primary text of this section, to claim a bigger political role for cities and launch a concept of citizenship founded not on nationality but on the diversity of city dwellers. I analyze this conception of citizenship as an ideological device of "urban cosmopolitanism." Finally, this chapter examines Francisco Casavella's 1991 novel *El triunfo*, which narrates the criminal endeavors of a group of small time crooks in pre-Olympic Barcelona. This novel portrays the ways in which the city hall's ideological maneuvers contributed to displace the underclasses and points at the social significance of the new African immigration.

The next two chapters focus on the most visible aspect of Barcelona's euphoric politics: the comprehensive urban renewal of the city. Chapter Three examines how the urban transformation during the years prior to the Olympics, from 1981 to 1992, intended two simultaneous things: to build the facilities needed to host the Games and to carry out a general reconstruction of the urban fabric. Oriol Bohigas, the municipal urban designer, conceived the general remodeling plan as a set of architectural interventions in specific sections of the city. Bohigas proposed a renewal rooted in the immediate realities of the street, the square, the neighborhood, and the park. These represented for him the fundamental elements that could generate urban compactness, good readability, mixture of uses, and public spaces.

I analyze this model in relation to two urban theories: Kenneth Frampton's program of Critical Regionalism, which endorses the forms of architecture that resist global homogenization through the care of local places, and Jane Jacobs' call for a new urbanism that combats the suburbanization and monofunctional zones of megacities. But, since the care for local differences is one of the main goals of corporate marketing, Critical Regionalism may collapse into the very global logic that it is trying to resist. Thus, I read the "Barcelona model" of urban transformation vis-à-vis the city's flourishing tourist industry to explore the relations between architectural works and marketing needs. By comparing the new Barcelona to (sub)urban phenomena such as the shopping mall, Disneyworld's EPCOT, or Las Vegas' hotels, I argue that Barcelona, like many European historic cities, might have imitated North American theme parks and thus become the imitation of their imitation. Here Quim Monzó's short stories provide a literary depiction of a generic, serialized Barcelona which reveals the ongoing commodification of the city produced by the Olympic urban renewal.

Perhaps in contradiction with the previous chapter, Chapter Four investigates how the urban transformation of Barcelona can represent an exemplary model for contemporary cities and even for the city of the future. I argue that two components of the Barcelona model are relevant beyond their original context: the master plan and public spaces. On the one hand, the general city master plan that orchestrated the variety of architectural interventions throughout Barcelona is a paradigmatic example of how to limit the capitalist logic of suburban expansion that determines the form of today's megalopolises. Master plans can ensure the implementation of the urban continuity needed to produce a cohesive city, or maybe a city as such. Following Rem Koolhaas' studies on urbanism, this chapter aims to contest the dominant view of the megalopolis as the inevitable form of the contemporary city.

On the other hand, the creation of multiple public spaces during the Olympic years corresponded to a conception of the city as the place of public encounter par excellence. But my reflection on public space aims to go beyond its common anthropological conception as a space of heterogeneity. Urban public spaces stand for the constitutive but unavailable essence of the city. A contradiction traverses this essence: the city is opened to virtually everyone, but this very openness makes possible the particular commercial, social, and political functions which take place in the city and which, inevitably, privatize it and commodify it. Given this contradictory constitution, the publicness of the city must be conceived negatively as the task to interrupt and dismantle the constant appropriations of the public itself. In this sense, even though Barcelona's public spaces have mostly served the tourist industry, they have also made possible a large set of urban heterogeneities and political actions, from antiglobalization movements to revolts against real estate speculation. These post-Olympic movements not only have revived Barcelona's past as an insubordinate city, but, most importantly, they have struggled against all particular appropriations of the city and have perhaps even pointed toward future emancipatory politics. Rather than describing the specific politics of Barcelona's social movements, the last section of this chapter analyzes the interdependence between official urban planning and the possibility of grassroots democracy.

Notes

1 As is known, when Saskia Sassen coined the term "global city" in 1991, she argued that we should reserve it for the three central financial centers of globalization: New York, London and Tokyo. See Sassen, *The Global City*.

2 In the early 1990s the term "global capitalism" was not as omnipresent as it is today. But "finance capitalism," "post-Fordism," or Ernest Mandel's "late capitalism" naturally describe the same phenomenon. Also, while Harvey uses "postmodernity" to describe this phenomenon as a historical situation (as his approach is mainly economic, sociological and geographical), Jameson uses the term "postmodernism" to emphasize the cultural, aesthetic, and superstructural logic of this historical situation. This explains why the two terms allude, respectively, to the historical process of modernity and to the aesthetic movement of modernism.

3 We find this viewpoint in Joan Busquets' *Barcelona: The Urban Evolution of a Compact City* and in Pep Subirós' *El vol de la fletxa*. These two books report, in great detail, the accomplishments of the renewal and launch Barcelona as a model of urban transformation.

4 Manuel Vázquez Montalbán's chronicle *Barcelonas* launched, in 1993, the first substantial critique of the Barcelona model. Donald McNeill's *Urban Change and the European Left: Tales from the New Barcelona* traces the economic interests and ideological investments of the main actors of Barcelona's local politics. John Hargreaves' *Freedom for Catalonia? Catalan Nationalism, Spanish Identity, and the Barcelona Olympic Games* analyzes the nationalist conflicts that took place during the preparation for the Games in relation to the display of symbols, emblems, flags, languages, and protocols. Manuel Delgado's *La ciudad mentirosa: Fraude y miseria del 'modelo Barcelona'* is a passionate critique of the municipal politics and a vindication of popular struggles and grassroots movements. Mónica Montserrat Degen's *Sensing Cities: Regenerating Public Life in Barcelona and Manchester* is a suggestive analysis of two regenerated neighborhoods – Barcelona's El Raval, and Manchester's Castlefield – through the prism of the senses; Degen investigates the ways sensory experience can resist power relations. Llàtzer Moix's *La ciudad de los arquitectos* is a precise and well informed chronicle of the development and contingencies of the urban renewal. Moix interviews the protagonists and narrates the difficult decision-making process regarding the transformation. From a more technical perspective, we find, among others, Francesc Muñoz's excellent *UrBANALización: paisajes comunes, lugares globales*, along with various related articles on what he terms "Brandcelona"; Jordi Borja's *Llums i ombres de l'urbanisme a Barcelona*; Josep Maria Montaner's *Repensar Barcelona*; Horacio Capel's *El modelo Barcelona: Un examen crítico*; Stefanie von Heeren's *La remodelación de Ciutat Vella: Un análisis crítico del modelo Barcelona*; and Francisco-Javier Monclús' article "The Barcelona Model: an Original Formula? From 'Reconstruction' to Strategic Urban Projects (1979–2004)." Also, the volumes *Transforming Barcelona*, edited by Tim Marshall, and *La metaciudad: Barcelona:*

Transformación de una metrópolis, edited by Mónica Degen and Marisol García, contain a variety of articles and critical perspectives on the city.

5 But see also Antonio Sánchez's *Postmodern Spain*, which analyzes, in one insightful chapter, the postmodern redevelopment of Barcelona.

6 All translations from Catalan, Spanish and French are mine, unless otherwise indicated.

7 For an illuminating analysis of the logic of sovereignty, see Rasch.

8 See Certeau 92.

9 Delgado specifically looks at the so-called "intifada del Besòs" (142–56), which took place in 1990, and which I also examine in Chapter Four.

10 The question of erection, as Delgado cleverly points out, also relates to sexual organs: while the city of power is visibly phallic, the multiple city of the people is "profunda y oculta... [l]o uterino de la ciudad" 'profound and unseen... [t]he uterine of the city' (127–28). Yet, again, the paradox is that the erection of the city is a necessarily phallic enterprise; without phallus, there would be no city. In any event, the city is always already phallic and uterine at the same time.

11 McNeill ("Writing" 243–44) refers to the models that have inspired him when writing on Barcelona: Mike Davis' *City of Quartz: Excavating the Future in Los Angeles*; Patrick Wright's *A Journey Through Ruins: A Keyhole portrait of British Postwar Life and Culture*; and François Maspero's *Roissy Express: A Journey through the Paris Suburbs*. These three books are remarkable sociological and ethnographic approaches to the most immediate street realities of cities.

CHAPTER ONE

Olympic Specters at the End of History

Barcelona's Olympic Vocation

In the opening ceremony of the 1992 Olympic Games, Barcelona's mayor Pasqual Maragall began his welcoming speech by retrieving an uncanny specter of the past. He referred to the city's attempt in 1936 to organize an alternative Games to the Nazi Olympics held in Berlin that same year. He also alluded to the president of Catalonia's autonomous government of the Generalitat de Catalunya, Lluís Companys, who would have inaugurated these Games if they had taken place. Maragall's exact words were "Senyors, ciutadants del món: fa cinquanta-sis anys s'havia de fer una Olimpíada Popular en aquest estadi de Montjuïc. El nom del president d'aquesta Olimpíada Popular és gravat allà dalt, a l'antiga Porta de la Marató. Es deia Lluís Companys i era el president de la Generalitat de Catalunya" 'Gentlemen, citizens of the world: fifty-six years ago, the Popular Olympics were supposed to open in this stadium of Montjuïc. The name of the president of these Popular Olympics is stamped up there, on the old Door of the Marathon. His name was Lluís Companys and he was the president of the Generalitat de Catalunya' (*Cerimònia inauguració*, TV3).

The purpose of these Popular Olympics was to organize a competition for the people against the Olympics that intended to glorify Hitler and the Aryan race. A tradition of alternative Games had already started in 1921 in Prague, when a group of mostly European unions and worker's associations created the Red Games in order to counteract the too aristocratic and elitist official Games founded in 1896 by Baron Pierre de Courbertin. Following Prague, the Red Games were celebrated in Frankfurt in 1925, in Moscow in 1928, and in Vienna in 1931. But, as Xavier Pujadas and Carles Santacana explain, the Barcelona Popular Olympics of 1936 were not exactly a new edition of the Red Games. Instead, multiple sport and civic associations, with the support of the Republican government of president Companys, organized them with the specific goal of counteracting the Nazi Games (79).

Opposition movements against the Berlin Games had already emerged in the United States in 1933, when the Amateur Athletic Union decided to boycott them for not allowing the participation of Jewish athletes. On behalf of the Olympic ideal of universal peace, this opposition to Berlin's racial policies continued throughout Europe, especially in Paris and Prague, where public speeches and street demonstrations abounded. Also, as the Games approached, Hitler's manipulation of the event as militaristic propaganda became an even more urgent concern than racial discrimination (Pujadas and Santacana 107–19).

As a result of this rising opposition, Barcelona's anti-Nazi Popular Olympics attracted sport associations from all over Europe and the United States, summoning up to 6,000 athletes – a lot more than the 4,106 participants in the Berlin Games (185). The progressive agenda of the Popular Olympics was unequivocal: not only did they aim to constitute a platform for the European and American movements united against Nazism, but they also contained an anticolonialist and nationalist subtext, as they admitted as separate teams countries and peoples such as Algeria, Spanish Morocco, French Morocco, Palestine, the Emigrated Jews, Alsace, Galicia, the Basque Country, and Catalonia.[1]

The Popular Olympics were aborted by the outbreak of the Spanish Civil War on July 18, 1936, the day before their scheduled commencement on July 19. General Francisco Franco took up arms in a coup d'état against the Republic the same day the organization was rehearsing for the opening ceremony in the stadium where mayor Maragall would make his welcoming speech 56 summers later. Remarkably, the Catalan and Spanish athletes, along with some groups of foreign athletes that became a precedent of the International Brigades, substituted guns for balls and barricades for jumping mattresses and joined the Republican forces in their resistance against the insurrected army.

In the Olympic ceremony in 1992, Maragall's brief tribute to president Companys was especially meaningful. At the end of the Civil War in 1939, when Franco's troops entered as winners in Barcelona, president Companys had already fled to France, where he worked for the continuation of the government of the Generalitat in exile. But on August 13, 1940, the Gestapo captured him and handed him over to Franco. He was later imprisoned in the castle of Montjuïc, located next to the Olympic stadium. In this castle, and after an unwarranted court martial, Francoist troops executed president Companys on October 15, 1940. This execution symbolized the disappearance not only of a representative of the Republic, but also of the political autonomy of the Catalan nation. In a heroic but also premeditated way, Companys' last uttered words before he was shot were: "Per Catalunya!"[2]

But what was the ideological content of Maragall's tribute to Companys in 1992? Maragall aimed to conjure a specter of the past, and when he mentioned Companys a spontaneous and intense ovation took over the stadium. How should we interpret this political and televised gesture?

The reference to Companys had at least three immediate political functions.

First, it was a way of acknowledging the experience of the Republic, the period when Catalonia had enjoyed the highest level of political autonomy in modern times; second, Maragall was symbolically aligning himself with the Republicans defeated during the Civil War; and, third, he connected the two Olympic events of 1936 and 1992 in order to present himself as the successor of Companys. His tribute in the inauguration of the Games implied that the mayor of Barcelona was acting as the equivalent to a president of Catalonia, which constituted a clear strategy to eclipse the president of the Generalitat de Catalunya, Jordi Pujol.

A more detailed text by Maragall can help us point at another, less visible meaning of his recollection of the 1936 Popular Olympics. In the introductory remarks for a symposium held in 1992 on the history of the Olympic Games, Maragall explained that Barcelona had already attempted to organize two Games: first in 1924 and later in 1936. For him, these attempts confirmed the city's early vocation to embrace the Olympic ideals. He said "Aquesta olimpíada popular és als annals dels arxius olímpics com un element molt singular de la seva història. No van ser uns Jocs oficials, però van ser la demostració d'una ciutat entestada a poder organitzar aquesta cita d'internacionalitat" 'These Popular Olympics are a very singular element in the annals of Olympic history. These Games were not official, but they were the expression of a city determined to organize this international event' (Castro Alcaide 12).

Maragall interprets the experience of 1936 as another episode of a collective long-lasting dream that finally comes true in 1992. In Maragall's narrative, the singularity of the Popular Olympics does not derive from their political significance and their oppositional content; instead, they represent another episode of Barcelona's early vocation to host the Olympics. Maragall performs a clear ideological operation: he appropriates the event while misrecognizing its singularity and downplaying the historical conflict from which it arose. Although the figure of Companys could still evoke the traumatic abolition of the Catalan government at the end of the Civil War, Maragall's allusion to him is also reinscribed in the narrative that turned the 1936 Games into a proof of the city's Olympic vocation. Furthermore, Maragall's writing of this vocation contains two symptomatic absences. In addition to the unsuccessful attempts of 1924 and 1936, Maragall could have reinforced his narrative by referring to the actual celebration of the II Juegos Olímpicos del Mediterráneo in 1955, or to the attempt to present a candidacy together with Madrid to host the 1972 Games. So, why did Maragall not make use of these two episodes?

These two episodes bring us to the other crucial figure of the 1992 Games: Juan Antonio Samaranch. Samaranch, who came from a very different political background than Maragall's, was the man responsible for the organization of the sports projects of 1955 and 1972. At the opening Olympic ceremony in

1992, Samaranch was standing next to Maragall when he gave his welcoming speech, as he was nothing less than the president of the International Olympic Committee (IOC). At the ceremony, following Maragall's speech, he made some brief congratulatory remarks to everyone who had participated in the organization of the Games, from the Spanish monarchy to the Catalan government, the city hall, and the IOC.

Samaranch was the son of a Catalan (but Spanish-speaking) bourgeois family of Barcelona. Born in 1920, he felt very early an inclination toward sports. After the Civil War, he became a hockey coach and at the same time began to run his family's textile company. Through hockey, he established a set of connections that helped him move up in the Francoist sports apparatuses. He founded and became president of the Federación Española de Patinaje in 1954. He was appointed Jefe Provincial de Deportes in 1956, Delegado Nacional de Educación Física y Deportes in 1966, and, in 1967, president of the Comité Olímpico Español. He left his position in the textile business and invested in property development in Barcelona. In 1963, he became the president of Urbanizaciones Torre Baró S.A., the company that built the area of Torre Baró, one of the areas at the outskirts of the city with cheap, state-subsidized housing that accommodated Andalusian immigrants. He also established close ties with the finance industry and was a member of Banco de Madrid's administrative board. His political career switched tracks in 1973 from the field of sports to the ruling of the provincial government, when Franco assigned him the presidency of the Diputación Provincial de Barcelona.

The fact that Samaranch was a Francoist politician and a real estate speculator earned him the profound dislike of the leftist movements of Barcelona. In 1977, after democracy had arrived, he left the Diputación after thousands of people led by Pere Portabella, film director and member of the newly legalized Partit Socialista Unificat de Catalunya (PSUC), demonstrated against him and tirelessly shouted "Samaranch, fot el camp" 'Samaranch, bugger off.' The new Spanish government sent him to Moscow as ambassador. But, in the meantime, he had already begun his meteoric career as a member of the IOC, the organization which, in the words of Vyv Simson and Andrew Jennings, "is one of the most secretive, powerful and lucrative interlocking societies in the world" (4). In 1980, he became its president.

In their biography of Samaranch, Jaume Boix Angelats and Arcadi Espada describe how his management of the Juegos Olímpicos del Meditérraneo in 1955 satisfied both the Franco regime for the political propaganda that they generated and Barcelona's rulers for the economic profits that they produced (176–83). Also, in 1965, when the Spanish government decided to present Madrid as an Olympic candidate for the 1972 Games, Samaranch, who was already a member of the IOC, insisted on making Barcelona a co-hosting city of the Games. He argued that Barcelona, unlike Madrid, was on the coast and could accommodate the aquatic sports. But, for multiple reasons (among them the eventual lack of support of the Franco regime itself), the IOC chose Munich as the Olympic city.

Samaranch was eager to bring the Games to Barcelona. And when, in 1979, the PSC won the local elections and Narcís Serra became mayor, Samaranch contacted him to lay out the project of an Olympic candidacy. The Olympic project thus brought together the odd couple of an ostracized ex-Francoist living in communist Moscow, and a socialist now in power. As Llàtzer Moix reveals, they even had to meet clandestinely (59–60); a very ironic fact, given that for a long time it was only the Left that had clandestine meetings in its struggle against Francoism.

Although he had to remain officially neutral, Samaranch, as newly invested president of the IOC, played an influential role in the decision of awarding the Olympics to his home city (Simson and Jennings 6). His preference for Barcelona, although it obeyed a presumable loyalty to his city and probable indirect economic gains, had one fundamental purpose: to reconcile himself publicly with the new democratic city. Indeed, the awarding of the 1992 Olympic Games to Barcelona led to this reconciliation, and his past as a Francoist politician and land speculator was conveniently overlooked by the main agents involved in the organization of the Games. He was such a central piece of the Olympic enterprise that none of these agents had the desire to recall Samaranch's infamous past and run the risk of jeopardizing the entire project.

When, at the opening ceremony, Maragall did not mention Samaranch's past travails for the city and the contributions to its progress in 1955 and 1972, Samaranch was probably not offended at all. On the contrary, one suspects that he very much appreciated Maragall's omission: these travails would have invoked the Francoist years from which he had worked on disentangling himself precisely through the project of the 1992 Games. We may also presume that, in turn, Maragall was glad to mention only the Popular Olympics of 1936. This event linked him directly to the Republican Left of President Companys and, at the same time, he could portray Barcelona's Olympic vocation as untainted by the Francoist episodes of 1955 and 1972.

The Olympic Games represented perhaps one of the final episodes of the ongoing reconciliation between ex-Francoists and the formerly clandestine Left during the Spanish transition to democracy. The so-called *pacto del olvido* had determined that, in order to make democratization effective, Spain should not undertake an examination of its past conflicts nor initiate any sort of postdictatorship judicial process. The democratic consensus resolved that the Francoist past should be forgotten and that Spain should move on and complete its process of democratization. The new official memory was, as sociologist

Salvador Cardús puts it, a "memory without a past" ("Politics" 25). As Cardús explains, "[t]he most comfortable approach was to keep talk about the past to a minimum, try to forget it, turn over a new page, or, up to a certain point, allow the veil of confusion to drop down over the question of responsibility" ("Politics" 26).

To these forms of erasure we should add yet another ideological practice, namely the retrieval of conveniently depoliticized past events. Maragall's retrieval of the ghost of Companys and the Popular Olympics at the opening ceremony is highly illustrative of this procedure: a procedure which, as Spanish democracy has progressed (and perhaps especially after 1992), has become more and more dominant, resulting in a new memory: not the transition's "memory without a past" but the memory of a past without conflict. At the Olympic ceremony on July 25, 1992, we can see a culminating and spectacular staging of the post-Francoist reconciliation: Maragall and Samaranch embodying the Left and the Right, the defeated Republicans and the victorious Francoists, who had buried their differences and worked together to launch Barcelona, Catalonia and Spain to the world. But in this staging we can also find the signals of an emergent, post-transition relationship to this past: that of commemorating the past while simultaneously suppressing its conflictual politics.

In addition to this internal reconciliation, the 1992 Games represented at the international level one of the first global mega-events (to use Maurice Roche's term) that epitomized the post-1989 reconciliation described by Francis Fukuyama as the end of history. In Barcelona, for the first time after the Cold War, previously antagonistic countries agreed to participate in a sports contest whose main motive was universal peace. Violence and boycotts had tainted most of the preceding editions of the Games: Mexico 1968 was associated with state repression and the killing of Tlatelolco; in Munich 1972, Palestinian terrorists attacked the Israeli teams; Montreal suffered enormous debts because of the ruinous 1976 Games; the USA boycotted the Moscow Games in 1980; in 1984, the USSR boycotted the Games in Los Angeles; and, even if the 1988 Games in Seoul enjoyed a large participation of countries, the conflict between South Korea and North Korea produced palpable tensions.

In 1992, the Olympic ideals seemed to materialize again, or perhaps for the first time, in a truly universal and conciliatory Games. A total of 172 national teams, the largest in history up to then, participated in the Barcelona Games, including post-apartheid South Africa, communist Cuba, and various ex-USSR republics. The 1992 Games provided the perfect frame to stage the new global geopolitics based on the supposedly definitive triumph of liberalism and democracy over the other two systems that had shaped twentieth-century history – fascism and communism. The euphoric ambiance of freedom and peace of the Games, spectacularly depicted by the media around the world, symbolized the post-Cold War triumph of neoliberal globalization at the end of history – a point that I will develop later.[3]

The 1992 Olympic official theme song was symptomatically called "Amigos para siempre (Friends for Life)," with music by Sir Andrew Lloyd Webber and lyrics by Don Black, and performed by Sarah Brightman and Josep Carreras at end of the closing ceremony. The song, which longs for an eternal friendship between Barcelona, the world, and all human beings, is a perfect example of this lavishly conciliatory agenda for a world that had seemingly begun its final stage of perpetual peace.[4]

In what follows I plan to analyze the hegemonic discourses of Barcelona's euphoric politics in relation to the global phenomena of the end of history and postmodernism, as well as in relation to the economic determinations of late capitalism. But to do so, we must first take a brief look at the turbulent history of modern Barcelona. This will allow us to see how this historical development was reinterpreted, if not openly falsified, in the postmodern context of the 1992 Games.

Class and National Struggle in Barcelona

Like any other industrialized city, Barcelona experienced constant and violent episodes of class struggle throughout modernity. In Catalonia, contrasting with the other parts of the peninsula except for the Basque Country, industrialization had transformed its agrarian society and had become the dominant form of production since the beginning of the nineteenth century. The textile industry was its most important specialization and it flourished in conjunction with the extraction of cotton from Cuba and Puerto Rico, the last Spanish colonies in the Caribbean. As in northern European countries, industrialization brought to Catalonia modernization, urban development and wealth, as well as social unrest and new class divisions.

Despite this economic progress, Catalonia had had no political autonomy since 1716. King Philip V, victor of the War of the Spanish Succession (1701–14), abolished the Generalitat de Catalunya and the Catalan institutions founded in the Middle Ages. Catalonia had maintained its institutions during the medieval period and also after the unification of the kingdoms of Aragon-Catalonia and Castille, upon the marriage, in 1469, of Ferdinand II and Isabel, the Catholic Kings. This unification (consummated after Isabel had become Queen of Castille in 1474, and Ferdinand King of Aragon-Catalonia in 1479) represented a union under the same monarchic sovereignty, and the two kingdoms remained politically independent to all purposes. However, during the War of the Spanish Succession, Catalonia aligned herself with England, Holland, Austria, and Savoy in their support of the Habsburg candidate, Archduke Charles of Austria, who opposed the Bourbon candidate, Prince Philippe d'Anjou, grandson of Louis XIV of France, endorsed by France and Castille. The Catalans fought against the Bourbons not only because a union of Spain and France would have produced a menacing hegemony over them (after all, the French and the Castilians had split the Catalan territory in 1659, when France took the area of the north of the Pyrenees, the Roussillon or North Catalonia, in exchange for military help to the Spanish monarchy), but also because England promised that, in case of victory, their autonomous institutions would be respected. But the Bourbons won the war and, when in 1716 Prince Philippe d'Anjou became King Philip V, he established the strongly centralist Decreto de Nueva Planta, the decree that abolished Catalonia's autonomy, imposed high taxes on the Catalans, and prohibited the official use of their language.

The end of the war brought a period of stability throughout the eighteenth century. During this period a process of primitive accumulation of capital took place in Catalonia. Several factors originated this process and established the bases for the industrial development of the next century. First, demographic growth together with the extension and intensification of agrarian production, especially of wheat and wine, increased the price of land and produced a general escalation of prices. Second, the peculiar feudal organization of the family, which prescribed that the oldest son, the *hereu*, inherited all patrimony, favored the industrialization process in two main ways. On the one hand, it established an accumulation of "un caractère lilliputien" 'a Lilliputian character' (Vilar II 580), that is, a system that neither dispersed the patrimony nor allowed the formation of big fortunes. On the other hand, this rigid, emphyteutic family structure compelled the younger brothers to leave the household and, therefore, they became free to work as proletarian workers or merchants.

Third, internal economic growth, as well as the relative stability of the Spanish empire, enabled the Catalan nascent bourgeoisie to begin to export goods – above all, wines, and later, manufactured textiles – to American colonies. The growing mobility of merchandise and people generated the commerce money that would intensify capital accumulation. At the same time, state protectionism provided by the Bourbon regime, especially against British textiles, played a crucial role in the development of Catalan factories. Throughout the nineteenth century, Catalan industries could keep their vital sales monopoly in the peninsular and South American markets, and they became the fourth largest producer of cotton textiles after England, France, and the United States. This prosperity symbolically culminated in the celebration of the Universal Exhibition of 1888, which brought international fame to Barcelona.

The penurious living conditions of Catalan workers, in turn, motivated the appearance of active syndicalist and socialist movements in urban centers and, above all, in Barcelona. These movements ranged from moderate unionizing for salary negotiation, to radical utopian projects such as the Cabetian Icarianism of Narcís Monturiol (who is also known for being the inventor of the submarine) and, as I will explain in Chapter Three, the Proudhon-inspired urbanism of engineer Ildefons Cerdà. By the turn of the twentieth century, more violent forms of class struggle altered Barcelona's social life. Luddite attacks on factories, anticlerical assaults on churches, and anarchist bombings, made Barcelona internationally famous as "the city of bombs." The most calamitous events took place in 1893 at the Liceu, the opera house, when an anarchist dropped a bomb from the upper circles into an audience composed of the wealthiest members of the bourgeoisie, and in 1909, in the episode known as the *setmana tràgica* or Tragic Week, when many churches and monasteries were burnt one after another during a whole week. Meanwhile, the Spanish state repressed these violent manifestations of class struggle, although, predictably, the brutal and arbitrary repression of the state only generated more violence. Along with this, several bourgeois families and factory owners, especially in the 1920s period of *pistolerisme,* hired assassins to commit crimes that would appear as if they had been perpetrated by anarchists. This strategy provoked a never-ending series of acts of vengeance and blood spilling.

At the end of the nineteenth century, another key element began to configure Catalonia's society, namely Catalan nationalism. While in the 1830s a cultural movement, the *Renaixença,* had already emerged to restore Catalan as a respectable literary language, it was not until the 1880s that Catalanism became politically articulated as a nationalist project. The origins of political Catalanism lie in the failed attempt to federalize Spain during the first Republic of 1873 and the subsequent neglect of the Federal Republicanism devised by Francesc Pi i Margall. Valentí Almirall, who had also belonged to Pi i Margall's federalist party, founded the association Centre Català in 1882 to bring together the collective of Catalans increasingly dissatisfied with the centralist state. The Centre Català held two conventions in 1880 and 1883. These conventions produced a variety of resolutions defending autonomous civil law, the co-official status of Catalan language, the prevalence of Catalonia as a common entity over the provincial divisions, and state protection of the Catalan industry. But Almirall looked too radical and separatist in the eyes of the bourgeoisie, and a new, more conservative group, the Lliga de Catalunya, was created to agglutinate their interests. In 1889, this new organization drafted the first statute for Catalan self-government, the *Bases de Manresa.* This document put forward the same points of Almirall's Catalanist conventions, but it avoided the republican undertones of the latter and stressed the unquestionable importance of the monarchy.

The disaster of 1898, and the loss of the colonial markets of the Catalan textile industries, prompted the foundation of an official political party: the Lliga Regionalista de Catalunya. Under the leadership of Enric Prat de la Riba, the new party united the industrial bourgeoisie to defend the Catalan national interests, while also respecting the unity of Spain – hence its "regionalist" ascription. In the following years, two internal dynamics of Catalan nationalism became evident: on the one hand, a clear division emerged between the more conservative regionalism with monarchical values, and the more progressive and republican nationalism; but, on the other hand, these two sides continued to defend Catalonia against the central state. This was especially clear in 1907, with the foundation of the coalition Solidaritat Catalana, which opposed the anti-Catalan military campaigns of the government. In 1914, a new political entity came to organize Catalonia's political life: the Mancomunitat de Catalunya. Under the presidency of Prat de la Riba, the Mancomunitat assembled the four provinces (Barcelona, Girona, Tarragona, and Lleida) and assumed a large number of state functions – from the construction of new infrastructures, to the creation of schools, libraries, cultural institutes, and multiple intellectual enterprises.[5]

Class antagonisms kept disrupting Catalan society until, in the 1920s and 1930s, authoritarianism appeared as the "solution" to this conflicting situation.[6] First in the figure of Primo de Rivera and his dictatorship from 1923 to 1930, and then with Francisco Franco, in power from 1939 until 1975, authoritarianism in Spain emerged as a unique form of regressive neo-imperialism equally opposed to communism and to capitalism. Primo de Rivera's and Franco's autocracies shared a Catholic, military, rural, centralist, and fundamentally reactionary conception of Spain. Thus, their ruthless repression of class struggle not only assisted the bourgeoisie and facilitated the exploitation of the working class, but was also part of their opposition to modernization and industry altogether. Given that the Catalans represented both the threat of modernity and the incomplete Castilianization of the Spanish state, Primo de Rivera and Franco were fiercely anti-Catalan and prohibited the language and any public display of nationalism.

The Catalan bourgeoisie always maintained an ambiguous relationship to the two dictators. On the one hand, they supported them because their military force promised to eliminate class struggle and could guarantee the necessary stability for their businesses; not coincidentally, Barcelona could hold another International Exhibition in 1929. But, on the other hand, the anti-Catalanism and irrepressible centralism of the dictatorships compromised their national identification and ultimately affected their economic interests as well. This situation generated constant clashes, not only between the state and the Catalan bourgeoisie, but also within the bourgeois classes themselves.

These classes attempted to handle this situation by displaying a distinctive ambiguity, but their unclear position became more and more untenable as the Civil War approached. During the Republic (1931–9), Catalonia enjoyed a stronger autonomy, but its ruling classes were not satisfied with the Republic's inability to reduce social unrest. For this reason, when the Civil War began in 1936, the position of the Catalan bourgeois classes collapsed: they were forced to take sides and privilege either their class interests (and support the Francoist rebels against the Republic) or their national affiliation (and defend a democratic government that had not prevented the emergence of a serious revolutionary threat). Eventually, neither their class interests nor their national affects were gratified, as Franco's victorious regime brought deep economic regression and applied a brutally repressive politics against Catalan culture.

We must also remark, however, that important sectors of this bourgeoisie had never been Catalanist and always refused to speak Catalan. These sectors did not have to face the dilemma between their economic interests and their nationalism, and their occasional tensions with the regime were caused by economic rather than cultural reasons. (The case of Juan Antonio Samaranch is very representative in this sense.) Moreover, after Franco had established his dictatorship, many bourgeois families adopted Castilian as their everyday language and embraced the Catholic and neo-imperial symbols of the regime.

The economic downfall of the postwar period ended in 1953 when Franco signed the Pact of Madrid with the United States. In exchange for four military bases for Cold War operations, the Franco regime received significant financial aid as well as its "strategic rehabilitation" (Payne, *Franco* 417). For the first time, the regime opened the country to foreign investment, first to American capital and later to the mostly European companies that wanted to take part in the new booming tourist industry. These circumstances had two main consequences. On the one hand, the alliance with the United States brought economic prosperity and political legitimacy to the dictatorship. The regime could launch in 1959 the *Primer plan de estabilización económica* and, in 1964, the *Segundo plan de desarrollo y estabilización económica*; in addition, the international boycott to the regime ended and Spain was accepted into the United Nations in 1955. But, on the other hand, the opening to international markets and institutions encouraged internal oppositional movements to fight against the regime. Now the protests of workers, students or Catalan and Basque nationalists could have a broader international impact. Even if the regime remained in many aspects untouched, and maintained torture and the death penalty until the very end, opposition grew stronger and brought together all types of groups and agendas, from leftist anticapitalists to countercultural revolutionaries to nationalist activists. Spain ranked as one of the top European countries in strike activity during the late 1960s and early 1970s.[7]

Catalonia prospered greatly during the 1960s, especially due to tourism. Large waves of immigrants coming from other parts of the peninsula moved to Catalonia in search of a better life. Between 1955 and 1975, about 1,800,000 people migrated to Barcelona (de Riquer 263). In general, Catalans, who occupied mostly the upper and middle classes, had a dubious relation with these immigrants. While, on the one hand, they certainly welcomed and took advantage of this provision of cheap labor, on the other hand the fact that immigrants were Spanish-speaking made them appear as another definitive threat to the already harshly oppressed Catalan culture. The derogatory term *xarnego* appeared in this context to designate the newcomers and differentiate them from autochthonous Catalan speakers. At the same time, language introduced a new division among immigrants. Since everybody in Catalonia knew, or was expected to know, Spanish, learning Catalan was optional to the Spanish-speaking population. Therefore, those who made the effort or had the opportunity to learn the minority language became more integrated into Catalan society, and the acquisition of Catalan at least potentially helped immigrants to prosper economically.

The situation of the immigrants or *murcianos* during late Francoism was famously portrayed by Jaime Gil de Biedma in his poem "Barcelona ja no és bona, o mi paseo solitario en primavera," published in 1966. In it, the poet is taking a stroll at the hill of Montjuïc, the emblematic park in the center of Barcelona, which contained the Olympic stadium of 1936 and also the military castle where Franco executed president Companys along with hundreds of prisoners after the war. The poet contemplates groups of young immigrants loitering in the dirty slopes of the hill and wishes that in the future these poor *murcianos* take over the whole city.

> Sean ellos sin más preparación
> que su instinto de vida,
> más fuertes al final que el patrón que les paga
> y que el *salta-taulells* que les desprecia:
> que la ciudad les pertenezca un día. (81)
> Let this city be theirs one day,
> with no better preparation
> than their survival instincts, stronger
> in the end than the bosses who pay them
> and the Catalan clerks who look down on them. (Nolan 29)[8]

Will the city belong to the immigrants some day, as the poet wishes? Or will the immigrants become a specter that haunts contemporary Barcelona?

The Context of Late Capitalism

Thirty years later, in 1996, writer Sergi Pàmies, too, set part of the plot of his short story "La gran novel·la sobre Barcelona" in Montjuïc. Here the mountain is no longer a filthy space as in Gil de Biedma's poem, but the clean, well-lighted area above the city that accommodated the main facilities of the 1992 Olympics.

The story, which tours different parts of the city from a plane and a taxi, includes a man who was murdered at the castle of Montjuïc after the Civil War and was buried in a common grave in the nearby cemetery:

> L'home que va ser afusellat prop del castell no s'avorreix. Després d'una llarga temporada de rutina, els últims anys li han regalat un renaixement acústic que no esperava. La proximitat de l'estadi li ha permès viure experiències sonores tan inteses com un concert dels Rolling Stones i bona part d'uns jocs olímpics. (Mai no oblidarà l'entusiasme dels seus companys de fossa quan, foradant un mur d'aplaudiments, la guitarra de Keith Richards va començar a tocar les primeres notes de "Honky Tonk Woman.") Els decibels... l'han ajudat a distreure's i a superar una de les temptacions més perilloses per l'home executat: la set de venjança. (115)

> The man who was executed near the castle is not bored. After a long period of routine, these last years have given him an acoustic renaissance that he did not expect. The nearby stadium has brought him sound experiences as intense as a Rolling Stones concert or a large part of the Olympic Games. (He will never forget the enthusiasm of his gravemates when, cracking a wall of applause, Keith Richards' guitar started to play the first chords of "Honky Tonk Woman.") The decibels... have helped him entertain himself and overcome one of the most dangerous temptations for the executed man: the thirst for vengeance.

Rock music and the Olympic celebrations block the return of the violent past: they keep the dead amused and harmless. This new literary portrait of Montjuïc perfectly conveys the situation of Olympic and post-Olympic Barcelona, one in which former class and political divisions have been, if not erased, at least repressed by the media spectacles and the culture industry that will rebuild Barcelona's contemporary economy. But I will return to Pàmies' short story later. Now, let us briefly look at some of the determinations that intervened in the restructuring of Barcelona's economy after Francoism. Three general factors must be analyzed here: the link between democracy and the free market in Spain; the consolidation of the new stage of capitalism; and the redefinition of space in postmodernity.

When Franco died in 1975, the process known as *la transición* began to establish the bases that transformed Spain into a parliamentary democracy under the reign of Bourbon King Juan Carlos I. Despite numerous street demonstrations and civil pressure for democratic reforms, the transition was not generated by a popular rebellion or a political coup d'état; rather, it remained at all times a process directed by the state. Also, the need to democratize led to the call for elections and the legalization of political parties and worker unions in 1977, but it also entailed a crucial change: the Left overtly abandoned revolutionary principles. Most noticeably, the PSOE held a special convention in 1979 to renounce their Marxist affiliations and embrace the values of social democracy.[9]

In this context, the will to appeal to the largest possible spectrum of voters made political parties adopt a conciliatory agenda. For democracy to be possible, both the autocratic and the revolutionary options needed to be dismantled. A tacit consensus was established determining that all political programs would assume the construction of democracy as their final goal. This points to a central aspect of the Spanish transition. As, again, Salvador Cardús explains, another characteristic of Spain's new memory was that it "had no clearly defined adversary" ("Politics" 25). The others of democracy were not the ex-Francoists, who were an essential part of the democratization process, but rather the "radicals" (25) who opposed the development of democracy. Parliamentary democracy was the self-fulfilling, all-encompassing model that only excluded those who refused to embrace it as the framework for their programs.

Yet the establishment of democratic rule was not a strictly political phenomenon. The real premise of the new model was that political freedom could only emerge within a free market economy. In this transition, the "radicals" were not only those who resisted change or those who demanded to impugn the Francoists; rather, the true others were those who refused to recognize the correlation between democracy and the free market. Therefore, the dismantling of the authoritarian regime and the Left's abandonment of Marxism constituted equivalent gestures from the opposite sides of the ideological spectrum.[10]

In order to understand better the nature of this link, we must examine the particular relationship that the state and the market have established in Western core states since the end of World War II. In this context, "neoliberal market" is a more precise term than "free market" to define this prevalent relationship. Giovanni Arrighi has explained how the neoliberal market, even if it appears to be based on the classic liberal conception of the self-regulating market as an invisible hand, in reality maintains such solid ties to the state that it is anything but a "free" market. Within neoliberalism, the market functions as an instrument "essential to non-totalitarian regulation of inter- and intra-state relations" (266). In Western core states after 1945, Arrighi continues,

> the visible hand of the state was assigned crucial tasks not only in creating and reproducing the global, regional, and national institutional arrangements that were necessary for the operation of a market economy. It was also attributed the role of setting developmental objectives and of supplementing, regulating, or even partially displacing market mechanisms in the pursuit of such objectives. (266)

In this sense, two main political and economic processes have taken place after World War II: first, the construction, or rather the intensification, of a world market economy through international organizational forms (NATO, the EU, the Marshall Plan, etc); and, second, the application of direct investment, in place of classic trade and territorial expansion, as the mechanism to compete and exploit at the transnational level. States no longer pursue territorial expansion to secure and enlarge their national markets, as happened during the imperial stage of capitalism. Instead, they focus on the regulation and management of the investments of multinational companies. To obtain wealth within the neoliberal market, states do not need to promote the development of a strong national industry; above all, they must work on creating the conditions to attract investments from transnational capital. The development of national industries is at all times dependent on the existence of multinational investments. At the same time, free competition is no longer the most important value that states need to ensure; on the contrary, the function of neoliberal statalism consists in reducing the autonomy of the market as conceived by classic liberalism. Corporations, the dominant organizational structure of production, do not aim to compete among themselves; their goal is rather to merge and form conglomerates to be able to manage large-scale production at the international level. Thus, states must assist corporations in realizing these goals in order to promote growth in their territories.

In Spain, the adoption of neoliberalism took place in a definitive way in the 1980s under the socialist government of Felipe González and the PSOE party. González's socialism, once disentangled from Marxist doctrine, pursued a "third way" that could balance capitalist development and social redistribution. The term "third way," theorized by Anthony Giddens, came later to characterize Tony Blair's politics in England during the 1990s. But PSOE's politics of the 1980s presented in substance the same type of neoliberal policies with a social democratic touch.[11] Coinciding with Arrighi's definition of neoliberal statalism, James Petras identifies five main points of the PSOE's state-directed policies:

> [PSOE's economic] restructuring was aimed at fitting Spain into the international division of labor as (1) a banking and financial center; (2) a low-cost resort center; (3) a supplier of docile labor for the subsidiaries of multinational capital; (4) a center for real estate and speculative capital; and (5) a means of deepening Spain's participation in such European and American military alliances as NATO. (121)

The new stabilized democracy, PSOE's neoliberal politics, and the admission of Spain into NATO and into the European Economic Community in 1986, stimulated an unprecedented economic growth. This growth fortified the state politics that had promoted it and reinforced the assumption that modernization necessarily required the overcoming of past ideological divisions. The economic progress throughout the 1980s was accompanied by a widespread euphoria sponsored, in turn, by the state itself. This progress culminated in 1992 when economic growth, state intervention, and collective euphoria became one and the same thing with the organization of three international events: the Barcelona Olympic Games, the Universal Exhibition in Sevilla, and the designation of Madrid as the Cultural Capital of Europe.[12]

While the transition from Francoism to democracy seemingly erased former class divisions, we must ask whether this process of erasure had not already begun in the 1960s, when Spain entered the *desarrollismo* years of euphoric consumerism and became a main tourist destination. Even though social antagonisms were very intense during Franco's dictatorship, they were ultimately articulated around the opposition to the regime, which resulted in the amalgam of workers, leftists, students, and nationalists fighting on the same side. But this political fight might have eclipsed the real change that was taking place in Spain, namely the conversion of the social space into a "postclass" consumer society.

Two processes of "reconciliation" or "erasure" overlapped during the Spanish transition: on the one hand, the most visible political process of reconciliation between ex-Francoists and the anti-Francoist Left; and, on the other hand, the economic, structural process of consolidation of the consumer society that had begun in the 1960s. The transformation of all things and events into commodities gradually traversed the political, social, and cultural spheres. While citizens evidently decided to act as political agents (of the Left or the nationalist struggles) and many cultural manifestations expressed collective hopes (such as the *nova cançó* in Catalonia), these actions took place in a social space more and more dominated by consumerism.[13] As a result, the various social spheres became dedifferentiated and political and cultural manifestations found themselves converted into other consumer options. This does not mean that politics or culture could no longer be significant and transformative in this context. The reality, however, was that the new consumer society, in conjunction with the media industry as one of its central parts, functioned as a structure that equalized the social meaning of all events and experiences.

"Reconciliation" or "erasure" must be understood here as this equalizing effect generated by the economic logic that transforms everything into commodities. In this respect, consumer society is a postclass society – not because social inequalities no longer exist, but because consumerism turns all individuals and social groups into customers. Social and individual differences appear as the result of consumer options or simply become indistinguishable from them. In a dialectical way, "postclass" also refers to the opposite but parallel effect that the phenomenon of mass consumerism has had on the people, namely the homogenization of taste and the elimination of individual differences in mass consumption. The extensive production of the same commodities homogenizes the social space and dilutes class distinctions.

Teresa M. Vilarós describes how the structural transition of Spain during the 1960s involved the development of the tourist industry. The Francoist Ministerio de Información y Turismo, created in 1951 and directed, from 1962 to 1969, by minister Manuel Fraga Iribarne, deployed a technocratic and media-based politics that transformed Spain "from a reactionary anomaly without circulation value into a tourist zone of prime economic interest" ("Lightness" 175). These state politics launched a new tourist industry and produced an image-commodity of Spain based on the country's sun, beaches, bullfighting, *fiesta*, *flamenco*, *sangría*, *paella*, etc. These exotic elements not only attracted masses of Northern European tourists eager to consume them, but also changed the perception that Spaniards had of themselves and of their country: the state promoted a new consumerism among Spaniards consisting in the joyful deployment of their own exoticism. A revealing component of this state ideology was the astute slogan, "Spain is Different," coined by Fraga Iribarne to advertise the country abroad. While Spain's "difference" had until then been associated with its economic backwardness and its regressive political regime, now the regime's technocrats began to use this difference positively in order to advertise the attractive, differential qualities of Spain. The deficiencies and shortcomings of modern Spain, vis-à-vis the industrialized countries of Northern Europe, were rapidly transformed into national virtues: what before had appeared as economic inefficiency, now turned out to be the relaxed lifestyle that made Spaniards enjoy their beaches and their *sangría*; what before could have looked like a country oppressed by a brutal regime, now appeared as the land of a violent and passionate people who expressed their personality through bullfighting, *flamenco*, and, well, the dictatorial regime itself.

Needless to say, this customized image of Spain largely succeeded in selling the country to tourists ready to have a bite of exotic otherness. What is still more interesting is to see how this state operation also succeeded in changing the self-perception of Spaniards and how the tourist industry introduced the rituals of mass consumerism among them. And yet, the insertion of Spain into a fully consumer economy, as Vilarós says, "was not evident until after the death of Franco" (175). In this sense, the critical articulations of the Left, focused on the urgency of the political struggle against the regime, generally failed to account for this structural transformation, or first transition, of the country. While the technocratic policies of the Ministerio de Información y Turismo cannot be considered to be yet fully neoliberal politics, they certainly constitute a precedent of the entrepreneurial role that will characterize state apparatuses in most Western countries from the 1970s on.[14]

This new entrepreneurial role gradually replaced the managerial functions of the Keynesian state. If the latter aimed at creating the conditions for full employment by means of extensive regulatory measures (and also intended, as Antonio Negri has shown, to deactivate the revolutionary threat of the working classes), after the 1970s the new dominant function of the state is to act as an entrepreneurial agent that competes to attract the investments from highly mobile capital.[15] The primary goal of the "managerial revolution," as James Burnham called it in 1941, was to create growth by ensuring that the market employed the maximum quantity of workforce; the neoliberal revolution of the 1970s, by contrast, proposed that the state itself should be a central producer of growth. Despite the free market rhetoric of neoliberalism, the new entrepreneurial functions of the state are part of the centralization of capital needed to operate on a global scale. Neoliberalism has led to the dismantling of Keynes' welfare state but not to the emergence of a more deregulated market; on the contrary, it has constantly pursued the fusion of the state and the market. For this reason, we must understand this change in the function of the state as connected to the structural shift in the development of capitalism: the shift from modernity to postmodernity, from monopoly capitalism to global capitalism, from a production-oriented economy to the consumer society.

The installation of the consumer society in the decades following World War II corresponded to the moment in which industrialized countries began to relocate their manufactures to the Third World. This relocation involved the detachment of capital from the sites of production and, in conjunction with the rapid dominance of the finance industry, ultimately entailed the detachment of capital from production itself. This set of inherently connected transformations inaugurated the third stage of capitalism, which Ernest Mandel defines as late capitalism to distinguish it from industrial or national capitalism and imperial capitalism. Mandel argues that, despite the dismantling of the manufacturing industries and their relocation to other emerging economies, late capitalism must not be interpreted as a post-industrial society. On the contrary,

> [f]ar from representing a 'post-industrial society', late capitalism thus constitutes a *generalized universal industrialization* for the first time in history. Mechanization, standardization, over-specialization and parcellization of labour, which in the past determined only the realm of commodity production in actual industry, now penetrate into all sectors of social life. (387)[16]

The unlimited commodification of all spheres of society is the most central component of late capitalism. This corresponds to the full automatization of the processes of production – the processes of extraction of raw materials as well as the manufacturing of all types of consumer goods. Over-specialization and generalized industrialization requires capital to be highly mobile, to the extent that productivity is less and less determined by territorial differences: "regional or international differences in levels of productivity no longer provide the main source for the realization of surplus-profits. This role is now assumed by such differences between sectors and enterprises..." (192). These sectors and enterprises are represented by the multinational corporation, which results from two dynamics of capital. On the one hand, capital expands internationally by diversifying and over-specializing the processes of production in search of higher surplus-profits, an expansion that, in turn, is made possible by the enormous development of technology and communication. On the other hand, this diversification of production requires larger volumes of capital investment, which causes the centralization of capital in multinational companies.

Since the extraction of surplus-profits initially comes not from territorial differences but from the constant and strategic restructuring of production processes, now territories have a new function: they must attract the production processes of transnational corporations. Given the continuous mobility of these processes, corporations can locate them wherever production generates the largest benefits. For this reason, territories must compete among themselves to attract these processes and the subsequent capital investments. Cities, states, or regions must make themselves attractive to capital in order to bring into their territory those headquarters, manufactures, services, events, tourists, or conventions that can potentially be placed anywhere. David Harvey has famously defined this new spatial work as an "active production of places with special qualities" (*Condition* 295). This production involves two main elements. On the one hand, the rulers of a certain space must invest in image-building, that is, they must highlight and manufacture the peculiar characteristics of the place and advertise them. On the other hand, they can assist multinational companies in making their investments profitable: "Local ruling elites can, for example, implement strategies of local labour control, of skill enhancement, of infrastructural provision, of tax policy, state regulation, and so on, in order to attract development within their particular space" (295).

This production of space involves a commodification of territories. While it is true that, as Mandel explains, territorial differences no longer determine the levels of productivity, it is also true that territories have had to develop and manufacture their own differential qualities in order to restructure themselves as new sites of production. Territorial differences no longer emerge from natural resources or geographical position, as in classic industrial capitalism; instead, these differences are the product of an active fabrication, to the extent that even natural resources and geographical locality must now be developed and advertised so that they function as strategies of territorial differentiation. The attributes that come to define territories are determined by their marketability rather than natural essences or a sense of authenticity. Indeed, by marketing their own special qualities, spaces create a simulacrum of themselves, and their image obliterates all sense of authenticity. Cities, states, or regions are defined by their visual double. As a consequence of being manufactured and sold like any other commodity, spaces become, so to speak, specters of themselves. In this respect, commodification has another inherent consequence for spaces: their entrance to the market as commodities entails their structural dedifferentiation. The development of differential qualities unifies them and turns them into equivalent, exchangeable objects like any other commodity. Their effort to be different ultimately makes all spaces identical. They become what Rem Koolhaas, as I will develop in Chapter Three, calls "generic" spaces (*Small* 1248).

In Spain, this postmodern commodification of spaces was already at work in the 1960s when Franco's Ministerio de Información y Turismo developed the tourist industry and began the process of packaging and selling the image of a country with the "special qualities" of beaches, bullfighting, *fiesta*, etc. Vilarós uses Harvey's terms to define Spain's entrance to postmodernity in the 1960s:

> Se puede afirmar por tanto que a pesar de las tensiones y chirridos que tal movimiento de integración en la nueva economía capitalista global necesariamente produjo al ser generado desde un régimen totalitario parcialmente desmarcado de las estructuras políticas exteriores, España entra de forma clara a partir de los años sesenta, y aun con el lastre de la dictadura, en el proceso competitivo estético-económico-social de producción activa de lugares con cualidades especiales. (*Mono* 79)

> We can thus affirm that, despite the tensions and frictions that the movement of integration into the new global capitalist economy necessarily produced for being generated by a totalitarian regime partially detached from external political structures, in the sixties Spain definitively enters, and despite the weight of the dictatorship, in the aesthetic-economic-social competitive process of active production of places with special qualities.

In this context, Catalonia also began to work to make the region attractive to international tourism. However, Catalonia in the 1960s and 1970s had only one possibility available under the dictatorship: to market herself as another Spanish region with the common characteristics of sun, bullfighting, *fiesta*, *sangría*, etc. Franco's centralizing politics would allow, at most, the display of regional folklore, traditional dresses, and the like. But on no account could regions – and least of all Catalonia – assemble and display special qualities that could dissociate these territories from the official imaginary of a united Spain.

For this reason, the particular image that Barcelona began to produce after the dictatorship had a further aspiration: the aspiration to break away from the homogeneity imposed by Franco's tourist politics. As I analyze further in Chapters Two and Three, the cultural and urban transformation directed by the city hall during the 1980s attempted to launch Barcelona as a singular city that worked, in some significant symbolic ways, to differentiate herself from the rest of Spain and even from the rest of Catalonia. The 1992 Olympics served as an incentive to carry out this deep transformation. In this sense, the Olympic Games perfectly epitomize the relationship between global capital and the spatial restructuring of localities in late capitalism. When cities prepare their candidacy for the Games, they initiate, above all, a process of restructuring of their spaces in order to produce an appealing image of the city. The cities that finally host the Games attract multinational companies that invest in the spatial renovation;

in return, cities obtain good publicity and intensify their processes of image-building, which soon attract more capital in the form of tourists, conventions, companies, study abroad programs, and all types of communication services.

To go back to Sergi Pàmies' short story, the Olympic Games as well as the concert by the Rolling Stones have an intriguing effect on the executed man buried in Montjuïc: the decibels of the events have helped the man overcome his thirst for vengeance. While the Games or the rock band can be read as unmistakable symbols of contemporary free-floating capital, we can find in the executed man one of the main effects that the arrival of global capital has on local spaces. This effect is the obliteration of local histories. In order to be attractive to capital, spaces must be safe and secure and, if possible, the social antagonisms and historical conflicts affecting them must be repressed or directly removed. The scene of the executed man in Pàmies' story reveals how late capitalist Barcelona and its spectacular events have appeased, or at least covered over, some of the haunting specters of the past. Let us now examine one of the principal ideologies that the city hall produced during the 1980s to contribute to the appeasement that would make Olympic Barcelona such an irresistible place.

The City of the People

The chameleonic figure of Juan Antonio Samaranch is highly representative of the new economy of contemporary Spain. In 1967, Samaranch abandoned the management of his family's textile factory, symbol of the industrial past, and pursued his career by combining, in a mixture of domains characteristic of late capitalism, real estate speculation, financial counseling, politics, and sports management. In the late 1960s, he also went from working exclusively at the national level in Barcelona and Madrid to developing international diplomatic relations, which eventually led him to the presidency of the IOC. Throughout the dictatorship, Samaranch searched for political power from the supposedly non-ideological field of sports, except for when, in 1973, he became the president of the Diputación Provincial de Barcelona. During this period as administrator his unpopularity grew incessantly until he had to flee the city. But he soon recuperated his neutral and adaptable position when he returned to the domain of sports, this time as the diplomatic president of the IOC that would help Barcelona obtain the Olympic Games.

Samaranch's performed neutrality is key to understanding how he could make a quite painless transition from being a member of Franco's government to being an international referent for democratic Barcelona. But a structural factor also intervened in this transition. The economic conversion to late capitalism that had begun in the 1960s had blurred former class antagonisms in a way that highly facilitated repositionings like Samaranch's. These reposition-

ings were common among the ex-Francoists, who, in the phenomenon known
as the *cambio de camisa*, quickly became advocates for democratization. Even
though these conversions were political, the structural condition that facilitated this process had an economic basis. The flexible and constantly mobile
nature of capital in late capitalism promotes all sorts of reassemblings of the
individual self. The market logic that has invaded all spheres of social life results
in the constant production of the new and the constant disposal of the old.
The *cambios de camisa* have become an established and even reputable practice.
Changing subject positions and reinventing oneself are not perceived as lack
of integrity but as signs of flexibility and progress. To this effect, Samaranch's
transition was not only possible but also admirable within the new dynamics
of the neoliberal market.

The passage to late capitalism is also crucial to understanding Maragall's
political career. Born in 1941, Maragall belongs to an illustrious bourgeois and
Catalan-speaking family of Barcelona; his grandfather was Joan Maragall, one
of the national poets of Catalonia. Despite his bourgeois origins, he soon got
involved with the leftist and anti-Francoist movements, in particular the Front
Obrer Català. After graduating in economy and law in Barcelona, he studied
urban planning in Paris and sociology in New York. In 1978, he was a Visiting
Lecturer at Johns Hopkins University.[17]

In 1965, Maragall began to work as an economist at Barcelona's city hall
and, in the 1979 municipal elections, he was elected number two on the list
of his party, the Partit dels Socialistes de Catalunya (PSC), the Catalan branch
of González's PSOE. PSC won the elections and mayor Narcís Serra designated
Maragall deputy mayor. In 1982, Serra departed to be named minister of Defense
in Madrid and Maragall replaced him. He remained mayor for the next 15 years,
until 1997, when, after having won the four elections in which he had run, he
resigned to prepare his way to the presidency of the Generalitat.

Donald McNeill explains that, when he studied in New York from 1971 until
1973, "Maragall became increasingly convinced that capitalism was capable of
surviving, and redeveloping, rather than lapsing into crisis. This ran contrary
to the analysis of many of his radical contemporaries, and would cement his
identity as a social democrat" (*Urban Change* 87). In the US, Maragall had the
chance to recognize what his leftist companions in Barcelona, fully focused on
the urgent struggle against the dictatorship, had not seen. He realized that the
real transition that needed to be addressed by the Catalan and the Spanish Left
was not only the path to democracy, but also the structural transition from an
industrial to a consumer society. Maragall understood (or rather decided) that
in this new context a leftist politics would only be possible by cooperating with
the new forces of the multinational market. He became, as McNeill observes, a
social democrat.

Maragall considered that social democracy offered the best compromise between the state and the market to satisfy people's needs. The "people" became the core of his program, a program that he identified with what was later theorized as the "third way." He expressed his affinities with Tony Blair in 1998:

> Blair's approach is the following: either the Left realise that the working class and a good proportion of the middle classes act together to follow a progressive politics, or there is no Left politics. If the middle classes continue to be seduced by multinationals and minimal social intervention, there is no citizenship, there is no progress, there is no democracy, there is no Left. Therefore, the Left to be left has to be centrist, has to position itself in the centre and has to capture the people there... statistically, and make their values the values of the people. ... I don't just agree with that, I practice it. (quoted in McNeill, *Urban Change* 90)

When Maragall, at the end of this statement, says that the Left has to "make their values the values of the people," one does not know in what direction this demand functions: is it the Left that must adopt the values of the people, or the people that must adopt the values of the Left? In fact, the sentence could even be interpreted as a tautology: "their" could also refer to "the people" and, therefore, the sentence would say that the Left has to make the values of the people the values of the people. In any case, these circularities reveal that the most central objective of Maragall's social democracy is to search for a politics that directly meets the real needs of the people.

The social democracy of the "third way" became PSOE and PSC's official doctrine, but Maragall put special emphasis on establishing a close, two-way connection between the political institutions and the citizens. For this reason, he believed that the framework of the city and its urban politics was more adequate than those of the region or the state to create a truly democratic politics. In the context of post-Francoist Barcelona, his political program also represented an effort to leave behind the autocratic practices of the dictatorship and, specifically, of Franco's appointed mayor in Barcelona, José María Porcioles, whose mandate lasted from 1957 to 1973. Porcioles constantly favored the ruling classes through underhanded policies, provided total immunity to real estate speculators, and administered the municipal government with autocratic rule. He represented the large period of Francoist nepotism known as *porciolisme*.[18]

Maragall's program, which he had already described in his investiture speech, "Per una Barcelona olímpica i metropolitana" 'For an Olympic and Metropolitan Barcelona,' consisted of three general projects. First, the local administration was divided into ten urban districts in order to decentralize and bring the municipal government closer to the citizens and their neighborhoods. Second, the city hall initiated a systematic revamping of Barcelona's public spaces and architectural heritage (which I will analyze further in Chapter Three). Finally, the prospect of hosting the Olympic Games sought to implicate the entire city in a collective enterprise. The aim of these three projects was to create a more cohesive city and a more democratic local administration.

The "gent" 'people' became an omnipresent word in Maragall's political rhetoric. As a newly appointed mayor in 1982, Maragall advertised his project for Barcelona with the slogan "Fent la ciutat de la gent" 'Making the city of the people.' Another slogan was "La ciutat és la gent" 'The city is the people,' which Maragall used as a logo for the 1983 elections. He later revealed that "un professor de Boston" 'a professor from Boston' told him that this logo was in fact a quote from Shakespeare (*Refent* 198). Indeed, the Roman plebeians in *Coriolanus* say the original sentence to protest against the election as magistrate of the arrogant and ruthless soldier Coriolanus. Thus, to introduce a parallel here, Maragall's slogan would represent the plebeians' "democratic" claims against the tyrannical Patrician Coriolanus, who, in the contemporary context, would evidently stand for the ghostly figures of Franco and his municipal delegate Porcioles.[19]

In Catalan, the word "gent" has a different connotation than the word "poble." The two meanings are contained in the English "people": "gent" as populace, community or multitude, and "poble" as the national people or *Volk*. As Brad Epps, following Joan Ramon Resina, observes, the political rhetoric employed in contemporary Barcelona relies, not on "la voluntat del poble" 'the will of the people,' but rather on "el que vol la gent" 'what people want' (*Modern Spaces* 192). Thus, the use of the term "gent" strategically avoids the nationalist (and perhaps also revolutionary?) connotations of the word "people," and it denotes a politics that responds to what common people really want.

Two main questions arise when examining the political content of Maragall's project of "the city of the people": one regarding its relationship with Catalan nationalism and the Spanish state, and a second question regarding the determinations of the economic structure over this democratizing project. So, first, was the symbolic content of "the city of the people" closer to the imagined community of the Catalan nation, or was it closer to that of the Spanish state? While Gil de Biedma's poem expressed the desire that some day Barcelona belonged to the *murciano* immigrants, the hegemonic discourse in democratic Barcelona emphasized above all that the city belonged to its citizens. The use of the word "gent" instead of "poble" in all political propaganda had a precise function: to avoid determining which national (Catalan or Spanish) "poble" Maragall's discourse represented. "La ciutat de la gent" provided a denationalized imaginary for the city, and both autochthonous Catalans and Spanish immigrants became primarily citizens of Barcelona. Given that the PSC has remained the most voted party in the city since the arrival of democracy, this integration of the two communities has seemed to satisfy most Barcelonans. In fact, Maragall's project ultimately consisted of extending these integrative city politics to the whole context of Catalonia. As he declares in *Refent Barcelona*: "Ens cal una Catalunya urbana, que sigui una síntesi de particularitats amb una identitat nacional basada en la diversitat" 'We need an urban Catalonia that constitutes a synthesis of particularities with a national identity based on diversity' (128).

Catalan politics had aimed to suture the gap between autochthonous Catalans and Spanish immigrants since the beginning of democracy. When Josep Tarradellas, the president of the Generalitat in exile, returned to Barcelona in 1977, he opened his first official speech with the famous words: "Ciutadans de Catalunya, ja sóc aquí!" 'Citizens of Catalonia, I am here!' His speech was addressed to the citizens of Catalonia instead of the Catalans in order to avoid excluding the mostly Spanish-speaking immigrant population.[20] Also, Jordi Pujol, the first elected president of the Generalitat de Catalunya, had coined a non-ethnic definition Catalan-ness: "Català és tot home que viu i treballa a Catalunya" 'Everyone who lives and works in Catalonia is Catalan' (*Immigració* 42).

However, Pujol and his conservative nationalist party Convergència i Unió (CiU) concentrated their policies on strengthening the public presence of the Catalan language at all levels. In opposition to Maragall's project of urbanizing Catalonia, Pujol wanted to "Catalanize" Barcelona and transform it primarily into the capital of the Catalan nation. CiU ruled the autonomous government of the Generalitat during the 1980s and 1990s and their focus on the revival of the Catalan language obeyed two main reasons. First, they claimed that the democratization process required the normalization of the minority languages and cultures that had been violently repressed by Franco's dictatorship. Second, they considered that the Spanish-speaking immigrant population should fully embrace Catalan because this would facilitate their integration into Catalan society.[21]

Maragall's and Pujol's different integrative politics – one that emphasized the denationalized, urban notion of citizen, and the other based on a flexible but rooted sentiment of Catalan-ness – were antagonistic only up to a certain point. Both pursued the cohesion of a society that had been linguistically and socially split since the 1960s, and, at the same time, in bigger or smaller proportions, both aimed to strengthen the presence of Catalan culture in the public sphere. The Spanish-speaking population did not always welcome this promotion, which was often perceived as an imposition of Catalan nationalism. Also, given that these politics resisted in one way or another the Madrid-centered Spanish state, Spanish immigrants tended to interpret Catalanism as a rejection of their ties with their native regions.

Pujol's Catalanist policies were probably not as effective as he proclaimed; in the same way, Maragall probably never embraced diversity as much as he advertised it. Pujol had in fact coined a previous definition of Catalan-ness different from the one quoted above. During his clandestine activism against Franco in the 1960s, he promulgated that "Català és tot home que viu i que treballa a Catalunya i que en vol ser" 'Everyone who lives and works in Catalonia, and is willing to become Catalan, is Catalan.'[22] Even if the definition does not specify how to prove one's willingness to become Catalan, it is implicit that one proves his or her willingness by speaking the language. Yet, the shortened version of the definition ("Everyone who lives and works in Catalonia is Catalan") became dominant. A good portion of Spanish speakers embraced this short version so that they could be considered Catalans while maintaining Spanish as their default language. Political parties, including CiU, were concerned that too much emphasis on language could alienate Spanish-speaking voters and they tended to remain ambiguous regarding the linguistic question; thus, the shortened definition of Catalan-ness also worked well for them. Yet, how should we interpret this ambiguity, especially in relation to Pujol's politics of gradual Catalanization? Was the omission of "the willingness to become Catalan" the sign that *pujolisme* began to consider Catalan and Spanish equally "proper" to Catalonia, or was the removed appendix a ghostly inscription within this process of Catalanization?

Teresa M. Vilarós argues that CiU's politics contain a neoliberal ideology of assimilation that aims to silence the Spanish immigrant or *xarnego*. The derogatory term *xarnego* was used in Catalonia in the 1960s and 1970s to designate Spanish newcomers. As Vilarós argues, the *xarnego* represents a historical figure of Catalonia's industrial past. This term virtually disappeared in the 1980s as the Catalan nationalist politics of assimilation began to operate. But, as Vilarós observes regarding literary and biographical accounts of *xarnegos*, "[g]hostly specters… vaguely reminiscent of the old *xavas* [or *murcianos*] of Biedma, of [Juan] Marsé's 'lumpen proletariats,' and of [Francesc] Candel's *xarnegos*, kept and keep haunting the deterritorialized scenery of the post-industrial age" ("Passing" 239).

However, the obliteration of the figure of the *xarnego* cannot be attributed only to the politics of assimilation of CiU's conservative nationalism. A more structural reason intervened in this elimination, and it is precisely in Maragall's project of the "city of the people" where we might get a glimpse of it. Given the denationalized frame of "the city of the people," Maragall's call to diversity detached the citizens of Barcelona from collective and national historical narratives. "The city of the people" posited an urban community disengaged from national paradigms. Its diversity, rather than represent a variety of identities and cultures, emptied out the historical content of the very identities that composed it. The diversity of the "gent" sought to replace the paradigm of the national community and, in this context, the term *xarnego*, as a linguistic trace of class and national struggles, had to be eliminated. *Xarnego* was the symptomatic and suppressed element that revealed that "the city of the people" had been built upon a nationally split city and had covered up a long historical conflict between two imagined communities.

The *xarnego* has not only emerged as a ghostly specter but has also been exploited as a full ideological device. As Josep-Anton Fernàndez notices, the distinction between *xarnegos* and Catalans has given way to new equivalents: "quillos" versus "catalufos," or "catalans" versus "catalans catalans." But the reproduction of this ethnic distinction is ultimately a sign, as Fernàndez observes, of "la reificació de la immigració com a posició subjectiva i de l'immigrant com a categoria ontològica i no com a estat transitori (és a dir, la immigració és una cosa que s'és, no una cosa que s'ha fet)" 'the reification of immigration as a subject position and of the immigrant as an ontological category and not as a transitory state (that is, immigration is something that one is, not something that one did)' (*Malestar* 260).

This reification of the *xarnego*-immigrant reflects in turn a further ideological short circuit. The transformation of the immigrant into a subjective condition serves two contrary purposes. On the one hand, underneath its civic postulates, Catalanism often contains an ethnic subtext that perceives the newcomer as a permanent immigrant. While for Catalanism the loyalty to the language is the central identity mark, the ethnic component (determined by the person's last name) is also often assumed as a sign of indubitable allegiance to the community. This discourse compels the immigrant (or, rather, the person with no "Catalan" last name) to provide constant evidence of her Catalanism (essentially by adopting the language at all times), whereas the Catalan-ness of the autochthonous Catalan is already certified and authenticated. But, on the other hand, a widespread state discourse also regards the *xarnego* (or the "quillo" or simply the "català") as an ethnic figure and not as the product of a particular act of immigration. But the goal here is to present the move of Spaniards to Catalonia not as an act of immigration, which would only occur between different states, but as part of the social dynamic of the same national collective. By considering the *xarnego* a social type, this state discourse enforces the view that Catalonia is part of the Spanish national body and compels the *xarnego*-immigrant to remain attached to her origin and language. Thus, as a result of the transformation of immigration into a subject position, Catalanism and the ideological apparatuses of the state reinforce their antagonism.

"The city of the people," which may also be defined, in opposition to CiU's ideology of assimilation, as the ideology of non-assimilation, aimed to cover up this major antagonism. Or perhaps we should say that Maragall's "postnationalist" discourse hoped to reconcile the two nationalisms of this antagonism. Indeed, as Eduard Company and Josep Maria Pascual have shown, Maragall has often employed a set of metaphors related to the family to promote this reconciliation. He said that Catalonia should have a fraternal bond with Spain; that Spain should be Catalonia's new daughter; or that Catalonia and Spain constitute a married couple (37–8).

Predictably, however, the discourse that proposed the possibility of surmounting this antagonism ended up favoring one of the two sides. Company and Pascual interpret Maragall's conciliatory position as sheer Spanish nationalism, but perhaps the most essential feature of Maragall's postnationalist ideology is not the recognition of Spain as the primary nation, but rather the wish to dismantle the option of Catalan separatism. In other words, Maragall's conception of Spain and Catalonia as compatible entities does not oppose Catalanism but rather opposes the possibility that the latter may turn into separatism, a possibility that Pujol also rejected at all times.

Maragall's postnationalism should not only be interpreted in political and ideological terms, but also as part of the obliteration of local conflict promoted by the logic of global capitalism. As we pointed out, the constant mobility of capital, the disconnection between production and territory, and the full commodification of the social space, entail the gradual loss of the sense of historicity and collective history. Global capitalism functions like the Rolling Stones in Pàmies' story: their international, free-floating music effaces local narratives and appeases the ghosts of the past. Thus, the "identity based on diversity" promoted by PSC (as well as the reconfigured Catalan identity of CiU's discourse, in which Catalan language, as a sign of historical and national conflict, also became a ghostly inscription) were also a product of the dehistoricizing effects of late capitalism.

This brings us to the second question regarding the link between "the city of the people" and the economic structure. A process simultaneous to the building of the democratic city of the people took place in Barcelona: the influx of global capital and the subsequent transformation of many urban spaces and economic actors. The entrance of multinational companies, the construction of communication infrastructure, the investments in image-building, and the enormous proliferation of service centers such as hotels, agencies, restaurants, franchises, retail stores, chains, megastores, and strip clubs, ran parallel to the political enterprise of "the city of the people." This conjuncture entailed a new relationship between the municipal government and the city's economy.

Regarding the function of public administrations in the global economy, Mandel explains how the state increases economic planning and socialization of costs to cope with three main demands of late capitalism: the shortening of the turnover time of fixed capital, the acceleration of technological innovation, and the increase in the cost of major projects of capital accumulation (483). But the state conceals its own management of capitalist development under the ideology of alliance and collaboration with the people:

> Socially, it [state management] involves a permanent effort to avert the growing crisis of capitalist relations of production by a systematic attack on proletarian class consciousness. The State thus deploys a huge machinery of ideological manipulation to 'integrate' the worker into late capitalist society as a consumer, 'social partner' or 'citizen'... (485)

State intervention is thus deployed as a caring politics for the citizens. The state aims at fully integrating the citizens into a participatory society, but this participation is the product of an ideological, phantasmatic effect produced by the state regulation of capitalism in its third stage.

"The city of the people" perfectly epitomized this new function of politics in consumer society. Even if Maragall was the mayor that fully implemented the agenda of "the city of the people," mayor Narcís Serra had already set its bases. When Serra became mayor in 1979, he declared that his office had four main objectives: "la humanización de la ciudad; la reforma democrática de la administración y de la Hacienda; la ordenación de la región metropolitana; y la descentralización del poder municipal y la participación ciudadana" 'the humanization of the city; the democratic reform of the administration and its treasury department; the planning of the metropolitan region; and the decentralization of municipal power and popular participation' (quoted in Subirós, *Vol fletxa* 33). This emphasis on popular participation, the humanized city, and the real needs of the people, attuned politics to the ongoing demand for democratization; but it was also a way of reducing politics to the management of the immediate needs of the citizens (transportation, urban equipments, social services, restoration works) and excluding more "abstract" and less "real" issues (such as, well, the possibility of implementing policies that could be radical or anticapitalist in any way).

The implicit objective of these managerial politics was to dismantle possible revolutionary threats. This postpolitical scene shut down the revolutionary possibilities that the democratizing process could have opened. The political was simply the regulation of the present state of affairs. To use Jacques Rancière's term, Barcelona's local politics were an exemplary case of "consensual postdemocracy."[23] But, while Rancière emphasizes the political ground of this contemporary conjuncture, we must also realize, following Mandel, that postpolitics are structurally determined by the economic logic of late capitalism, which attacks class consciousness by celebrating the integration of the citizen into the state.

In this respect, the type of postpolitics that we encounter in Olympic Barcelona may be understood as an attempt to blend Keynesian managerialism and neoliberal entrepreneurialism. The managerial task of fulfilling people's needs, and the enterprise of transforming the city to attract global capital, became an indissoluble mixture. This fusion of the two tasks was key to achieving a hegemonic consensus regarding the urban renewal of the city. Managerialism on behalf of democratization, and entrepreneurialism on behalf of economic growth, composed the successful formula by which the city hall integrated Barcelonans into its particular form of consensual postpolitics.

In Olympic Barcelona, the blending of public politics and capitalist interests took place in multiple but concrete ways. The initial idea of hosting the Games was provided by Samaranch to mayor Narcís Serra and, therefore, since the beginning the process of municipal democratization went together with the preparation of the Olympic candidacy. The Olympic project, as well as "the city of the people," were possible thanks to the previous reconciliation between the mostly Francoist ruling classes and the new Left embodied in the figures of Samaranch and Serra, respectively. This political reconciliation, in turn, must also be understood in relation to the convergence of private economic interests and public administrations within late capitalism.

In *Barcelona, cap a on vas?*, Manuel Vázquez Montalbán and Eduardo Moreno explain that, when PSC won the 1979 municipal elections and took over Barcelona's city hall, many builders and speculators were scared (58). They were afraid that they would have to account for all the cheap, poor-serviced construction that they had promoted since the 1960s. The closing of factories and the loss of manufacturing jobs during the 1970s, as well as the deteriorating living conditions produced by this cheap construction, marked the beginning of a period of unrest and protest among the working classes. Once democracy had arrived, developers and factory owners feared that a socialist party ruling the city hall would defend the interests of the workers. The last time a leftist party had been in power was during the Republic, when efforts of collectivization and large expropriations took place. The ghosts of these revolutionary actions were very present during the transition to democracy. But, as Vázquez Montalbán and Moreno observe, the ruling classes soon realized that the political change and the postmodern model for Barcelona was going to benefit their interests more than ever (62–3).

Ironically, with the notorious exception of Samaranch, the politicians of the new Left had to struggle to convince the ruling classes to invest in the urban transformation that would provide them so many profits. The bourgeois classes had prospered during decades of industrial production, and the city hall's task of "fent la ciutat de la gent" or the prospect of investing in image-building did not captivate their industrial mindset. Why would the creation of public parks or the restoration of Antoni Gaudí's buildings be profitable for them? In this context, a concrete project was needed to convince everybody of the possibilities of the new economy and to incorporate private capital into the general transformation of Barcelona. This project was, of course, the Olympic Games, which, again, was not originally devised by the new Left, but by "revamped" ex-Francoist Juan Antonio Samaranch.

At this point, other important figures in Barcelona undertook acts of conversion less conspicuous than Samaranch's, but equally strategic. Builder Josep Maria Figueras, who had promoted many degraded complexes for immigrants during the 1960s (with the support of the Banco Catalán de Desarrollo, of which Samaranch was an executive member,) became the president of one of the city's most dynamic commercial fairs, the Fira de Barcelona. He was also the president of the Cambra Oficial de Comerç, Indústria i Navegació de Barcelona and of the foundation Barcelona Promoció, which certainly did not promote the areas that Figueras had built 20 years before. Román Sanahuja, a builder too, undertook in 1986 the creation of one of the main shopping centers – L'Illa Diagonal, designed by Rafael Moneo and Manuel de Solà-Morales – included in the urban renewal of the city. Josep Lluís Núñez, another prominent builder, became the president of Futbol Club Barcelona. From the Left, members of the Communist Partit Socialista Unificat de Catalunya (PSUC) soon recycled themselves as less radical figures. Famous cases were those of Josep Miquel Abad, who became the president of the Comitè Organitzador Olímpic de Barcelona (COOB' 92), and Jordi Borja, who was one of Maragall's assessors in local urbanism.[24]

The Olympic Games, the city fair, a shopping center, a soccer club, or being a consultant for the city hall, are economic activities neither completely private nor entirely public. These are representative individual cases that reveal how the transition from a national-industrial to a late capitalist economy dissolved the distinction between private and public interests. The production of textiles or automobiles no longer dominated Barcelona's industry. Now the major commodity that the city began to produce was the city itself: its image, its spaces, its history. This change blurred the difference between public space – comprising, in its largest sense, streets, squares, civic institutions, historical monuments, etc – and private capital. While public spaces and institutions had become part of the city's active production of special qualities, private capitalists, in turn, no longer properly owned the means of production. Samaranch, Figueras, and Núñez did not own the IOC, the Fira de Barcelona, or the Barça club. Nobody fully owns these corporations; but neither are they genuinely public institutions. Samaranch was the most extreme example of this blurring between public interest and private profits: he was never paid a salary as president of the IOC, but the organization covered the entirety of his expenses (housing, travel, health care, clothes, and food).

This dissolution of the public and the private was evidently not a specific phenomenon of Barcelona. The economic logic that determines that territories must compete to attract global capital entails the fusion of the two spheres. This fusion results from the confluence of public agents that work to make their locality attractive and corporations that decide to invest in a specific place. Simultaneously, these dynamics of late capitalism have another key consequence: the local ruling classes are no longer exclusively local. In Barcelona, multinational capital began to dominate the local economy in the 1980s. While, during late Francoism, the state had established that foreign investments could represent up to a maximum of 50% of Spanish companies, when this limitation was lifted in 1977 foreign capital began to enter massively into Spain. Or, rather, as Francesc Cabana reveals, foreign capital had already controlled big fractions of Catalan and Spanish companies since the late 1950s, but this reality had been concealed by special agreements among stock holders. Thus, in post-Francoism, the massive selling of Spanish companies to foreign investors was not a new phenomenon but rather the juridical recognition of the economy's real organization.[25]

In Barcelona and in Catalonia, a large amount of companies became part of multinational corporations. Cabana gives a detailed account of these movements of capital. These were some notorious cases: Nissan bought 80% of Motor Ibérica in 1982; Volkswagen acquired 51% of Seat in 1986 and 99.9% in 1990; Japanese companies in electronics – such as Sanyo, Sharp, and Sony – absorbed the previous manufacturers in the early 1980s; the French corporation SBN acquired the water company Font Vella; Carrefour supermarkets arrived in 1976 and have continued to expand until the present; etc.[26]

In this context, the Olympic Games played a central role in the globalization of Barcelona's economy. The very project of the Games came from the multinational institution of the International Olympic Committee, based in Lausanne, Switzerland; the most visible skyscraper built during the Olympic years, the Hotel Arts, belonged to Texan promoter G. Ware Travelstead; Florentino Pérez's Madrid-based construction company built many of the Olympic facilities; NBC's investments in the broadcasting of the Games resulted in the development of the technological infrastructure of Barcelona and the subsequent process of image-building; etc. Finally, another key component of the city's globalized economy corresponded to the establishment of multinational chains. Emblematically, the first McDonald's opened in Barcelona in 1981. After McDonald's, many other chains opened their local "embassies": Burger King, Pizza Hut, Kentucky Fried Chicken, Planet Hollywood, Fashion Café, Virgin Music, Hard Rock Café, the Body Shop, etc.[27]

Saskia Sassen, in her analysis of the effects of the global economy on cities, observes that "the denationalizing of urban space and the formation of new claims by transactional actors and involving contestation, raise the question – whose city is it?" (*Globalization* XX). The presence of global businesses represents the end of the traditional exclusive ownership of Barcelona by its local rulers. Thus, the question "To whom does the city really belong?" becomes unanswerable. Or, at most, the question can only be answered by tracing the networks of private capital of multinational companies, whose capital, nevertheless, is not entirely private, as public spaces, historic monuments, or photographic images of the city also function as assets with exchange value. In Barcelona, this (im) material indetermination of capital finds a superstructural correspondence in the denationalized political discourse of "the city of the people." The multicultural and undefined "city of the people" is the ideological result of this diffusion of global capital. In this respect, perhaps the correct answer to Sassen's question is that the city ultimately belongs to the spectral category of "la gent."

The Ghosts of the Universal and International Exhibitions

Let us now explore other spectral phenomena of Olympic Barcelona through one of the most celebrated literary portraits of the city: Eduardo Mendoza's *La ciudad de los prodigios*. Mendoza published his novel in 1986, the same year in which the International Olympic Committee chose Barcelona to host the 1992 Games. Although written when the city hall undertook the comprehensive urban renewal that would make Barcelona an appealing candidate for the Olympics, the novel does not refer to this contemporary moment. Instead, Mendoza's novel is set in the period between the Universal Exhibition of 1888 and the International Exhibition of 1929.

La ciudad de los prodigios fictionalizes the muddy world made of speculation, corruption and crime that surrounded the Exhibitions. The novel tells the story of Onofre Bouvila, a teenager who leaves his hometown in the Catalan Pyrenees for Barcelona because he is attracted by the work opportunities generated by the first Exhibition and who, during the inauguration of the second Exhibition, leaves the city having become its richest man. During this trajectory, Bouvila progresses from distributing anarchist pamphlets and being involved in petty gangsterism, to being a true mafioso, real estate speculator, arms dealer, and film producer. Thus, despite his economic progress, the nature of his businesses requires him to maintain a close and predatory relationship with the city's underworld.

Mendoza portrays throughout *La ciudad de los prodigios* the contrast between the happy image that the city depicts to the world in both Exhibitions, and the corruption and social divisions hidden underneath these events. Mendoza tells us the illustrative case of a construction worker who died while building a pavilion in 1888 and whose body, for lack of time, was buried under it – a case that "no salió a la luz pública y los visitantes de la Exposición nunca supieron que bajo sus pies había un cadáver" 'was kept secret, and visitors to the fair never suspected there was a body under their feet' (91; Molloy 95). At the same time, Mendoza describes the deplorable living conditions of the (both Catalan and Spanish) immigrants that arrived in Barcelona to build the infrastructure of the second Exhibition: "Sobre este entramado de agonía, depauperación y rencor Barcelona levantaba la Exposición que había de sorprender el mundo" 'Upon this foundation of misery, bitterness, and humiliation, Barcelona was building the fair that was to astonish the world' (357; Molloy 380). In fact, the evolution of Bouvila, from the poor underworld to a position of power and wealth, corresponds to the city's own economic dynamic in the sense that the "production" of the city begins with the work of the exploited immigrant population and ends with the opulent spectacle of the Exhibitions. Thus, if during the Exhibitions the local authorities "se habían comprometido a limpiar la ciudad de indeseables" '[were prepared] to weed out all Barcelona's undesirables' (104; Molloy 110), Mendoza's novel does the opposite: it brings back the proletariat and the rabble that not only lived in the same city where the Exhibitions were held, but also provided the workforce and illegal means that made them possible.

Mendoza portrays another main element of the process of production of Barcelona and its Exhibitions, namely the conflictive relationship with the Spanish state. The local authorities conceived and managed the first Exhibition, whereas, in 1929, dictator Primo de Rivera organized the Exhibition for the megalomaniac propaganda of his regime. But Mendoza shows how, in both cases, the alliance between Barcelona and the Madrid-centered state remained distrustful and hostile. According to Bouvila, the root of this permanent conflict was that the Spanish government dealt with Catalonia's internal problems "como si se tratara de otro problema colonial: enviaba al principado militares trogloditas que sólo conocían el lenguaje de las bayonetas y que pretendían imponer la paz pasando por las armas a media humanidad" 'as if Catalonia were just another colony. It dispatched military troglodytes who knew only the language of the bayonet and whose idea of imposing peace was putting half of mankind to the slaughter' (163; Molloy 173).[28]

At the end of the novel, Bouvila, tired of his life, family and businesses, flees the city with his lover María Belltall in a blimp conceived and built especially for them. They escape at the precise moment when King Alfonso XIII and dictator Primo de Rivera are at the hill of Montjuïc inaugurating the 1929 Exhibition. To the amazement of the authorities and the crowds that attended the inauguration, Bouvila's blimp takes off from one of the pavilions. The people recognize Bouvila, who, from above, feels omnipotent, looks over the entire city, applauds the King, and yells contemptuously at the dictator: "¡Hala, que te frían un paraguas, borracho!" 'Go jump in the lake, you old drunkard!' (391; Molloy 414). Finally, the blimp keeps moving until it crashes into the Mediterranean. Although, apparently, Bouvila commits suicide, or dies in a predictable accident, a rumor spreads through the city claiming that the accident was simulated and that now he and his lover live somewhere remote. Whichever the case may be, Mendoza emphasizes that, in Bouvila's escape, "se realizaban los sueños de todos, por su mediación se cumplía una venganza colectiva" 'in him the dreams of every man were realized, in him a collective revenge was achieved' (390; Molloy 413). But, who is this collective that Bouvila symbolizes? And, against what are they taking revenge?

Joan Ramon Resina understands this culminating scene as the moment in which Bouvila signs a Faustian pact with Primo de Rivera's dictatorship. Money has made it possible for him to break away from the historical conjuncture of the dictatorship and also realize his desire of escaping with his lover Belltall, whose last name means "beautiful cut," with obvious sexual connotations. Resina interprets Bouvila's pact as a symbol of Barcelona's bourgeois class: "The historical event (or series of events) that the concept of the Faustian pact alludes to is the Catalan bourgeoisie's betrayal of the revolutionary impulse of Catalan nationalism in exchange for the Madrid government's guarantee of bourgeois class domination" ("Money" 954).

The bourgeoisie faced a dilemma: should they remain faithful to the Catalan national project, or should they support a dictatorship that opposed Catalanism but also defended their class interests and repressed social struggle? They ended up acquiescing in the dictatorship, but this outcome was not particularly advantageous, as Primo de Rivera dismantled Catalonia's political institutions (especially the Mancomunitat de Catalunya, founded in 1914 to enhance the country's material and cultural infrastructures) and implemented a fierce state repression against Catalan culture. The bourgeoisie's ultimate wish might have been to elude these defeating historical circumstances and avoid this tragic dilemma altogether. According to Resina, this is what Bouvila, in his heroic trajectory, could accomplish, as the Faustian pact that he could sign with the dictatorship, thanks to his economic power, allowed him to escape from turbulent Barcelona.

Resina explains how Bouvila embodies the figure that fulfills the collective desire of plenitude reachable through, and also posited by, economic progress. Thus, since Bouvila succeeds in escaping this tragic historical dilemma, he accomplishes a collective vengeance of the Catalan people against the dictatorship. Nevertheless, there is also another possible interpretation that complements Resina's insightful reading. That is, what if Bouvila's trajectory from the city's underworld to the city's sky, which lifts him above the historical conditions that are constricting the Catalan bourgeoisie, represents a vengeance of the lower classes affected by the repression exercised over class struggle by the dictatorship, but also by this bourgeoisie? Here, the collective vengeance would consist of a class vengeance directed against the ruling classes, namely the Catalan bourgeoisie and the Spanish dictatorial state. Mendoza, however, leaves this point undetermined. He avoids turning Bouvila into a symbol of class struggle, although he does not eliminate this possibility either. Mendoza presents Bouvila as an exemplary and successful specimen of the "raza eminentemente mercantil" 'eminently mercantile breed' (185; Molloy 197) of Barcelonans. But, by the same token, Bouvila's success can be interpreted as the vengeance of the lower classes against the rulers of this mercantile people and by means of their own mercantile methods and schemes – an undecided point, to which I will return later.

The conflict between Barcelona and the Spanish state, and the distance between the official image of the city in the Universal and International Exhibitions and its real historical struggles, anticipate the similar historical oppositions that will preside over the contemporary Olympic city. In 1986, Mendoza's novel throws the specters of past struggles over the euphoric Olympic discourses that the city hall had already put to work since the early 1980s. The novel shows how the collective euphoria and social consensus generated by the city hall and Barcelona's ruling classes to pave the way for a successful candidacy for the Olympic Games might be replicating the same dynamics of the Exhibitions. By recalling the historical situation of these past events, *La ciudad de los prodigios* contests the new hegemonic narratives of contemporary Barcelona, namely Maragall's postpolitical call for a "city of the people" and Pujol's nationalist reconstruction of Catalonia, which assumes Barcelona as the capital of a nation without a state. Specifically, the novel confronts the new Barcelona with the fact that the city would have never known historical splendor without two key historical processes: the exploitation of the immigrant underclass and the Faustian pact with the Spanish state. In the pre-Olympic 1980s, these processes were equally crucial for Barcelona. They corresponded, on the one hand, to the Spanish immigration that had arrived in Catalonia in the 1960s and 1970s and, on the other hand, to the alliance between the PSC and Felipe González's PSOE. Along with this, Mendoza reveals through the precedents of the Exhibitions how the production of the image of a neat and well-designed Barcelona ready to host the Olympic Games entails the existence of an underworld made of real estate speculation, political corruption, and repressed class struggle. When the Olympic project was just starting to become reality, *La ciudad de los prodigios* aimed to haunt the preparation for the Games with the specter of this underworld.

Now, my question is: how could a novel so critical of contemporary Barcelona become an immediate bestseller that in fact contributed to promote the city? Was its confrontation with official politics eclipsed, or even neutralized, by its success?

Many commentators have invariably interpreted *La ciudad de los prodigios* as a new version of *picaresca* literature, or "neopicaresca," as Herráez calls it (65),

with Bouvila as a modern *Lazarillo*. Some of them have also read it as a historical novel related to Pérez Galdós' *Episodios nacionales* (Saval 39–45), as a *bildüng-
sroman* (Giménez Micó 132–9), or as a parody of detective fiction (Knutson
65–92). Therefore, most of the scholarship on *La ciudad de los prodigios* has been
devoted to searching, in an ahistorical fashion, for genre affiliations and literary
precedents that inscribe it in a national Spanish canon.

Mendoza's novel, however, has been incorporated into another canon – what
we could call the (Anglo-American) tourist canon of Barcelona's fiction, as "built"
by the various guidebooks on the city. The guidebook *Lonely Planet* recommends
"top five books" to understand Barcelona: Mendoza's *La ciudad de los prodigios*
and *La verdad sobre el caso Savolta*; George Orwell's *Homage to Catalonia*; Carlos
Ruiz Zafón's *La sombra del viento*; and Mercè Rodoreda's *La Plaça del Diamant*
(Simonis 29–30). The *Rough Guide to Barcelona* also recommends *La ciudad de los
prodigios*, or rather *The City of Marvels*, together with other books: Manuel Vázquez
Montalbán's Carvalho detective novels, Colm Toibín's *The South*, John Bryson's
To the Death, Amic, etc (Brown 273). The Australian *AA KeyGuide* also recommends
Mendoza, along with Javier Cercas' *Soldados de Salamina*, Colm Toibín's *Homage to
Barcelona*, or John Richardson's *A Life of Picasso* (45). So, *The City of Marvels* is the
only book that is recommended in all guides: in this tourist canon, it is the book
that comes closer to what would be the great novel of Barcelona.[29]

But let us now go back to Sergi Pàmies' short story, ironically titled "La gran
novel·la sobre Barcelona," which is part of a collection from 1996, eponymously
titled *La gran novel·la sobre Barcelona*. Most of the stories of the book depict
lonesome couples and domestic troubles with no allusions to Barcelona, and
only "La gran novel·la sobre Barcelona" actually refers to the concrete spaces of
the city. These references, however, are never explicit. The story describes Barcelona's spaces with generic terms such as the square, the castle, the Roman wall,
or the monument, with no further specifications.

Pàmies' story begins, like Mendoza's novel, with a quick panoramic view of
Barcelona. Then it mentions the animals inhabiting the city, mostly pigeons,
dogs, and rats. After this, it lists the different regimes that have ruled the city:
the Romans, the Visigoths, the Muslims, the Frankish counts, the various Kings.
It recalls how, when the city was bombed during the Civil War, couples were
killed in bed because, when the sirens went off, they decided to keep making
love instead of running to the bunkers. A divorced father spends Sunday with
his son playing at the park and watching a movie. An old woman walks up to
the castle on top of the mountain to contemplate the place where her husband
was executed 50 years before and buried in a common grave in the nearby
cemetery. As I quoted above, a concert by the Stones and the Olympic Games
have entertained the murdered man and have helped him forget past crimes.

To understand the ultimate implications of Pàmies' story we must look at two of its formal features. First, the pace of the narration is strikingly fast. This allows Pàmies to jump quickly from one episode to another without developing them in a "realistic" manner. Second, the verbs of the story are exclusively in the present tense, which produces the effect of blurring any distance or substantial difference between past and present. Through these formal features, the story presents a series of situations emptied of their historical content. The habits of domestic pets are equalized with the killing of Republican prisoners, or going to the movies seems as significant and at the same time as inconsequential as the mourning of a widow. Correspondingly, the spaces in which these situations take place become dedifferentiated: the castle or other historical buildings are depicted as spaces as generic and flat as movie theaters or fast-food chains.

Pàmies' story is evidently not the great novel of Barcelona but a compendium of the stereotypes and clichés that any candidate for the great novel of Barcelona should have. The story resembles a quick tour around Barcelona in one of those two-storey red buses with the inevitable tour guide who provides, via a microphone, brief descriptions of the city's highlights and spices them up with funny and dramatic historical anecdotes. Similarly, the story can be read as an abridged version of Mendoza's novel or of any other of the contemporary novels that aim to represent certain historical periods of Barcelona. In fact, in the last few years Barcelona has generated a large quantity of novels that use historical monuments and periods as appealing backgrounds of suspenseful and thrilling plots. These are novels that seem to compete to become (and appear in guidebooks as) the next and definitive "great novel of Barcelona." Some examples are *La sombra del viento* and *El juego del ángel*, by Carlos Ruiz Zafón, *La catedral del mar*, by Ildefonso Falcones, *La ciudad sin tiempo*, by Enrique Moriel, or *La clave Gaudí*, by Esteban Martín and Andreu Carranza. But what is crucial about this serialized production of literary entertainment is not only that it appeals to tourists that want to complement their visits to the city's monuments with exciting historical novels; the key point is that the massive consumption of these books by Barcelonans, and Catalans and Spaniards in general, reveals how natives also establish a merely "tourist" relationship with their own city and its past.

Not coincidentally, these tourist "great novels of Barcelona" were all written in Spanish. Catalan, as a minority language, appears to be a less effective platform for best-selling novels. However, one of the preoccupations of Catalan writers and intellectuals throughout the twentieth century has precisely been the production of a solid and emblematic "great novel of Barcelona." The debate around the symbolic importance of such a novel for the construction of the Catalan nation emerged in the 1920s. The debate dealt with the cultivation of the novel in general, but, in fact, it was assumed that Barcelona ought to be the setting and the theme of this fiction. The articulation of the Catalan nation as a "Catalunya-ciutat" with metropolitan Barcelona at its core was one of the central premises of *noucentisme* – the hegemonic cultural and political movement of Catalonia during the first two decades of the century. But the *noucentistes* proclaimed that poetry was the most adequate literary genre to create an edifying imaginary for the Catalan people. It was only within the so-called *postnoucentista* period that writers such as Josep Pla, Josep Maria de Sagarra, and Josep Carner realized that the cultural construction of Catalonia could not be completed without the cultivation of prose. In fact, Paul Valéry instigated this debate when, in 1924, he gave two conferences in Barcelona and stressed the importance of writing prose if Catalan culture wanted to avoid its "provençalization." The problem of Provençal literature was that it possessed a great medieval tradition of poetry, but had no modern prose to keep it alive as a present-day literature. This was the danger that many influential Catalan writers were determined to overcome.[30]

In addition, prose, and the novel in particular, could help Catalan culture dissociate itself from its rural and provincial connotations. Prose would bring forth the "civility" and "urbanity" that *noucentisme* had envisioned since the beginning of the century. As Josep Carner affirmed in 1928, "La nostra literatura es donà vivament compte que no podia aspirar a un veritable to metropolità sense reeixides invencions novel·lístiques" 'Our literature fully realized that it could not aspire to have a true metropolitan style without the creation of excellent novels' (quoted in Yates 201).[31] At the same time, as Alan Yates explains, a specific material reason determined this preoccupation with the novel in Catalan: "El debat sobre la novel·la conté el primer plantejament públic, seriós i sostingut, del tema de la professionalització de la literatura catalana" 'The debate around the novel contains the first public, significant and continued confrontation with the matter of the professionalization of Catalan literature' (204). The novel was the literary genre that could prompt the emergence of a wide readership and the subsequent opportunity for Catalan writers to earn their living through writing. As a result of these efforts, Catalan culture developed during the late 1920s and 1930s a complex publishing industry that, in turn, generated a large production of fiction.

This national enterprise was brutally interrupted by Franco and his systematic repression of Catalan culture. In this context, writing fiction in Catalan remained an uncertain, clandestine, and exiled activity.[32] It was not until the 1960s that the publishing industry could be re-established, little by little, in a process that culminated in the arrival of democracy, when this industry could receive the financial support of the reinstated Generalitat de Catalunya. In the meantime, authors in Spanish such as Juan Marsé, Manuel Vázquez Montalbán, and later Eduardo Mendoza, became the most prominent fiction writers in Barcelona.[33] Their success must obviously be attributed to the merits of their works, but the fact that they chose Spanish instead of Catalan was also a key factor toward the dissemination and canonization of their fiction. Given that many contemporary "great novels of Barcelona" have been written in Spanish, Pàmies' short story implicitly plays with this haunting ghost of the Catalan nation – the ghost of the great metropolitan Catalan novels as they were devised in the 1920s and 1930s. It seems as if Pàmies is ironically but also dramatically stating that, after Francoism and the intense Castilianization of Barcelona's literary production, the "great novel of Barcelona" in Catalan has turned into no more than a brief short story: this is all that the Catalan nation can produce or, perhaps, this is all that is left of the Catalan nation. Whether this is a form of mocking the cliché of the great novel of Barcelona and the attribution of a nationalist function to Catalan literature, or whether it is a way of lamenting the Castilinization, or rather the "de-Catalanization," of Barcelona's literature, is ultimately ambiguous, although one is tempted to deduce that Pàmies is affirming both things at the same time.[34]

But, leaving aside these cultural and political subtexts, Pàmies' ironic distortion of the fictional representation of the past ultimately reveals how our – not only literary but also properly epistemological – access to any previous historical period has become totally mediated by a variety of stereotypes and clichés, starting in this case with the cliché of the great novel of Barcelona itself. In postmodernity, "historical" novels are subjected to the conditions of representation established by the media and the tourist industry. All historical accounts necessarily fall prey to these structural conditions that turn seemingly realist depictions of history into generic stereotypes.

Pàmies allows us to push this interpretation further, as in his story the obliteration of the past even reaches the potential return of its ghosts and specters. That is, even the inexpressible traumatic and repressed experiences of the past have become stereotypical components of the new representations of history. Or, at least, it has become impossible to decide whether the traces of traumatic events are easily incorporated into present narratives, or whether they (still) suppose a break, a disruptive syntactical lapse in the discourses of the present. In other words, the potential haunting of past specters over the present seems to be exorcized and neutralized by the very equalizing serialization with which ✓ Pàmies narrates all historical events. For example, referring to the bombing of the city during the war (during this unspecific war that the reader might still associate with the Spanish Civil War of 1936 to 1939), Pàmies simply makes a cold and unaffected list of their effects on people's bodies: "A sota, mentrestant, l'esclat s'especialitza en diverses menes de dolor. El més còmode és la mort... Pel que fa a les ferides, tenen l'inconvenient de la seqüela. En el millor dels casos, una o dues cicatrius, però també ortopèdia, malsons, metralla al cervell" 'Meanwhile, the explosion on the ground develops into different forms of pain.

The most comfortable is death... As for wounds, the trouble is that they have consequences. At best, one or two scars, but also orthopedics, nightmares, shrapnel in the brain' (113).

This fast account of the tragic consequences of the war not only blocks any possible emotional identification of the reader with the narrated events, but also makes it impossible to know what kind of impact the war had on its victims. One is left wondering whether this analytical distance aims to underscore the large amount of suffering generated by the war by contrasting it with a seemingly unaffected account (as if the traumatic pain could not be narrated and therefore the only way to approach it was by coldly dissecting it), or whether this distance conveys the general indifference that past events produce in the present. In any case, Pàmies reveals how personal and collective memory has turned into a random set of stereotypes. These stereotypes maybe incorporate, or maybe dismantle, the latent traumas that return from the past and the specters that the war still engenders.

Now, is this transformation of the past into a series of disconnected events and generic stereotypes not an evident symptom of commodification, of a twofold commodification of the aesthetic representations of history and therefore of history itself? Commodification is the erasure of the traces of production of manufactured goods and of the social labor embodied in them. Or, as Marx says, "the commodity reflects the social characteristics of men's own labour as objective characteristics of the products of labour themselves, as the socionatural properties of these things" (*Capital* 164–5). Thus, the transformation of history into stereotypes denotes how struggles, traumatic experiences, and tumultuous events of the past are not erased by aesthetic representations, but, even worse, are turned into seemingly objective components of these representations. And, as a result of this objectification, we lose the possibility of establishing a meaningful connection between the present situation and the past. In other words, the real "process of production" of history, its social antagonisms and forms of class struggle, are incorporated into the literary representations of history as the autonomous and "fantastic" play between stereotypical characters, plots, and settings – in the same way that the capitalist relations of production are objectified and finally erased in the so-called fetishism of their product, that is, the commodity form.[35] In this sense, while the fetishism of the commodity entails the elimination of any social relation that is not established as an act of exchange, and therefore of any relation that is not mediated by capital, the transformation of literature into a set of stereotypes is a symptom of its loss of social meaning beyond its existence as a product of consumption. Consequently, the sense of historicity is obliterated, time and history are "alienated" from themselves, history turns into a screen on which to project ready-made plots, characters, words, and images, literature becomes another commodity, and the aesthetic experience, pure entertainment. This contemporary literary production corresponds, in turn, to the writing of a past without conflict that, as we said above, has become prevalent in post-transitional Spain.

The Euphoric Gospel of the End of History

The supposed overcoming of class antagonisms is one of the central components of the neoliberal narrative of the so-called end of history. As is well known, Francis Fukuyama's *The End of History and the Last Man*, published in 1992, announces the arrival of a system that has finally reconciled the antagonist forces that have shaped human history up to the present. This system is the tandem composed of liberal democracy and the free market.

Fukuyama states two main points. On the one hand, he asserts that human beings have undeniable material needs, and also have an evident desire for recognition (which connects to Plato's idea of *thymos*). Fukuyama proclaims that a functional society must offer the possibility of satisfying these two desires. But, on the other hand, he shares with Marxism the will to fight against inequality – the inequality produced by the very desires for material comfort and social recognition that drive people's lives.

Given that these two structuring principles – the individual "pursuit of happiness" and the concern for social equality – are in conflict with each other, Fukuyama argues that the combination of free markets and democratic states constitutes the best imaginable arrangement. Even if these principles are ultimately irreconcilable, the tense balance of the two remains the insuperable ideal for human societies. For Fukuyama, free markets naturally work to satisfy all imaginable human needs. At the same time, some of the components of the "free world" – such as entrepreneurship, electoral politics, and athletic competition (as in the Olympic Games) – offer the platforms where human beings can search for social recognition while complying with the democratic precept of human equality. In this narrative, political practice and economic processes are fused in an ideal social whole.

Among the numerous examples that illustrate the "tight relationship that exists between economic development, educational levels, and democracy" (110), Fukuyama refers to the case of Southern Europe and, specifically, to Spain's transition from Francoism to democracy. He interprets Spain's transition as a process of democratization generated by ongoing economic progress. Spain proves the assumption that, on a global scale, economic and political progress are not only possible, but also interconnected. Strikingly, this neoliberal interpretation of Spain's transition coincides with Marxist approaches in one basic point: they find in the economic structure the determining instance that made political change possible. However, while the neoliberal viewpoint interprets this process as a proof that economic growth brings political and social freedom, Marxism shows how freedom can never be complete or universal within capitalism, as economic growth within this system necessarily comes at the expense of other agents of its structure.[36]

Fukuyama's celebratory account of liberal democracy arrived shortly after the fall of the Berlin Wall and the resulting disenchantment of the Left. The end of the Cold War and the triumph of Western capitalism seemed to denote the end of the possibility of systemic change. Although this abandonment of revolutionary and utopian goals had already occurred during the 1980s, the disintegration of the USSR corroborated that communism was no longer a viable alternative. Most leftist parties decided that, given the apparent unavoidability of capitalism, all they could do was work to reform the system and establish different degrees of social democracy.

Marxist theorists, most notably Perry Anderson and Fredric Jameson, quickly opposed Fukuyama's liberal dismissal of revolutionary designs. In *A Zone of Engagement*, Anderson historicizes Fukuyama's proclamation of the end of history by relating it to previous proclamations announced by Hegel, Antoine-Augustin Cournot, and Alexandre Kojève. He presents three main counterarguments. First, there is no material possibility for the Second and Third Worlds to reproduce the level of wealth enjoyed in the First World. Capitalism inevitably produces oligarchic wealth, as the amassment of power and capital of today's corporations demonstrates. Second, globalization requires aggressive control measures on oil supplies, immigration, and armaments: three fields of permanent conflict between peoples, nation-states, and corporations. Finally, Anderson shows how Fukuyama's idea of democracy is nothing more than today's electoral system, and the legitimacy of this system is being seriously undermined by widespread abstentionism and indifference.

Jameson, in turn, historicizes Fukuyama by relating him to Frederick Jackson Turner's 1893 essay "The Frontier in American History." Jameson explains that Fukuyama's notion of the end of history does not obey a temporal logic but rather expresses "the feeling of the constriction of Space in the new world system" (*Cultural Turn* 90). Thus, Fukuyama's book constitutes a triumphant ideologeme that redirects or simply masks the anxiety of which it is itself a symptom: the anxiety about the further expasion of capitalism in a fully commodified globe. In other words, by interpreting the present situation as the positive moment in which fundamental antagonisms have been overcome, Fukuyama appeases the anxiety produced by the presence of unsurpassable global limits. The task of perfecting the established system aims to displace this anxiety and conceal it under a positive and celebratory scheme.

However, strong attacks on this neoliberal narrative came not only from Marxist scholarship but also from deconstruction. Jacques Derrida's *Specters of*

Marx, published in 1993, addresses the self-proclaimed triumph of neoliberalism and establishes, perhaps for the first time in such an explicit way, the inherent political content of deconstruction.

Derrida analyzes Fukuyama's argument as a symptom of the post-1989 conjuration against Marxism. He describes *The End of History and the Last Man* as a "gospel" (56) which claims to demonstrate that History has necessarily led humanity to liberal democracy but does not interrogate the assumptions of its own reasoning. Derrida shows how this gospel advances according to a twofold procedure. On the one hand, Fukuyama claims that the union of liberal democracy and the market, as found in Western Europe and the United States, embodies the last stage of History, a stage in which economic and political freedom and personal thymotic desires are the pillars that sustain a contentious but ultimately reconciled society. On the other hand, however, when empirical evidence indicates that contemporary liberal democracies also generate inequality, starvation, pollution, violence, and oppression, then Fukuyama strategically transforms liberal democracy into a goal to be pursued, a regulative idea, or a promised land. That is, depending on the case at stake, liberal democracy is presented as a consummated reality or as a project to be accomplished.

In this sense, Derrida unfolds the double meaning of Fukuyama's oracular "good news has come" (XIII). With this declaration, Fukuyama implies that he is reporting the positive events that have already taken place, and also that he is announcing the coming of a harmonious world, which, nevertheless, will always remain future. (In a similar way, Derrida could have also exploited the obvious implied meaning of the "end of History" in the title of the book: here, liberal democracy is the system where History culminates and ends, but it is also the regulative end or final goal of History.) In this respect, Derrida demonstrates how the narrative of the end of history is ultimately an idealist and Christian teleology: "The model of the liberal State to which [Fukuyama] lays claim is not only that of Hegel, the Hegel of the struggle for recognition, it is that of a Hegel who privileges the 'Christian vision.' ... This end of History is essentially a Christian eschatology" (60). The ultimate purpose of this eschatology is to get rid of the "Hegelian Left," that is, of Marxism: since History's final end is liberal democracy, History can no longer be conceived dialectically as class struggle. In Fukuyama, History has become a series of empirical contingencies that do not affect the transhistorical and naturalized ideal of liberal democracy. The end of History is simply the realization of this ideal.

To break, or rather to radicalize, this dilemma between actuality and ideality, Derrida proposes that we explore the logic of the specter. The specter or the ghost – this "paradoxical incorporation, the becoming-body, a certain phenomenal and carnal form of the spirit... some 'thing' that remains difficult to name:

neither soul nor body, and both one and the other" (6) – inhabits the gap between what exists and what does not. In political terms, this gap defines the essence of democracy. For Derrida, democracy is essentially democracy to come, a notion that does not refer to a future realization of democracy, but to the very conditions of possibility of democracy:

> Even beyond the regulating idea in its classic form, the idea, if that is still what it is, of democracy to come... is the opening of this gap between an infinite promise... and the determined, necessary, but also necessarily inadequate forms of what has to be measured against this promise. (65)

The gap of democracy to come is the (non-)place of the opening to the Other, the opening to what is to come, to the event that cannot be anticipated or recognized as such. It is the permanent deferral of the ideal of democracy while it is simultaneously its realization in multiple forms and political practices. Democracy to come is the place of spectrality: what is there (the ideal of democracy and its actual manifestations) but that is nevertheless not there (as this ideal can never be fully realized in the multiple, real practices, and for this reason democracy remains a promise and a horizon).

Derrida's spectral democracy radicalizes Fukuyama's project in two directions deduced from Marx. First, even within the idealist logic that considers democracy the ideal that societies must pursue, one must continue the Marxist critique of the conditions of production "in order to adjust 'reality' to the 'ideal' in the course of a necessarily infinite process" (86). But, second, one must also permanently question the ideal of democracy and the existing institutions, discourses, economies, and laws deployed on its behalf. In this sense, Derrida links democracy to those overdetermined material conditions that constitute History as much as to its idealist or spiritual definition. In his thinking on democracy, Derrida rearticulates the Spirit of History as both spirit and specter, as both ideal and material, present and absent, one and the other, and also as neither one of these pairs.

One may say that Derrida retrieves the materialist task of Marxism against Fukuyama's idealism in the same sense that Marx himself retrieved the materialist basis of Hegel against the Hegelian Right, for which the Absolute Spirit could be identified with the Christian God. For the Right, Hegel's Absolute Spirit would be a *Wirklichkeit*, that is, a reality already taking place in nineteenth-century Prussia; for the Left, on the contrary, the Absolute Spirit would be a *Realität*, a tangible reality, but not necessarily existing anywhere yet. Thus, Fukuyama would be an interpreter of the Right and Derrida, a thinker of the Left.

Olympic Specters

Before returning to Olympic Barcelona, we must further understand this rethinking of History as spectrality, which will result, as we will see below, in a redefinition of the ontology of the present as a hauntology. In short, we must explore the question of the meaning and nature of the ghosts of history. In our postmodern situation, how can we recognize the appearance of an invisible ghost from the past? How can we distinguish between a reference to the past that is integrated into a new narrative, in which case the past becomes properly narrativized and therefore idealized or spiritualized, and the return of a (repressed) specter from the past that supposes a fundamental break in the narratives of the present? Is it possible to distinguish between these two cases? Can we differentiate the specters that move along with history (the references to the past that become components of the present) from those that suspend it? This is the suspension caused by the ghosts that haunt the present and keep it from overcoming the past, the ghosts that stand for the very conditions of possibility of history.

To address these questions, we can return to Derrida's re-examination of history as spectrality by looking at Jameson's historicization of it in his essay "Marx's Purloined Letter." Jameson's essay contains, among others, three crucial observations in relation to Derrida: the question of mourning, the context of late capitalism, and the opening to the messianic or the utopian.

Jameson affirms that, even though Derrida follows Marx when he stresses that specters can contest the idealization of history and the dominance of institutional narratives, Marx is probably more aware than Derrida of the malevolent effect that the past and the dead have over the present. This malevolence does not only mean that the ghosts of the past, like Hamlet's father, compel the living to commit crimes and continue the never-ending chains of revenge. Rather, this malevolence also comes from the very impossibility of mourning and remembering the past in a proper way. "To forget the dead altogether is impious in ways that prepare their own retribution, but to remember the dead is neurotic and obsessive and merely feeds a sterile repetition. There is no 'proper' way of relating to the dead and the past" (58–9).

Jameson interprets Derrida's vehement call for this necessary, albeit impossible, mourning as a reaction against the current posthistorical situation in which all ghosts have been exorcized and late capitalism has become the new ontology of the present. This is the situation that Fukuyama paradigmatically exalts as culminating and definitive. While Fukuyama embodies the apocalyptic Right that forecloses the possibility of systemic change, Derrida attempts to envisage a messianic Left based on the impalpable figure of the specter. His thinking on the messianic or "messianism without messianism" consists in the opening to the possibility of radical change, a possibility that is inscribed into the spectrality of history. As Jameson writes, "[t]he messianic is spectral, it is the spectrality of the future, the other dimension, that answers to the haunting spectrality of the past which is historicity itself" (64). The messianic emerges here as the possibility of revolution in times when radical change seems inconceivable, like in the "end-of-history" years of the 1980s and the 1990s.

However, Derrida explains that messianism without messianism, as the opening to the possibility of the arrival of an altogether Other and of an unforeseeable and non-conceptualizable event, stands for the impossible itself: the impossible that constitutes the conditions of possibility of historical events as well as their conditions of impossibility (*Specters* 65). The articulation of this (im)possibitity aims to go beyond historical time as the ultimate horizon of ontology itself. Derrida, as we have seen with his notion of a democracy to come that is not "a *future* democracy in the future present" (64), refuses to consider historical time the ontological limit that permits time and history to be constituted as such. To remain open to the spectral Other of ontology is a way of recognizing spectrality as the constitutive impossibility of present historical situations and of presence itself. For Derrida, one must always avoid the foreclosure that determines history as the ultimate horizon of being and time. He calls for "another opening of event-ness as historicity that permitted one... to open up access to an affirmative thinking of the messianic and emancipatory promise as promise: as *promise* and not as onto-theological or teleo-eschatological program or design" (75).

In this sense, whereas Jameson interprets Derrida's "messianism without messianism" as a form of utopia that hopes for the arrival of a revolutionary event that changes the current historical situation in a radical way, Derrida rejects utopia because it "would still retain the temporal form of a *future present*" (65). In "Marx & Sons," he replies directly to Jameson that the messianic cannot be understood as a longing for a utopian future version of the present (249). The messianic must be conceived as the impossible beyond time and history, and beyond ontology and being.

In turn, Jameson, for whom utopia appears in allegorical form as a glimpse to a future historical situation that is unimaginable within the structure of the present (a situation that is also often insufferable, so that utopia quickly folds over into dystopia), refuses to talk about impossibility. Jameson wants to avoid the "theoretical defeatism" that the word impossibility entails, as "the minute you say that [impossibility], then you feed into some other ideologies about silence, ultimate unknowability, the chaos of the world, unrepresentability, indeterminacy, and so forth in all kinds of undesirable ways" (*Jameson* 195–6). Thus, the crucial difference between the two thinkers is that, while Derrida thinks through the (im)possibility of an externality to the ontology of historical time, Jameson's thinking of utopia as the potential emergence of the future within the present assumes history as the ultimate horizon of ontology. Jameson writes:

> The presumption is that Utopia, whose business is the future, or not-being, exists only in the present, where it leads the relatively feeble life of desire and fantasy. But this is to reckon without the amphibiousness of being and its temporality: in respect of which Utopia is philosophically analogous to the trace, only from the other end of time. The aporia of the trace is to belong to past and present all at once, and thus to constitute a mixture of being and not-being... (*Archaeologies* xv)

Jameson understands the aporia of the trace (the trace of the past, but also the glimpse at the future, which are both simultaneously present and absent in the present) within the horizon of historical time. He identifies being with the present and not-being with the past and the future. In him, being and time continue to be the pillars of the ontology of the present, even if throughout his work he makes it clear that historical situations can never be represented as such, as they can only be grasped allegorically. For Derrida, on the contrary, the aporia of the trace could never be inscribed into historical time and being. For him, the trace is the sign that "must be absolutely excessive as concerns all possible presence-absence, all possible production or disappearance of beings in general, and [that] yet, *in some manner* it must still signify, in a manner unthinkable by metaphysics as such" (*Margins* 65).

The trace can only be thought as an erasure of the trace itself. But this erased trace is not the trace of the differentiation of being from non-being, or of what is present from what is absent. This erased trace is even more unthinkable: it is the trace of the very possibility of this differentiation between being and non-being. For the difference between being and non-being, and between presence and absence, to arise, there must be the unthinkable and unnameable condition that makes possible difference itself. In this respect, being and presence must not be understood as the ultimate content of our language and thought, but as "the trace of the trace, the trace of the erasure of the trace" (66). This "trace of the trace," which constitutes language and metaphysics, is the sign of the erasure of the very possibility of difference, the possibility without which no being could emerge from non-being and no presence could appear as such. In other words, being and historical time are not original horizons of ontology but they are after-effects (but not in any temporal sense) of the Other, of the infinitely different condition of difference, which is "ceaselessly differing from and deferring (itself)" (67). Thus, the presupposition of a horizon that encompasses the metaphysical realm of being and time becomes an insufficient conceptuality: the conceptuality of the Western metaphysics of presence that closes off and forgets the most original event of its incessantly different (non-)origin.

Despite their fundamentally distinct theoretical frames, Derrida and Jameson coincide in at least two key points. On the one hand, Jameson acknowledges too that the "traces" of utopian futures are never present, or that they are present in their absence in the present. While he embraces history as the last ontological horizon, his thinking of utopia attempts to escape a reassuring metaphysics of presence. His analyses of aesthetic or philosophical works continuously seek for the (non-)appearance of what remains absent in the present. On the other hand, while Derrida refuses to consider history the last horizon of thought, he very much attempts to describe the historical specificity of the present, especially in *Specters of Marx* and afterward, when Derrida realizes his *Kehre* toward more explicitly political and social texts.

Derrida and Jameson agree that the new global order – characterized by Derrida as "the fantastic, ghostly, 'synthetic,' 'prosthetic,' virtual happenings in the scientific domain and therefore the domain of the techno-media and therefore the public or political domain" (*Specters* 63), and identified by Jameson as late capitalism and its cultural logic called postmodernism – corresponds to a situation in which History has been obliterated by a world of sheer simulacra and full commodification. As is known, Marx already linked capitalist commodification and the spectralization of reality when he defined the objectivity that congeals human labor in the commodity as a "phantom-like objectivity" (*Capital* 128). But Derrida remarks that the commodity is not the only ghostly element of this logic. Within capitalism, human beings also become spectral beings, as they "no longer recognize in... [the commodity] the *social* character of their *own* labor. It is as if they were becoming ghosts in their turn... These ghosts that are commodities transform human producers into ghosts" (*Specters* 155–6). For this reason, Derrida defines the ontology of the present as a "hauntology" (51), that is, as a general, haunting spectralization of all beings, past and present, generated by the media and the unavoidable technologies of telecommunications and integrated in the very logic of commodification.

Derrida's crucial point is that the very obliteration of history and its ghosts in contemporary society has caused a general spectralization through which this repressed history returns. That is to say, the return of historicity must be found in the spectral materiality that crosses today's social, economic, political, public, and individual spheres. In the postmodern or "end-of-history" context, historicity returns, but perhaps not in the form of traumatic ghosts or syntactical short circuits, but in the very ghostly constitution of the contemporary simulacrum. Thus, to paraphrase Jameson, the messianic or the utopian in these apocalyptic times are potentially in front of all of us, like Poe's purloined letter.

Now we can see how the answer to the question about the recognition of the ghosts from the past in a situation in which spectrality is constitutive and omnipresent is found in the very terms of the question. In the spectralizing media society of late capitalism, ghosts are everywhere, so to speak. But, for this reason, it has become undecidable whether a ghost from the past is integrated into the narratives that structure the present, or whether it breaks them – whether it is a spirit or a specter. Ghosts are no longer unrepresentable traumas that cannot be incorporated to the existing historical narratives; rather, they are part of the very simulacrum that has obliterated the sense of historicity to begin with. And yet, in this context, historicity must be found in this very undecidability, in the hesitation between spirit and specter, and in the very structure that spectralizes all beings, subjects and discourses.

This brings us back to some of the specters that haunted the euphoria of Olympic Barcelona: the ghost of President Companys, the ghosts of the *xarnegos*, or the ghosts of the Universal and International Exhibitions. Mayor Pasqual Maragall retrieved the uncanny ghost of Companys at the opening ceremony of the Olympics, but one suspects that the executed president appeared simply as another character of the spectacle. Naturally, the reference to Companys and the 1936 Popular Olympics was part of the ceremony's script. This reference did not constitute an unexpected break in the narrative of the event, nor was it an abrupt eruption of haunting specters from the past. However, another haunting spectrality can be detected in them, namely the very spectral nature of the entire spectacle itself. The retrieval of the historical figure of Companys epitomized the spectrality of the medium itself: an Olympic ceremony that was in turn the perfect epitome of the contemporary society of the spectacle.

The most symptomatic part of the appearance of Companys' specter, the moment in which his specter really emerged, came after mayor Maragall mentioned him and the audience in the stadium began to applaud enthusiastically. This applause was a precise illustration of the undecidability of the contemporary simulacrum. The question is: why did people clap so enthusiastically? On the one hand, the applause might have been a collective tribute to a tumultuous episode of the past and the sign that people had not forgotten the struggles of the Civil War nor the state repression infringed over Catalonia. The fervent applause would have intended to exorcize Companys' specter in the double sense of acknowledging all the things he represented and at the same time expelling them. This applause would have been a symbolic burial and an act of memory and forgetting.

However, on the other hand, this frank homage also functioned as one of the conventional ovations that televised ceremonies require. The people in the stadium were also the audience of a TV set, and it is likely that they clapped intensely because they knew that it was the appropriate time to clap intensely in the mediatized ceremony, in the same way that TV programs determine with canned laughs and clapping when it is the appropriate time to laugh. This undecidability between reality and the media, between what was scripted and what was unanticipated, between history and simulacrum, between the traces of trauma and their banal reproduction, traversed the brief commemoration of the executed president. The euphoric ovation of the audience was haunted by its own mediatization in the spectacle. But it is precisely here, in this spectral shadow that appeared from within the euphoric ovation itself – the shadow of its own mediatization – where we must find the truly disruptive eruption of the specters of history.

Hence, historicity is not recaptured in commemorations and ceremonies that have turned into a simulacrum of history. Instead, in postmodernity, the past emits its signals through the (absent) space between the real and the image: this is the space that reveals postmodernity as the historical period of sheer simulacra and full commodification. The sense of historicity repressed by the late capitalist society of the spectacle returns in the form of the very spectrality of the spectacle. In Barcelona's Olympic ceremony, we can say that the ghost of Companys haunted the present, not directly through Maragall's reference and the subsequent ovation from the audience, but by emerging as a symptom of the impossibility of "appearing" outside this structure of the spectacle.

Another revealing case is the form in which "the city of the people" both integrated and spectralized the linguistic and cultural differences of the citizens of Barcelona. The city and the people constituted the empty signifiers that attempted to hegemonize the social space by interpellating both Catalan-speakers and Spanish *xarnegos* as citizens and not as "natives" and "immigrants." Their linguistic "identity" turned into their double, their haunting double, the (historical) shadow of their (posthistorical) belonging as citizens. What matters here is not only that "the city of the people" served as an ideology to exorcize the specter of the *xarnego* immigrant and also to "de-Catalanize" Barcelona and launch a more multicultural imaginary. Rather, the discourse of "the city of the people" and its attempt to detach the citizens of Barcelona from national histor-ical narratives also reproduced this logic of spectrality: the imagined diversity of "the city of the people" coopted the various "identities" of the citizens. To put it bluntly, one could not not be part of the diversity of the people, as this discourse served to represent whatever "identity" citizens might embrace. The difficulty, if not the impossibility, of establishing a distance between this official discourse and the "real" social space of the people resulted in spectrality between the two, between the official picture and the street, between the people and... the people.

Similarly, Mendoza's *La ciudad de los prodigios*, by retrieving the ghosts of the Universal and International Exhibitions and the political corruption, the class struggle and the state repression that they entailed, aimed to counteract the celebratory spirit of the Olympic project and the political consensus that the city hall could establish thanks to this project. But these ghosts seemed to be quickly exorcized as the novel became a successful contribution to the tourist and Olympic promotion of the city. Specifically, the novel connected well with the new tourist exploitation of the past by encapsulating a series of representative scenes, characters, and events of Barcelona's history. The historical period portrayed in the novel (1888–1929) not coincidentally corresponds to the moment of emergence of *modernista* architecture, as well as to the formative years of Picasso, Dalí, and Miró in Barcelona: as is known, these are the architectural style, and the three artists that have been most exploited by the city's tourist industry.

Despite this process of commodification of *La ciudad de los prodigios*, it still remains undecidable whether Mendoza's retrieval of the tumultuous past consisted of an entertaining reproduction of a series of clichés about a historical period, or whether this retrieval could constitute a truly disruptive intervention in the city's triumphant present. But what matters here is this very undecidability. The hesitation between these two options is what truly disrupts the present, as it makes evident the unremitting commodification and spectacularization that traversed the Olympic event, the staging of political reconciliation, and the entire city with its history and its literature.

Mendoza's novel uncovers the spectralization of the present, but not because it retrieves the specters of the two Exhibitions: after all, this retrieval meshed well with the interests of the tourist and cultural industries of the city. Instead, the novel reveals the present spectralization by precisely failing to retrieve these historical specters outside the official promotion of the city. Its hesitation between the intended retrieval and its inevitable commodification turns this great novel of Barcelona into a spectralizing mirror of the Olympic city. The novel casts the specter of history over "posthistorical" Barcelona to the degree that it fails to bring back the Universal and International Exhibitions as haunting ghosts. This failure to escape the extensive commodification of Barcelona paradoxically uncovers this commodification as the constitutive feature of this historical period.

Similarly, the undecidability about whether Bouvila embodies a collective vengeance of the lower classes can also point to the fact that, in the present context, class antagonisms have supposedly been overcome and that any meaningful representation of them has become impossible. Paradoxically, again, the disclosure of this impossibility can be a way of invoking these antagonisms. *La ciudad de los prodigios* occupies the same position of its main character: in the same way that Bouvila can be read as a successful specimen of the eminently mercantile breed of Barcelonans and simultaneously as the avenger of the lower classes, the novel can be read as a successful exemplar of tourist literature and simultaneously as the advocate of past class struggles, the advocate that brings these struggles back by using the same commodifying methods that have obliterated them and the past altogether.

This inquiry on the inherent hesitations of certain phenomena of postmodern Barcelona aims to supplement one of the principal critical approaches to the Spanish transition. This approach, notably represented by Teresa M. Vilarós, Joan Ramon Resina, Cristina Moreiras-Menor and Jo Labanyi, among many others, examines the tensions between the official *pacto del olvido* and the ghosts of the past that irrepressibly returned and disrupted the historical amnesia of this period. As Vilarós states,

> El momento transicional, tensado por diferentes y opuestas fuerzas, se revela como un agujero negro, una fisura o quiebre en la sintaxis histórica que si bien permite por un lado iniciar en el posfranquismo una nueva escritura, agazapa en su seno todo un pasado conflictivo que el colectivo "pacto del olvido" reprimió. (*Mono* 20)

> The transitional moment, tensed by different and opposing forces, emerges as a black hole, a fissure or a break in the syntax of history, which, while on the one hand it prompts a new writing in post-Francoism, also gathers in its core the conflictive past repressed by the collective "pacto del olvido."

This critical approach explores significant cultural products of the transition in search of the fissures and syntactical lapses through which the repressed conflicts from the past returned. These interstices destabilized the new transitional narratives in multiple and oblique ways and left residual excesses that symptomatized this repression of the past. Moreiras-Menor writes

> Estos residuos ocultos y no simbolizados, impensables desde las políticas culturales, van dejando así estelas incorpóreas (no inscritas en la narrativa, pero contenidas en sus intersticios) que surgen a modo de fisuras sin suturar cuyas cicatrices se imprimen con fuerza desestabilizadora. ("Agonía" 101)[37]

> These hidden, non-symbolic residues, which cultural politics cannot explain, leave incorporeal trails (not inscribed in the narrative but contained in its interstices) that emerge in the form of unsutured fissures whose scars are imprinted with destabilizing force.

As we have seen in some examples from Olympic Barcelona, a parallel "return of the repressed" can be found at the very spectral and spectacular core of postdictatorial narratives. The collapse of the boundaries between the real and the virtual, between the image and the referent, or between spirit and specter as a result of the full commodification of the social space, brings forth the constitutive spectrality of history. In this posthistorical deadlock we find the possibility of historical change: the messianic and the utopian dwell in the very difficulty to imagine a radically different future, in the spectral hesitation of the commodity form, in the (non-)space of the Other, of the Other as specter, the Other of historicity itself, a non-commodifiable Other and an Other to capitalism. This critical possibility, at least, has permitted us to identify the hegemonic appropriations of the democratic impulse, the forms of domestication of historical ghosts, the design of de-historicizing representations of the people, and the subsumption of literature under the tourist industry. Ideological vigilance can be a first step in the search for a different systemic situation.

Notes

1 See also Krüger and Murray 233.
2 For a political biography of Lluís Companys, see Vila; for accounts of his imprisonment and execution, see Solé i Sabaté and Güell.
3 For complete accounts and data of media coverage and the technological resources used during the 1992 Games, see Moragas et al., *Television in the Olympics*; Roche 143–54; and Castro Alcaide.
4 Its main stanzas say:

> Amigos para siempre
> Means you'll always be my friend
> Amics per sempre
> Means a love that cannot end
> Friends for life
> Not just a summer or a spring
> Amigos para siempre
> I feel you near me
> Even when you are apart
> Just knowing you are in this world
> Can warm my heart
> Friends for life
> Not just a summer or a spring
> Amigos para siempre. (*Cerimònia clausura* 42)

5 I further explain the components of Prat de la Riba's nationalism and the tasks of the Mancomunitat in relation to *noucentisme* in Chapter Two.

Contemporary historiography has largely debated whether political Catalanism can be considered a bourgeois project, or whether it emerged as a transversal phenomenon that crossed many layers of Catalonia's civil society. Some historians have argued that the bourgeoisie "invented" Catalan nationalism to defend their corporate interests, and also to control the social unrest of the working classes. From this perspective, Catalanism functioned as an ideological device that redirected the anger produced by class antagonisms against Madrid and the centralist state. But other historians have argued that, even if it eventually gained hegemony, bourgeois Catalanism was only one of various types of nationalism. Indeed, the popular classes also strongly identified with Catalan cultural markers and political claims against the multiple forms of repression of the central state. (For arguments of the first position, see Solé Tura or Marfany. For a vindication of the second position, see Termes, and Termes and Colomines, which contains an introduction with an exhaustive bibliography on the subject.)

Even though this second position seems to be historically more accurate, it is crucial to realize that, from a more conceptual viewpoint, both positions are simultaneously right. While Catalanism may have been present in most spheres of Catalan society, it was only when bourgeois Catalanism could articulate a hegemonic position that it became an effective and central political force. Given that, as Gramsci taught us, hegemony is the necessary function of civil society (12), any account of the origins of Catalanism must assume these two premises: that a variety of particular forms of Catalanism were present before the bourgeoisie may have appropriated or overpowered them, and that Catalanism came into full political existence only when the bourgeois classes launched it as the principal transformative force of Catalan civil society.

6 For excellent cultural and social analyses of Barcelona in the 1920s and early 1930s, see Davidson and Ealham.

7 For a fundamental bibliography on Franco's regime, see Payne, *The Franco Regime, 1936–1975*, *Fascism in Spain, 1923–1977*, and Preston, *Franco: a Biography*. For a study of labor movements in Barcelona during Francoism, see Balfour, *Dictatorship, Workers, and the City*.

8 Notice, in passing, the politico-linguistic subtext of the word "salta-taulells," which is a derogatory term in Catalan for "clerk" or "shop assistant." By using this term, the poem implies that those who despised Spanish-speaking immigrants were the Catalan-speaking natives, as Nolan's translation makes explicit ("the Catalan clerks"). Biedma's ideological move here consists in creating an opposition between, on the one hand, the Castilian of the (powerless) immigrants and the Castilian of his own poem and, on the other hand, the Catalan of the (dominant) natives. This opposition simplifies the more complex power relations between the two languages, and it conceals two things: the fact that Barcelona's upper classes, who exploited the *murcianos* (and to which Biedma belonged) also mainly spoke Castilian, and the fact that Castilian was also the language imposed by the Franco regime over Catalonia. While Biedma is eager to repudiate his upper class origins and to identify with the destitute immigrants, he does not problematize the potential contradictions of his own linguistic position; instead, he redirects them toward a simple antagonism between Castilian and Catalan.

9 After Francoism, unions also entered a period deep crisis. As Sebastian Balfour explains, three main causes provoked this crisis: the relocation of companies and the subsequent high unemployment, which made workers distrustful of the force of unions; the widening gap between workers and union leaders, who seemed more occupied in gaining political power from the new legalized parties; and, finally, the shadow of the dictatorship, which had imprinted the common perception by which the state could have a paternal role and protect the worker from the employer, thus making the mediation of unions unnecessary (*Dictatorship* 243–48).

10 For a fundamental bibliography on the Spanish transition, see Powell; Preston, *The Triumph of Democracy in Spain*; Prego; Tusell; Muniesa.

11 See Anthony Giddens' *The Third Way: The Renewal of Social Democracy*.

12 For a comprehensive economic analysis of Spain's new economy, see Etxezarreta; and Recio and Roca.

13 The movement of the *nova cançó*, or new song, emerged in the late 1950s and early 1960s to demand the normal use of Catalan and protest against Francoism. The best-known folk singers and songwriters of the movement were Lluís Llach, Raimon, Joan Manuel Serrat, Maria del Mar Bonet, and Ovidi Montllor. See Pujadó.

14 As Justin Crumbaugh observes, two writers, Juan Goytisolo in *El furgón de cola* (1967) and Max Aub in *La gallina ciega: Diario español* (1969), had already unmasked the depoliticization (or "microfascistization" [8]) of Francoism through consumerism and the tourist industry (7). For analyses of Spain's tourism during the 1960s, see Crumbaugh; Pack; and the collection of essays in Martí-Olivella and Afinoguenova.

15 See Negri's analysis of Keynes' capitalist theory of the state in Hardt and Negri 22–50.

16 "Post-industrial society" is the term that Daniel Bell popularized in 1976 in *The Coming of the Post-industrial Society*.

17 The fact that he could witness first-hand the urban transformation of Baltimore and its waterfront probably gave him many ideas for the renewal of Barcelona, as I will show in Chapter Three.

18 For detailed accounts of Porcioles' corrupted nepotism, see Genovès; Marín; and McNeill, *Urban Change*, 114–17.

19 In fact, the original quotation from *Coriolanus* says:
SICINIUS: What is the city but the people?
CITIZENS: True, the people are the city. (*Coriolanus* 3.1.198–200)

20 As I explain in Chapter Two, the waves of non-European immigrants did not begin to arrive in Catalonia until the late 1980s.

21 Pujol's political programs can be found in his *Entre l'acció i l'esperança* (volumes 1 and 2) and *Antologia política de Jordi Pujol*. For a study of Catalonia's linguistic politics, see Woolard.

22 He also conceived analogous definitions: "Català és tot home que viu i que treballa a Catalunya i que, de Catalunya, en fa el seu país"; 'Everyone who lives and works in Catalonia, and makes Catalonia his country, is Catalan'; "Català és tot home que viu i que treballa a Catalunya i que amb el seu treball, amb el seu esforç, ajuda a fer Catalunya"; 'Everyone who lives and works in Catalonia and contributes with his work and efforts to build Catalonia, is Catalan'; and "[És català qui de Catalunya] en fa casa seva, és a dir, que d'una manera o una altra s'hi incorpora, s'hi reconeix, s'hi entrega, no li és hostil" '[Everyone who makes Catalonia] his home, who embraces it, who recognizes himself in it, who devotes himself to it, and who is not hostile to it, is Catalan.' See Pujol, *Entre l'acció i l'esperança/2*, 20, and *La immigració, problema i esperança de Catalunya*, 70.

23 This is Rancière's definition of "consensual postdemocracy":
The term will simply be used to denote the paradox that, in the name of democracy, emphasizes the consensual practice of effacing the forms of democratic action. Postdemocracy is the government practice and conceptual legitimization of a democracy *after* the demos, a democracy that has eliminated the appearance, miscount, and dispute of the people, and is thereby reducible to the interplay of state mechanisms and combinations of social energies and interests. (121)

24 For a detailed account of these dubious metamorphoses, see McNeill, *Urban Change*, 41, 43, and 127.

25 See Cabana, *Multinacionals*, 43–4; and *25 anys*, 33.

26 See Cabana's *25 anys de llibertat, autonomia i centralisme (1976–2000)*, in which he offers a comprehensive economic history of contemporary Catalonia.

27 For accounts of Barcelona's economic growth, see, in addition to Cabana, Roca i Albert's *La formació del cinturó industrial de Barcelona*; and McNeill, *Urban Change*, 49–50.

28 The allusion to "el lenguaje de las bayonetas" is symptomatic as it avoids the reference to the state imposition of another language, that is, Castilian, over the "principado" or the "colonia" of Catalonia. In other words, to talk exclusively about "el lenguaje de la bayonetas" is a way of avoiding the thorny question of whether the presence of Castilian in Catalonia is a product of a state implementation (as most Catalan nationalists would argue), or whether it is mostly a result of immigration and the voluntary adoption of Castilian by certain classes of Catalan society, especially the upper ones. In any event, by making Bouvila affirm that the imposition of military force is the real cause of the hostilities between Catalonia and the Spanish state, Mendoza, who does not refer to any case of linguistic conflict in the novel, does not take into account the planned and deliberate repression of Catalan language executed by the state throughout modernity.

29 *Time Out* is the only major guidebook that does not refer to *La ciudad de los prodigios*. The only literary references in this travel guide are the two chapters in which Don Quixote visits Barcelona. According to the guidebook, these chapters should suffice to see how the city still maintains what Don Quixote admired, as, in them, "one gets a glimpse of a city that survives to this day: 'A home to foreigners, a refuge to the poor... unique in position and in beauty'" (17).

30 Many writers referred to the significance of Valéry's remarks on the issue of Catalan

prose. For example, Josep Pla:

> Valéry, el 1924, digué a Barcelona: cultiveu la prosa!, cultiveu sistemàticament la prosa!... i en el moment de dir-ho recordà el precedent impressionant de la decadència de la literatura de llengua d'oc, la fulminant caiguda d'un moviment literari que del cantó de la prosa fou deficitari i del cantó poètic tingué una brillantor d'esperit i de mitjans tècnics absolutament importants. (Pla, *Les escales de Llevant* 67)

> In 1924, Paul Valéry said in Barcelona: you must cultivate prose!, you must cultivate prose systematically!... and he recalled the striking precedent of the decadence of the literature written in langue d'oc, the sudden fall of a literary movement with a deficient prose on the one hand and, on the other hand, a poetic tradition with a brilliant spirit and a set of technical resources absolutely important.

Another example is poet Carles Riba, who recalled in 1927: "Paul Valéry també ens ho deia: 'Feu prosa, sobretot prosa. Els provençals han vist morir llur literatura per manca d'una prosa.'" 'Paul Valéry told us too: "Write prose, above all prose. The Provençals saw their literature die due to the lack of prose."' (quoted in Xavier Pla, *Josep Pla* 364). For the reception of Valéry in Catalonia, see Llanas; and Xavier Pla 363–66.

31 I will further explain the characteristics of *noucentisme* in Chapter Two. For the debates around the production of Catalan novels, see Yates 109–200.

32 For general studies of Catalan literature during Francoism, see Manent, Triadú or Samsó. Josep Benet's *L'intent franquista de genocidi cultural contra Catalunya* and *Catalunya sota el règim franquista* are the most comprehensive accounts of Franco's repression of Catalan culture.

33 Some of their most celebrated works were Marsé's *Últimas tardes con Teresa* (1966), *Si te dicen que caí* (1973), *El amante bilingüe* (1990), Vázquez Montalbán's *El pianista* (1985), Mendoza's *La verdad sobre el caso Savolta* (1975), and *La ciudad de los prodigios* (1986).

34 The anxieties about writing fiction in Catalan also involved recurrent hesitations regarding the linguistic model that should be used. A fascinating account of these hesitations can be found in Pericay and Toutain. Also, for a recent, and more reactionary, text lamenting the lack of a great Catalan metropolitan novel, see Puig 88–90.

35 The adjective "fantastic" of course refers to the way Marx defines the form of appearance of the commodity: "It is nothing but the definite social relation between men themselves which assumes here, for them, the fantastic form of a relation between things" (*Capital* 165).

36 Fukuyama's interpretation of Southern Europe's progress contrasts with analyses such as, for example, Immanuel Wallerstein's notion of "semiperipheral development." In "The Relevance of the Concept of Semiperiphery to Southern Europe," Wallerstein exposes how Southern European states occupy a semiperipheral position in the world system. Although this position is unstable, and countries might move toward the core or toward the periphery of the world economy, there must always necessarily be a set of states that remain in the semiperiphery and the periphery so that the global lines of production can operate.

37 See also Moreiras-Menor's *Cultura herida*; Resina, *Disremembering*; and Labanyi 1–21.

CHAPTER TWO

The City Where Europe Meets the Mediterranean

This chapter analyzes three specific ideological aspects of the politics of postmodern Barcelona. While the previous chapter contextualized the 1992 Olympic Games in the global moment of the end of history, here I focus on the calculated use of the notions of the Mediterranean, Europe, and the city to deploy a specific hegemonic definition of Barcelona. I will describe this ideological redefinition as Barcelona's "urban cosmopolitanism." Therefore, while Chapter One inscribed our object of study in a temporal frame, this chapter focuses on the spatial imaginary of Barcelona's euphoric politics during the Olympic years. My aim is to undertake a critique of some of the specific ideologies that composed this imaginary. (In Chapters Three and Four, I will inspect the physical embodiment of these new imagined spatialities in the urban renewal of the city.)

Two main sociological studies have examined at great length the political discourses at work in Olympic Barcelona. John Hargreaves' *Freedom for Catalonia?* analyzes the nationalist conflicts between the Spanish state and the Catalan government of the Generalitat and, less directly, the conflicts between these two and the city hall. Hargreaves describes the multiple battles that took place during the organization of the Games regarding the display of symbols, emblems, flags, languages, and protocols. He also shows how, in spite of continuing mutual antipathies, the battles for the Catalanization versus the Spanishization of the Games eventually found a quite satisfactory compromise for all parts, as the Olympic ceremonies and other main events included an equal number of Catalan and Spanish identifying marks.

Donald McNeill's *Urban Change and the European Left: Tales from the New Barcelona* perfectly complements Hargreaves' book, and focuses not on the nationalist conflicts, but rather on the "citizen-based pragmatism" (91) of mayor Pasqual Maragall, which created a model for the new European Left. McNeill's comprehensive study examines the relation between Maragall's urban politics and the numerous neighborhood movements and popular demands that emerged during the transition to democracy. His analysis demonstrates how it became impossible to decide whether this relation was one of cooperation, or whether the city hall subtly coopted and deactivated the political claims of the people.

Given that these two sociological studies have already accounted for the "real" battles of the period, in this chapter I aim to complement McNeill and, more tangentially, Hargreaves, by looking at the ideological constructs that sustained the politics of the city hall during the Olympic years.[1] This set of ideological constructs were also part, or maybe even an original cause, of these battles. To search for concrete evidence of these nebulous constructs, I will focus on two main documents: the script of the ceremony of the reception of the Olympic flame, and the political manifesto "The Rio–Barcelona '92 Declaration," signed by the city halls of Rio de Janeiro and Barcelona. I will supplement these documents with mayor Maragall's own programmatic texts. Also, Francisco Casavella's novel *El triunfo* will allow me to point at the darker side effects of this ideological work and the neglected social sectors of Olympic Barcelona. Casavella's novel is an acute portrait of the ways in which the city hall's maneuvers contributed to displace Barcelona's underclasses. Even though I could have examined many other materials, I chose these texts not only because they can help us represent the ideologies of the city, but also because they were among the most sophisticated political and cultural articulations of the period. This variety of texts will hopefully offer us a glimpse at the tortuous deployment of a hegemonic ideology that fused the categories of the Mediterranean, Europe, and the city.

The Olympic Flame and the Mediterranean

The lighting of the Olympic flame and the torch relay is likely the best-known ritual of the modern Olympics. The ritual always begins in Olympia, Greece, where a torch is lightened with the concentrated rays of the sun symbolizing the ancient Olympian gods. Then a series of athletes, celebrities, and volunteers carry the torch for several weeks throughout the territory of the country hosting the Games. Finally, the last torchbearer ignites the Olympic flame at the stadium.

This emblematic ritual was not introduced by the founder of the modern Olympics, Pierre de Coubertin. Although Coubertin was naturally inspired by the Greek Olympic precedent, many components of the modern Games are quite dissimilar from the ancient ones. Indeed, the central element of the Greek Olympics – namely the religious honoring of the gods – was totally absent from Coubertin's conception of the Games. For him, the Games should embody the values of international peace and cosmopolitan fraternity achieved through fair competition and individual effort. In his own words, he "revived" the Olympic Games to institute them as a religion, but not in honor of the gods as in ancient Greece; instead, the modern athlete honors his country, his race, and his flag. Therefore, I believe that I was right to restore, from the very beginning of modern Olympism, a religious sentiment transformed and expanded by the internationalism and democracy that are distinguishing features of our day. (580)[2]

Given that honoring the gods was not the purpose of modern Games, the ritual of the fire, as a ritual that symbolized the connection with the Olympian gods, was initially not included in the modern ceremonies.

But, in 1936, the Nazis instituted the ritual of the Olympic flame at the Games held in Berlin. These Games were awarded to the German capital in 1931 and, even if Hitler abhorred the Olympics and the enlightened ideals with which Coubertin had infused them, he was later convinced that he could use them to deploy propaganda for his regime. With this purpose in mind, Carl Diem, secretary of the German National Olympics Committee, invented the torch relay from Olympia to Berlin in order to underscore the distinctive and unique link between ancient Greece and modern Germany. The Nazis emphasized the Greek origins of the Games precisely against Coubertin's internationalism: their goal was to de-internationalize them and turn them from a celebration of the all-too-French ideals of fraternity and democracy into an affirmation of Germany's unique relationship to ancient Greece.

The Nazi reappropriation of Greece connected with a long tradition of graecophilia that opposes the French neoclassic version of Greece, and runs from Hölderlin to Nietzsche and Heidegger. As Philippe Lacoue-Labarthe and Jean-Luc Nancy explain, modern German nationalism identified with the mystical, archaic Greece to oppose the bright and civic Greece promoted by French neoclassicism (301). German thought contested the French *lumières* and their picture of Greece as a classic model by retrieving the less enlightened dialectics between night and day, darkness and light, and myth and reason of archaic Greece. The Aryan myth was adopted because, as Lacoue-Labarthe and Nancy state, the Aryans are "the bearers of the solar myth... which causes forms to come forth as such" (309). In other words, the solar myth causes forms to emerge from unformed darkness. In this respect, the ritual of the Olympic flame is inscribed in this German (or perhaps primarily anti-French) mythology of light and darkness and humans and gods: fire connects these opposites in the same way that it symbolically connected Germany and Greece.

Even if the torch relay had a specific ideological function in the Games that staged the idolization of the Nazi regime and the Aryan race, this ritual has been enacted in every posterior Games. We can find the reason for this continuation in the same Berlin Games, where, as is known, the first torch relay was recorded by the most celebrated and also the most controversial documentary ever made about the Olympics: Leni Riefenstahl's 1936 *Olympia*. The film, an unsettling piece, both an aesthetic monument and an ideological monster, effectively exploited for the first time the immense visual attraction of the torch relay and the torch-lighting ceremony. *Olympia* inaugurated the transformation of the Games into visual spectacle.[3]

Thus, the incorporation of this ritual in post-World War II Games was not a further attempt to highlight their Greek origins or to invoke any divinities; rather, it was a sign of the gradual spectacularization of the Games in the media society. The ritual of the Olympic flame became a key element of the manufacture of the Games despite the disturbing, and rapidly forgotten, circumstances of its creation. But the origin of this ritual can at least make us aware of one thing, namely the ways in which other Games have reappropriated and deployed the mythologies of ancient Greece. The torch relay has provided a perfect occasion to generate appealing images for the global media, but it has also given the opportunity to cities and countries to promote themselves by fabricating an interested relation with ancient Greece.

At least this was the case in 1992, when Barcelona took enormous advantage of the ritual of the flame and the Greek origins of the Olympics. On June 12, 1992, the Olympic Committee (COOB' 92) organized a long ceremony at the coastal town of Empúries, north of Barcelona, to receive the flame lightened in Olympia. The flame had traveled across the Mediterranean on a boat named "Catalunya." The ceremony was staged in Empúries, where the ancient ruins that correspond to *Emporion* are located. *Emporion* was the first settlement founded by the Greeks on the Iberian peninsula in the fifth century BC. Two centuries later, it became the colony where the Romans began their conquest of the peninsula then renamed Hispania.

The reception ceremony, conceived by Catalan cultural critic Xavier Rubert de Ventós (born 1939), aimed to reproduce this initial arrival of Graeco-Roman civilization to the Iberian peninsula. An assemblage of texts related to the Olympic world and interwoven with quotations by authors from ancient Greece, German Romanticism, and Catalan *noucentisme* structured the ceremony. The script, which was recited by well-known Catalan, Spanish and Greek actors and actresses, also included various theatrical performances and musical pieces, as well as conventional political speeches. The performances comprised the Catalan national dance of the *sardana*, the traditional folklore of *gegants* (giant dancing figures) and *capgrossos* (individuals wearing big masks shaped like a head), and a series of contemporary dances honoring Greek gods. The musicians played different instruments such as the Greek *sirtaki*, the Spanish *bandurria*, and the Catalan *tenora*, and various ensembles and choirs played baroque music as well as the Catalan anthems "Santa Espina" and "Cant dels ocells." But the texts composed and compiled by Rubert de Ventós reveal more evidently than any other component of the ceremony how, in 1992, this Olympic ritual became a marked occasion to deploy a calculated linage between

Catalonia and Greece, a lineage which, by extension, linked Catalonia, Europe, and the Mediterranean.[4]

The script of the ceremony is divided into six parts: two initial speeches and a dramatized dialogue, which is in turn divided into four topics and staged by a narrator, a philosopher, a poet, a foreign hero, and, like in a Greek drama, a choir. The first speech, read by Greek actress Irene Papas, is titled "D'on venim" 'Where We Come From,' and it recalls, through various quotes by Lysias, Pausanias, and Isocrates, how the ancient Games served to establish peaceful relations between the Greek cities. The speech argues that the Hellenic cities correspond now to the entire world and calls for a continuation of "l'antiga ensenyança de lluitar amb les persones sense perdre les formes" 'the old lesson of fighting with people without ever losing good manners.'

Secondly, Catalan actress Núria Espert read a speech titled "On arribeu" 'Where You Arrive,' which already contains *in nuce* most of the themes of the ceremony. The text begins by asserting that, thanks to the carrying of the Olympic fire, "Ara la nostra història és gairebé la vostra, portadors dels déus primigenis" 'Now our history is almost yours, carriers of the primeval gods.' It remains initially undetermined whether the subject of "our history" are the Catalans, the Spaniards, or even the whole humankind. But a correspondence is later established between Greece and the Empordà, the "comarca" or county that surrounds Empúries. The Empordà is "un país tancat i acabat, tal i com els grecs imaginaven la República" 'a closed and finished country, as the Greeks imagined the Republic.' Etymology here reinforces this correspondence, as "Empordà" originally derives from the Greek *Emporion*, which was later transformed through the Latin *Emporitanu*. Thus, we find a perfect enactment of the Greek Republic in the very geography of this "comarca" situated between the Pyrenees and the Mediterranean.

This geographical self-enclosedness allows its inhabitants to recognize the county, which the text quickly proceeds to call a country, as a full entity: "Un país cenyit... un país amb principi i final, emmurallat de muntanyes que vénen a ensumar el mar, un país del qual els seus habitants poden parlar d'una manera concreta i precisa" 'An enclosed country... a country with a beginning and an end, walled up by mountains that come to smell the sea, a country about which its inhabitants can talk in a concrete and precise way.' We must notice how the affirmation that the enclosed geography of this country allows its inhabitants to talk about it in a concrete and precise way avoids one classical nationalist trope: the trope of identifying a certain territory with a certain language and presenting the latter as an organic emanation of the former. Rubert de Ventós does not link the geography of the country to its "natural" language; rather, he delimits the country by observing that it can be named and perceived in a concrete and precise way.

A long tradition of Catalan writers have portrayed the Empordà as a synec-dochical equivalent to Catalonia. Most notably, *modernista* poet Joan Maragall (1860–1911), who was the grandfather of Barcelona's mayor Pasqual Maragall, wrote in 1908 the famous poem "L'Empordà," which constitutes a milestone of Catalan literature; poet Jacint Verdaguer (1845–1902) wrote two other national anthems: "L'Empordà" and "A la Verge del Mont;" and Josep Pla (1897–1981) also wrote extensively about the inhabitants and places of the Empordà as representative of Catalonia.[5] Similarly, in *Refent Barcelona*, mayor Maragall (who was a close friend of Rubert de Ventós) wrote about the symbolic significance of the reception of the Olympic flame in Empúries and the Empordà: "L'Empordà no és tan sols una part de Catalunya, diu el poeta, sinó el cel d'una certa carac-terística de catalanitat. Si Catalunya quedés reduïda a l'Empordà – diu el seu poeta – Catalunya sencera podria tornar a existir, l'Empordà podria tornar a generar Catalunya" 'The Empordà is not only a part of Catalonia, the poet says, but also the sky of a certain characteristic of Catalan-ness. If Catalonia were reduced to the Empordà, the poet says, Catalonia could be resurrected, the Empordà could generate Catalonia again' (148).[6]

In this synecdochical use of the Empordà, we encounter one of the most subtle ideological devices of Catalanism. This consists in presenting the most immediate surroundings and landscapes as one's true fatherland. Thus, the "comarca" or county, the valley, or the city that one inhabits, are perceived as the real "pàtria" or homeland. This perception has three main ideological implications. On the one hand, by circumscribing one's homeland to a specific geographical place, one avoids recognizing the territory of the state – that is, Spain – as an effective nation. Since the state defines its members as Spaniards, this cultural and affective attachment to a "personal" landscape is a way of eluding this official interpellation. However, on the other hand, this type of patriotism also avoids endorsing Catalonia as the ultimate "pàtria." The reason is that such an endorsement could entail an implicit call for independence from Spain. Even if this patriotism can be defined as a synecdochical form of Catalan nationalism, which claims the nation through one of its parts, in the end its ambiguity distinguishes it from the open forms of Catalan separatism.

Finally, this specific type of Catalanism differs from the classic nationalism of both nation-states and stateless nations in one crucial point. While nationalism aims at unifying its members into the national body of the people, this type of patriotism promotes the individual identification of oneself with one's most particular, almost private, surroundings. That is, this form of imagining the community does not intend to create a unified collective body, but rather stresses the individual relationship with one's territory, even though this relationship does assume a sort of collective ritual and communal practice.

Given these various implications, we can interpret this ambiguous but rooted form of patriotism in connection with an economic factor. This patriotism is perfectly compatible with the class interests of a Catalan bourgeoisie that wanted to have a good relationship with the Spanish state, whose protectionist measures secured the marketplace for the Catalan industries, while it also wanted to maintain a special status as a different culture, given that, after all, the defense of Catalan culture could often serve to establish social consensus and tame class antagonisms. Indeed, as I will explain below, the Catalan bourgeoisie has always aspired to transform and federalize the state without dismembering it. For this reason, a form of patriotism that embraced neither the Spanish nation nor Catalan separatism was adequate to their calculated ambiguity vis-à-vis the political structure of the country. Similarly, this type of cultural patriotism that gave priority to the individual sphere over the articulation of a unified national body can also be interpreted in relation to the classic individualistic values of the bourgeoisie. Again, the target of this patriotism would be the collective separatist movements that were often intermingled with the workers' movements.[7]

After describing the unified wholeness of the Empordà, Rubert de Ventós continues his Empúries script by asserting that we – it still needs to be determined who is comprised within this "we" – decided to go north and "construir el nostre ordre romànic i cristià, que va derivar fins a esdevenir romàntic" 'to build our Romanesque and Christian order, which evolved until it became Romantic.' This single sentence draws a long and direct genealogy that goes from Greece to the expansion of Christianity and the emergence of Romanticism: three moments that indicate that "our... order" refers to Europe, to a certain hegemonic configuration of Europe as a Graeco-Christian continent.

But the speech finishes with an invocation to Venus by Catalan philosopher Eugeni d'Ors: "petita testa de Venus, que potser ets una petita testa d'Artemisa, trobada a Empúries: vulgues, per record i per amor de la vella Catalunya grega, donar un sentit clàssic a la moderna Catalunya confosa..." 'small head of Venus, which may be a small head of Artemis, found in Empúries: may you give, for the memory and the love for old Greek Catalonia, a classic path to this confused modern Catalonia...'[8] Here, the "we" of the narrative, and the pertinence of "our... order," no longer correspond to Europe, but are specifically redirected toward Catalonia and the Catalan people.

Up to this point, the speech has established a chain of equivalences that define the place where the Olympic flame arrives and the collectivity that is invoked. As this final allusion to Catalonia makes explicit, Empúries and the Empordà function synecdochically to represent Catalonia as a whole. This chain of equivalences is articulated through the different terms that refer to the place receiving the flame: first, the term is an unspecified "terra" 'land;' then, it becomes the "contrada" 'county' of the Empordà; and, finally, it jumps to a "país" 'country,' which is repeated a total of six times. Thus, this chain of spatial terms – "terra," "contrada," "país" – is interweaved with the determination of "our order" as Romanesque, Christian, and Romantic. This blending of "spaces" and "orders" articulates a collective subject initially identified with the barbarians civilized by the Greeks, and later with the original Empordanesos, the Christians, the Romantics, and, finally, the Catalans.

The quotation by d'Ors establishes a direct connection with the previous and prominent effort to construct a Greek genealogy for modern Catalonia. This effort is an important precedent that deserves a brief digression, which should help us historicize Rubert de Ventós' script. During the first two decades of the twentieth century, Eugeni d'Ors (1881–1954) led the movement of *noucentisme*, composed of a group of writers and artists that launched a program of cultural and political action for Catalonia and Spain. Specifically, *noucentisme* came together as a movement in 1906, the year in which d'Ors began his daily column or "glosa" at the newspaper La Veu de Catalunya. This column appeared until 1921 and functioned as the main source of indoctrination for the whole movement. *Noucentisme* gathered, most notably, writers Josep Carner, Jaume Bofill i Mates, and Carles Riba, painters Joaquim Sunyer and Joaquim Torres-García, sculptor Josep Clarà, and architect Rafael Masó, among many others. The movement officially ended in 1923, when the dictatorship of Primo de Rivera abolished all Catalan institutions as well as the public use of the language.

Noucentisme promulgated the aesthetics of Graeco-Roman classicism and turned them into a full cultural and political program to build a new national personality for Catalonia. One of d'Ors' first columns of 1906, "Empòrium," retrieved Empúries as a foundational origin of Catalonia. For him, Empúries was the evidence that the essence of Catalonia should be found in its Mediterranean psyche and its link to the Greek and Roman empires. In the column, d'Ors declares: "penso que tot el sentit ideal d'una gesta redemptora de Catalunya podria reduir-se avui a *descobrir el Mediterrani*. Descobrir lo que hi ha de mediterrani en nosaltres, i afirmar-ho de cara al món, i expandir l'obra imperial entre els homes" 'I think that today the ideal meaning of a redeeming endeavor of Catalonia could be reduced to *discovering the Mediterranean*. To discover the Mediterranean in ourselves, and announce it to the world, and expand the imperial task amongst mankind' (18). This inner, but also rediscovered, Mediterranean-ness of the Catalans would be expressed through the aesthetic qualities of classic Graeco-Roman art. The characteristics of measure, proportion, and harmony constituted the programmatic values of the *noucentistes* and infused each aspect of their "imperial" task, from literature and art, to politics.

The reference to this so-called imperial task points at the close link between *noucentisme* and the political program of Enric Prat de la Riba and his conservative party of Lliga Regionalista, mainly supported by the Catalan bourgeoisie.

Also in 1906, Prat de la Riba published his influential essay-manifesto *La Nacion-alitat Catalana*, in which he advocated a Catalan imperial intervention in Spain so as to transform the centralist state into a federal one. Prat's imperialism aimed to enlarge the self-government of the Catalan nation and simultaneously encourage all Iberian peoples to gain more autonomy.[9] His program reacted against a demoralized post-1898 Spain which had lost not only the Spanish-American War along with the rest of its colonies and external markets, but also its national self-esteem and its glorious imperial imaginary. For Catalanism (and for the *regeneracionistas* of the *Generación del 98*), the attachment to this past imperial glory had caused Spain's present backwardness. Prat argued that the Catalan industrial model and civil society should replace Castile's agrarian order controlled by rural oligarchies and the army. The task of bourgeois Catalanism was to lead the transformation of the state and initiate a path to modernization.[10]

Modernization and the reform of the state were constructive and necessary tasks, but another underlying goal of Prat's imperial program was the economic control of the peninsula. And "imperial" was indeed the most precise term to define the task of bourgeois Catalanism: as Lenin analyzed in his famous essay, imperialism is the "monopoly stage of capitalism," which involves the establishment of capitalist monopolies as well as the pursuit of exclusive colonial possession.[11] Thus, Catalan imperialism results in a unique and often contradictory mixture of federal reform and capitalist control, of national liberation and raw colonization. Somewhat ironically, bourgeois Catalanism ultimately hoped to replace one form of imperialism with another: the old imperialism of Spain with modern capitalist imperialism.

In this context, *noucentisme* provided an alternative imaginary for Catalonia and Spain, a fresh symbology centered on the classic Graeco-Roman Mediterranean and detached from the decadent emblems of Castile and the Spanish empire. *Noucentisme*'s neoclassicism propagated an aesthetics of urban civility and metropolitan refinement that aimed to supplant the rural and archaic social forms of Castile.

This imaginary, however, also involved a definite investment in class politics. As Josep Murgades explains, *noucentisme* represented the ideological state apparatus of a Catalan bourgeoisie that not only hoped to redefine the political structure of Spain, but also wanted to domesticate Catalonia's internal social antagonisms. The classic aesthetic qualities of measure, proportion and harmony entailed an ideal of civil order intended to contain and ultimately suppress class struggle. This containment was twofold: it was motivated by a set of predictable economic class interests, but these interests also included a political aspect. Specifically, Murgades argues that the imperialist project, despite advocating for Catalan supremacy, directly opposed Catalan separatism. He writes: "[e]n tant que a quest mot s'associa amb la idea d'assimilació, d'annexió, parlar d'imperialisme era demostrar explícitament l'antiseparatisme inherent del programa burgès, frenar els desviacionismes d'un catalanisme de base popular progressivament radical-itzat i combatiu" 'As this word is associated with the ideas of assimilation and annexation, the reference to imperialism explicitly demonstrated the inherent antiseparatism of the bourgeois program and its determination to halt the devia-tions of a popular Catalanism progressively radicalized and combative' ("Assaig" 46). Thus, the political antiseparatism of the bourgeoisie should ultimately be connected again to their class interests and their attempt to control the Spanish market with the help of the state.

The *noucentista* aesthetics of Mediterranean classicism assisted the political ambitions of the Catalan bourgeoisie in three main ways. First, these aesthetics could help distinguish Catalonia from Castile, as Castile could not embrace notions of Mediterranean-ness for obvious geographical reasons. Given that the dry *meseta* would never enjoy the crystal-clear waters of the Mediterranean, *noucentista* aesthetics can be interpreted as the cultural expression of the wish for Catalan supremacy and capitalist monopoly in Spain. Second, even if these aesthetics were devoted to the construction of Catalonia, their Mediterranean and Graeco-Roman scope kept them from appearing too openly nationalist. This way they could contribute to disband the potential attempts of Catalan radical separatism to configure a clear-cut nationalist culture and symbology.

Finally, the classicist values promoted by the *noucentistes* – measure, propor-tion, harmony – could effortlessly serve as a cultural and aesthetic justifica-tion of the established civil order and class hierarchy. In fact, the *glosa* "Petita Oració" by d'Ors, from which Rubert de Ventós extracted the quotation for his script, is one of the most rampant examples of how d'Ors used classicist values to demand social order. The head of Venus to which he appeals and asks for protection and guidance belonged to a statue that was excavated in Empúries in August 1909, during a summer full of violent episodes of class struggle and anticlericalism. The *setmana tràgica* or Tragic Week, when many churches in Barcelona were burnt, had just taken place a month earlier, in July. D'Ors hopes that Venus will give a "classic path to this confused modern Catalonia," and adds: "[p]rotegeix-la [la nostra ciutat] dels greus perills que l'amenacen... Fes que la governació d'ella tota sencera, no pugui pus apertànyer sinó als vers ciutadans, i lliura-la de les mans dels barbres, dels esclaus, dels afranquits i dels metecs" 'May you protect [our city] from the serious dangers threatening it... May you ensure that its governance belongs to its real citizens, and keep off of it the hands of the barbarians, the slaves, the freed slaves, and the foreigners' (106). It is not too difficult to find modern correspondences for these classic figures. Thus, while the dominant classes and the conservative Lliga would embody the "real citizens," the hordes of barbarians, slaves, freed slaves, and foreigners could easily correspond to the communists, anarchists, anticlerical-ists, and immigrants that are disturbing the social order.

While the reader may find the inclusion of immigrants in this diatribe not only racist, but also, and especially, incongruous, we must refer to the next *glosa*, published three days later, on December 14, 1909, and titled "Els metecs." In it, d'Ors affirms that French nationalists are wrong when they complain about the presence of *métèques* in France. When they arrive in France, the *métèques* – which was the name for foreigners in ancient Athens – quickly adopt French and adapt themselves to their new milieu. In Catalonia, however, the "factors d'origen múltiple no s'equilibren" 'the factors of multiple origins do not find an equilibrium' (108). Specifically, this means that the presence of (mostly Spanish-speaking) immigrants may frustrate the efforts to strengthen Catalan language and culture. Thus, while the chauvinist undertones of the *glosa* are undeniable, d'Ors is pointing here at a crucial problem: that of the different cultural effects that immigration has in different contexts.

Given Catalonia's lack of political autonomy, Catalan does not appear to immigrants as the official, "natural" language of the land where they now live and, for this reason, the requirement to speak it is often perceived as a gratuitous imposition. In France or in other sovereign states, by contrast, state apparatuses have naturalized this imposition and turned it into a logical and beneficial expectation. In this sense, when comparing Catalonia with France, d'Ors had two possible "solutions" to the language problem: either to blame immigrants and their lack of interest in learning Catalan, or to propose that Catalonia should strive to become an independent state. Given the antisepara-tist stance of the Catalan bourgeoisie, it is not surprising that he chooses the former and does not even mention the latter as a possibility.[12]

Leaving aside their class affiliations, the *noucentistes* undertook for the first time in modern Catalonia the creation of numerous cultural infrastructures, including schools, libraries, art centers, book collections, academies, and founda-tions. They founded, among other institutions, the Institut d'Estudis Catalans, the Biblioteca Nacional de Catalunya, the Estudis Universitaris Catalans, the Escola Superior dels Bells Oficis, and the Cercle Artístic de Sant Lluc. These institutions, organized through the central Mancomunitat de Catalunya (1913–25), have sustained the country's cultural life up to the present. The Mancomunitat, under the presidency of Prat de la Riba first, and of architect Josep Puig i Cadafalch from 1917 until dictator Primo de Rivera abolished it in 1925, functioned not only as a cultural institution, but also as a pseudo-state that worked on the improvement of Catalonia's technological and industrial infrastructure. For this reason, *noucentisme*'s task, as Murgades writes, has "cristal·litzat en unes pràctiques d'integració social que resulten altament operatives i eficaces en l'àmbit institucional, cultural i científic" 'crystallized in numerous practices of social integration that are highly operative and effective in the institutional, cultural, and scientific fields' ("Assaig" 42). During the Republic, and again in the post-Franco period, the cultural and social work of *noucentisme* has continued to shape Catalonia's civil society.

However, the original class ideology of the movement has equally traversed many Catalanist projects, resulting in intricate clashes between class and nation. Specifically, two conflictive aspects of the promotion of Catalan culture derive from the *noucentistes'* affiliation with the bourgeoisie. On the one hand, this promotion has tended to be identified with class politics and interests. This association is still often invoked, especially by Spanish anti-Catalanists, to dismiss the advancement of Catalan culture altogether. But, on the other hand, when materialist analyses of Catalan cultural artifacts detect class ideology in them, such analyses tend to be interpreted, especially by Catalan nationalists, as motivated by anti-Catalanist sentiments. Thus, the often distrustful relationship between Catalan and Spanish cultures frequently emerges through one of these two forms of ideological short circuiting.

This brief incursion into the significance of *noucentisme* should allow us to examine the rest of Rubert de Ventós' script for the Empúries ceremony and shed light on its historical and ideological implications.[13]

The second part of the script includes the four sections of the dramatized dialogue. The first section presents the "Admiració i nostàlgia" 'Admiration and Nostalgia' that ancient Greeks have aroused among modern peoples. The dialogue, which includes quotes from Schiller and Schlegel, laments, in a Romantic fashion, that the modern rational world, unlike the Greek cosmos, is fragmented and emptied of all essence. The text also affirms that in Greece, sports were not a mere "rècord quantitatiu" 'quantitative record,' which of course implies that the modern Olympics, as a product of enlightened rationality, have little in common with the ancient Games. But, after having recalled this fundamental difference between the Greeks and the moderns, the text carefully establishes continuity between the two. That is, the script first presents the Greek world as an invaluable and irreproducible precedent, and then posits the possibility of reviving it in Empúries. The choir declaims at the end of this section:

> Empúries Port, vell bressol de fragments, quan els grecs arribaren, tot era espera en l'esguard d'un encalçat horitzó. Els noucentistes, més tard, per fundar al seu redós una idea exultant d'existir d'un país, l'han revifat en triomf.

> Empúries as Port, old cradle of fragments, when the Greeks landed there was only waiting and looking at a limited horizon. Later, the *noucentistes* founded on it the exultant idea of the existence of a country and succeeded in reviving it.

This intervention of the choir, which loosely follows the format of Greek tragedies and serves as a comment on the dramatic action, refers to the fragmented nature of Empúries itself. This can be understood in two ways: either that the ruins of Empúries comprise a fragmented collection of the Greek past, or that Empúries was a fragmented world before the coming of the Greeks. If we follow this second option, a correspondence is established between the indigenous peoples of Empúries, who waited (for the Greeks) while looking at the horizon, and the *noucentistes*, who created an ideal for the country that revived this act of waiting. That is, in the same way that the Greeks brought unity to the dispersed pre-Hellenic territories, the *noucentistes* provided an ideal of triumphant plenitude to a fragmented country, a country that, thanks to this ideal, is now waiting for the end of its incompleteness. Thus, another loose but unmistakable chain of equivalences is articulated here between the dispersed modern world, the fragmented pre-Hellenic Empúries, and the political incompleteness of Catalonia. In the same way that Romanticism longed for unity amidst modern rationality, and Greece provided a unifying horizon to Iberian Empúries, the idea of Catalonia devised by the *noucentistes* brings unity to this expectant country. Whether the initial arrival of the Greeks to Empúries would here correspond to the coming of Catalonia's independence is left undetermined, as the text calculatedly lays emphasis on the act of waiting. Once again, we encounter the same ambiguity that *noucentisme* embraced: there is the hope that Catalonia will some day be autonomous, but there is no confrontation with the Spanish state with a blunt call for independence.

The second part of the dialogue comprises a series of ancient sayings about "Jocs i esports" 'Games and Sports.' We find quotes by Aristotle or Philostratus determining the qualities that athletes must possess in order to compete. Among these references, there is also an old saying found in Quintilianus and Petronius that encourages athletes: "Qui ha aixecat un vedell podrà aixecar un toro." 'If you can lift a calf, you can lift a bull.' Despite the classic origin of the reference, and the fact that the bull is a central character in ancient mythology, the bull has also a specific connection with the contemporary context: it has been employed for a long time, and especially under Francoism, as a symbol of Spain. Is it too far-fetched to read in this encouragement to lift a bull a veiled political meaning – namely, that Catalonia should lift the governing rule of the Spanish state? Given the Catalanist stance of so many parts of the script, these connotations should not be excluded.

At the end of the second part, the choir declaims:

Empúries Pacte, que aquells que vivien apart uns dels altres, grecs, indiketes, romans, vas ajuntar, com d'antic diu Estrabó, en una sola llei, per conviure i per créixer, past dels seus bàrbars costums, grega la mira del temps.

Empúries as Pact, which brought together, as old Strabo says, under one single law those Greeks, Indiketes, and Romans who lived apart, so they could live and grow, nourished with their old barbarian customs and having acquired the Greek vision of time.

This characterization of Empúries as the place in which successive peoples have made pacts to coexist in a peaceful manner directly connects with a long tradition of modern Catalan historiography: that of identifying pactism as a psychological and social trait of the Catalan people. Let us also examine, in a short digression, the different historical imaginaries of Catalonia and Spain vis-à-vis the question of pactism.

The structure of feudalism in Catalonia – based on the pacts established between lords and peasants, as well as between Barcelona's ruling classes of merchants and the aristocracy, and even the Catalan kings – has often been interpreted as the reason why pactism evolved into a spiritual trait of the Catalans. As Robert Hughes writes:

> The feudal institutions of medieval Catalunya developed out of a healthy concern for the mutual rights and obligations of nobles, clerics, peasants, burghers, and workmen. And Catalunya's particular feudalism was the core of its national identity... Feudalism, with its corporate loyalties and its belief in negotiation – "pactism" was the key word – would transform itself in the Catalan political world straight into modern capitalism... (94)

In addition to explaining the emergence of industrial capitalism in Catalonia, the historiographic focus on pactism has had another, more political function. The proclamation of pactism as a national trait ultimately proposes that the Catalans, if they want to remain faithful to their historical identity, must seek to establish a pactist relationship with the Spanish state that supersedes the current subordinate or colonial bond. Given that the premodern practice of pactism ended with the abolition of the Catalan institutions in 1716 after the War of the Spanish Succession, when Catalonia was integrated to the centralist state through Philip V's Decreto de Nueva Planta, the interpretation of Catalan feudalism as a pactist society aimed to project this social practice on a modernity in which pactism was no longer possible for a region subordinated to the central state. Thus, this projection of pactism as a national feature implicitly contained a call for a future redefinition of Catalonia's relationship to the state.[14]

Rubert de Ventós' categorization of ancient Empúries as a place of pactism can be read as a continuation of this historiographic tradition. However, the tracing of the origin of pactism back to the initial coming of the Greeks contains a further ideological move. While the feudal origin of pactism served to claim the redefinition of the internal relationship between the Spanish state and Catalonia, the location of this origin in Graeco-Roman civilization can be interpreted as an attempt to project Catalonia beyond Spain and connect it with the larger entities of the Mediterranean and Europe. On the occasion of the Olympics, Barcelona and Catalonia wanted to "sign a pact," so to speak, with the Mediterranean and Europe, in order to gain visibility on a more transnational scale. Naturally, this embrace of the Mediterranean and Europe did not cancel the aspiration to reform and decentralize the Spanish state; on the contrary, it perfectly complemented it. (I will further develop this point later.)

The third section, "Foc i crítica" 'Fire and Criticism,' includes the symbology of fire in Greece, as well as critical comments made by some classic authors against the Olympics. The narrator explains how Prometheus stole the fire from the gods and how fire is an element that may illuminate the world or that may destroy it: "[l]a torxa olímpica, que duem avui de mà en mà, és la conservació i alhora la domesticació d'aquest foc que simbolitza la transformació de la guerra en esport" '[t]he Olympic torch, which today we pass on from hand to hand, preserves and domesticates the fire that symbolizes the transformation of war into sport.' The text proceeds by quoting Heraclitus' dictum, "War is the father of all," and emphasizes again that sport contests exemplify the way in which civilization tames the essential combat of all things.[15] Then, Euripides and Xenophanes are quoted criticizing the Games as a fruitless and pompous spectacle. But they are counterbalanced by the Persian soldier Trigames, who exclaims in fear that, if the Greeks are willing to fight among themselves for a mere laurel wreath, they must be terrifying when they fight an enemy. And the choir declaims:

> Empúries Porta, en l'herència d'aquell esperit de riquesa
> que a la península ha dut grecs averanys, i més tard
> la romanització, el bressol d'Hispània, la copa
> que amb el temps ens havia de ser Seu del menar Episcopal,
> Comtat d'Empúries fins al gresol que alentà Barcelona,
> prínceps i comtes-rei que la memòria en té l'abast.

> Empúries as Door, inheritor of the rich spirit that brought Greek signs to the peninsula, and later Romanization, the cradle of Hispania, the cup that afterward became Episcopal See, the Count of Empúries and the crucible that inspired Barcelona, princes and king-counts recalled by our memory.

This paragraph repeats some of the ideas that have already been discussed. Empúries here represents the door through which Romanization and Christianity, the fundamental pillars of (European) civilization, entered. We may notice that Rubert de Ventós employs "Hispània" to refer to Roman Spain, but that he states that Romanization and Christianization culminated in the successive counts of Barcelona, that is, the medieval dynasties of Catalan kings who ruled while Catalonia was still a sovereign territory.

The fourth and last section, "Lletanies i poemes" 'Litanies and Poems,' leaves behind the allusions to ancient Greece and overtly refers to Catalonia. An officiant of the choir recites a poem by Joan Maragall. The poem, "Expedició de Catalans a Orient" 'Catalan Expedition to Orient,' evokes the medieval period when Catalonia conquered several territories throughout the Mediterranean, including Greece. Maragall's poem glorifies the conquering spirit of the

Catalans, which enabled them to seize the birthplace of the ancient Mediterranean empires: Athens. The poem says:

> Arreu cercant guerres – sis mil catalans
> se'n van cap a Grècia – a on no aniran?
> Salvaran imperis – n'enderrocaran;
> entre ells faran Guerra – si amb altres no en fan,
> i a bots i a empentes – la Grècia espantant,
> fins dalt de l'Acròpolis – pendó plantaran.

> Seeking wars – six thousand Catalans
> go to Greece – where will they not go?
> They will save empires – and overthrow others;
> when they have no enemies, – they will fight among them,
> and advancing by fits and starts – frightening Greece,
> on top of the Acropolis – they will put in a pennon.[16]

Indeed, during the thirteenth and fourteenth centuries, the Catalan–Aragonese kings expanded their dominion over different areas of the Mediterranean. The expansion, carried out either by force or through marital alliances, took control of Mallorca (1229), València (1238), Sicily (1282), Sardinia (1323), and Athens and Neopàtria (1311–88). This so-called Catalan Mediterranean empire has largely been idealized by various Romantic historiographers eager to envision a magnificent past for the Catalan nation. But, in contrast to most modern nationalisms, which appropriate imperial pasts to exhibit the unremitting and transhistorical power of their nation, this historiographic tradition, notably represented by historians Joaquim Miret i Sans, Antoni Rubió i Lluch, and Ferran Soldevila, recognizes that the Catalan empire did not consist in a fully military, political, and cultural domination over the Mediterranean. Instead, the Catalan empire has been defined as a commercial empire, that is, as an enterprise driven not by the need to accomplish glorious deeds and subjugate foreign peoples, but rather by the will to control sea routes and various strategic ports.

However, as J. N. Hillgarth has argued, the expansion of Catalonia fundamentally consisted in a series of dynastic occupations often also conceived as religious crusades. These occupations were too eclectic and circumstantial to be part of a well-defined expansionist project. Given the internal limitations of the Crown (an undeveloped economy, political divisions, limited naval and military resources), along with the struggles with other powers such as France, Castile, or the Italian republics, Catalan invasions ended up forming a rather weak and unstable dominion over the Mediterranean. This dominion certainly favored Catalan trade, but on no account were Barcelona's merchant classes prosperous enough to finance a full commercial expansion. Despite all these limitations, Hillgarth concludes, the Catalan–Aragonese Crown did achieve a real control over a substantial part of Mediterranean commerce during the thirteenth and fourteenth centuries. This control greatly benefited Barcelona and turned Catalan into one of the languages of diplomacy and trade (54).

After Hillgarth's analysis, we can see how the stress on the commercial nature of the Catalan Mediterranean Empire found in modern Romantic historiography had one key ideological motive: the attempt to present Catalonia as a country that had always been characterized by its trade and industry. In this respect, this depiction of the Catalan empire aimed to contrast with the picture of the Spanish empire as a military, cultural, and religious venture. As we have seen, for Catalanism these characteristics had given way to an imperial imaginary based on military glory and religious causes that had put modern Spain in a marginal world position. The Catalan empire of trade opposed the Spanish empire of honor and religion and thus contained a clear reformist subtext. Rather than different imperial forms, what we encounter here are competing nationalist representations of former imperial enterprises.

We find parallel ideological mystifications in the relationship between modern Spain and its former empire. Spain's marginal position in the nineteenth century has been attributed to two main complementary causes related to its empire. First, the cost of fighting the wars of independence in Latin America, and loss of trade and customs revenues largely impoverished the state and made it very difficult to launch a process of modernization. Second, the past possession of a glorious empire also thwarted the impulse needed to modernize the country in more ideological and socio-psychological ways. As Martin Blinkhorn explains,

> in Spain's case the very possession of an empire and the values which it encouraged probably acted as a brake on industrialization – and on the modernization of rural society – rather than as a stimulant towards these mutually related processes. Easy colonial wealth, it has been argued [by Jordi Nadal in "Spain, 1830–1914"], contributed to the Spanish bourgeoisie's persistent lack of economic enterprise and its ready acceptance of rural-aristocratic values. (7)

But the relationship between Spain's modernization (or its lack thereof), and its former empire, can be more complexified if we learn from the groundbreaking work of Henry Kamen, *Empire: How Spain Became a World Power, 1492–1763*. In this book, Kamen demonstrates how the representation of the Spanish empire as a full military, cultural and religious conquest of America and other territories was a product of modern nationalist Spanish historiography, rather than a historical reality. Kamen departs from the fact that it was materially impossible that a rural and underpopulated Castile could conquer a vast amount of territories with millions of inhabitants in less than a hundred years. Thus, the Spanish empire was made possible by "the combined resources of the Western European and Asian nations, who participated fully and legally in an enterprise that is normally thought of, even by professional historians, as being 'Spanish'" (xxv). For Kamen, the empire must be described as a "transnational organization" (491) that combined and mobilized Portuguese navigators, Genoese financiers, African settlers, and Chinese traders. The Castilians could, at most, be seen as the "managers" (493) of the organization, but, as is known, the profits rarely went to Spain. Similarly, Castilian did become the "language of the empire," but only for administrative tasks; on no account did the peoples who lived under the rule of the Spanish monarch adopt Castilian as their everyday language. In Europe, Italian as a language of cultural exchange was much more predominant than Spanish (500); in Asia, the lingua franca of commerce was Portuguese (501); and, in Latin America, Spanish only became the primary language in the nineteenth century, when the new independent states enforced it as part of their nation-building processes.

Kamen shows how the Spanish empire established a much weaker dominion over its territories than it is usually assumed. The representation of the Spanish empire as a full conquest corresponds to a modern nationalist projection of Spain over its past, a projection that also fitted well with the interests of other states: the new Latin American states (and here perhaps we could include the Catalan nation too) could portray themselves as the former victims of, and the new liberators from, the imperial legacy. Yet, one of Kamen's final conclusions is even more startling:

> we are accustomed to the idea that Spain created its empire, but it is more useful to work with the idea that the empire created Spain. At the outset of our historical period 'Spain' did not exist, it had not formed politically or economically, nor did its component cultures have the resources for expansion. The collaboration of the peoples of the peninsula in the task of empire, however, gave them a common cause that brought them together and enhanced, however imperfectly, peninsular unity. (xxv)

For the assessment of the nature of Spain's modernity, the consequences of this statement are immense. While it is commonplace to say that Spain's lack of modernization was caused by the decline of the empire (and the psychological block that this produced, the false sense of wealth, the military and religious archaic values that the empire entailed, etc), after Kamen's analysis we can propose a supplementary thesis: that Spain's modernization unfolded precisely as a "non-modern" project by means of the representation of a lost empire. That is, the empire did not prevent Spain from modernizing itself; instead, modern Spain was constituted by (mis)representing itself as a once glorious and powerful empire, an empire that had established military dominance, the Catholic faith, and the Spanish language in multiple parts of the globe. The purpose of this modern ideological representation is that it could articulate in an effective way the military and religious values of the Castilian rural oligarchies and the centralist hierarchies of the state.[17]

Spain's modernity should no longer be interpreted only as a failed or incomplete process due to internal cultural traits, religious fervor, and persistent backwardness. Instead, the characteristics of Spain's modernity seem to be more determined by its position in the capitalist world system as a country with "semiperipheral" development, to use Immanuel Wallerstein's terms. Thus, the archaic values of the Castilian oligarchies, the representation of past imperial glory, centralist power, or *caciquismo* do not constitute remnants of the past, but truly modern phenomena that have configured the country as semiperipheral. Indeed, these phenomena are the very expressions of Spain's modern semiperipheral condition.

This point of view also sheds light on the motives behind Catalonia's imperial project over Spain. While, in principle, this project wanted to modernize Spain and free it from its oligarchic politics, we must also recall that it was the state's oligarchic structure that had permitted Catalonia to develop its textile industry and enjoy the protectionist measures that a more "modernized" state would probably not have implemented. In *Spain, 1808–1939*, Raymond Carr describes the continuous efforts of the Catalan bourgeoisie to obtain strict protectionist measures from the state against the liberals' attempts to liberalize the state (277–90). Carr affirms that, in the nineteenth century, "Catalan industrialists and intellectuals, for three generations, were to defend protection by variations on the single theme that it was a *national* necessity, not a Catalan interest" (279). At the same time, however, the liberal politicians who advocated free trade did not strictly pursue the modernization of the country. In reality, they were more sensitive to the interests of the rural oligarchies, who extracted their benefits from a still agrarian economy:

> the products of the soil not only provided most Spaniards with a living but the state with most of its income and the economy as a whole with its purchasing power abroad. It is easy to see why most finance ministers were free traders at heart and unresponsive to the claims of industry for continued high protection at the expense of export staples. (278–9)

In any case, without state protectionism, the much more developed core industries of England or France would have easily taken over Catalonia's Spanish market. Thus, contradictorily, the very protectionist measures that made Catalonia's industry possible also inhibited its competitiveness; a contradiction directly related to the semiperipheral position of Spain and Catalonia within the structure of capitalism. Given this situation, we can say that, despite the different levels of industrialization, Catalonia needed to modernize as much as Spain did. The Catalan bourgeoisie knew this, and the "imperial" work of the Lliga, *noucentisme*, and the Mancomunitat intended to create the infrastructure and social institutions that could realize a more effective process of modernization, that is, the process of making Catalan industry more competitive and less dependent on state protectionism. In this context, the historiographic representation of the Catalan medieval empire as a commercial expansion constituted an empowering figure for a modern Catalonia striving to reform Spain and establish a more "pactist" relationship to the state.

These are some of the ideological and historical subtexts contained in the pactism of Empúries in Rubert de Ventós' 1992 script. Yet, at the Empúries ceremony, the insertion of Joan Maragall's poem, and its glorification of the Catalan Mediterranean empire, points at a further use of this past. The poem focuses on the fact that the Catalans arrived in Athens, a city that is at the opposite side of the Mediterranean or, more specifically, at the opposite side of the Northern and European shore of the Mediterranean. Thus, such a retrieval of the conquest of Athens seems to fit well with the political attempt of Barcelona's city hall to launch the Catalan city as one of the capitals of the Mediterranean.

In 1986, in his initial program, *Refent Barcelona*, mayor Pasqual Maragall stated that his goal was to transform Barcelona into a "pivot d'aquest 'Nord del Sud' europeu" 'a pivotal point of this "North of the European South"' (91). He defined this "Nord del Sud" as the region that comprises the Spanish Mediterranean, the French Midi, and "quasi" 'almost' Northern Italy (91). In 1991, in *Barcelona, la ciutat retrobada*, mayor Maragall slightly reduced this North of the European South: the region that Barcelona should articulate comprised the cities of Toulouse, Zaragoza, València, Palma de Mallorca, and Montpellier (101–3). But, in any case, this area largely coincided with the territorial boundaries of the Catalan–Aragonese Crown, and the call for a restitution of the alliances among these cities sought to transform Barcelona into a key port in the Mediterranean, as it had been in the Middle Ages.

Barcelona aspired to become a financial and economic capital for companies operating in the Western Mediterranean, and one of the main materializations of this plan began in the early 1990s with the exploitation of Barcelona's port as the departure point and final destination of countless holiday cruises along the Mediterranean Sea. The port has currently the largest transit of passengers in Europe, and it ranks number five in the world.[18] Thus, the cruises of Royal Caribbean Cruises, Norwegian Cruise Lines, Costa Cruceros, or MSC Cruises, which have weekly departures from Barcelona, may represent the contemporary equivalent to the ships and vessels of medieval Catalan merchants. These cruises seem to follow the same medieval routes along the Western Mediterranean: Palma de Mallorca, Nice and Montecarlo, Livorno (from where passengers can visit Pisa and Florence), Civitavecchia (Rome's port), Naples, Palermo, Messina, or Venice. From here, cruises depart toward the East Mediterranean, Dubrovnik, Athens, and the Greek Islands being their major stops. Cruises very rarely approach other cities or countries, except for rather occasional stops at Istanbul, Alexandria, Haifa, Cyprus, and the Tunisian coastal resorts.[19]

Symptomatically, the itineraries of these cruises are almost always limited to the European shore of the Mediterranean; they follow the ideological map that divides the sea into the European (and Graeco-Roman, Christian, more affluent) side and the African and Asian (and Oriental, Islamic, poorer) sides. This was also the map of Barcelona's city hall when they sketched their plan to transform the city into an economic center of the European Mediterranean. In this context, Joan Maragall's poem "Expedició de Catalans a Orient," even if it describes Athens as the Orient, provided the glorification of a historical episode that meshed perfectly well with the ideological premises of this plan.[20]

The allusion to the imperial past in the Empúries script is followed by the choir's oration:

Empúries Pont que recull la cultura dels clàssics vinguda
camí de l'aurora sagnant, cap al ponent prosseguint
una manera de ser, barrejada la forma cristiana
amb la de l'àrab sapient, la del jueu atzarós,
cap al nou món, cap a Amèrica rica en futurs i miratges
de l'avenir que amb treballs prova que ens ha dut fins avui.

Empúries as Bridge, gathering classic cultures
coming from the bloody dawn and taking Westward
to the new world, to an America full of future and mirages,
a way of being that mixes Christian forms, Arab wisdom
and Jewish wandering, and that proves with difficulty
that it has sustained us until today.

This oration transfers to the trans-Atlantic context the cultural intermingling that has taken place in the Mediterranean throughout its history. The text mentions, for the first time, the existence of non-Christian components, and the conquest of America is depicted as an expansion of Graeco-Roman civilization mixed with Arab and Jewish cultures. This multicultural definition of civilization, however, keeps intact the conception of the civilizing path as the expansion of a "way of being": a "way of being," the being of civilization itself, that has spread over uncivilized peoples and territories, from the Iberian peninsula to America. Thus, the multicultural glaze of the paragraph can hardly conceal its classic Eurocentrism.

Similarly, this fourth section expresses at the end the wish to project the Olympic values, inherited from Greece onto the new European context, "cap a la renovada Europa, més oberta i plural" 'toward the renewed, more open and plural Europe.' Hence, the section ultimately contributes to the configuration of a tolerant and multicultural new Europe.

The four interventions of the choir provide the script with a sense of cohesion by defining Empúries as port, as pact, as door, and as bridge. Given that Empúries functions as an evident synecdoche of Catalonia, these four terms

suggest a conception of the country as a meeting point of various Mediterranean traditions. As we have seen, this conception connects with previous
idealizations and theories of Catalonia, especially those produced within the
noucentista movement. But many other Catalan intellectuals have envisioned a
similar conception. For instance, Jaume Vicens i Vives' 1960 *Notícia de Catalunya*
presents negotiation, exchange, and pactism as the main transhistorical forms
of interaction of the mercantile Catalan people. Or Josep Ferrater Mora's *Les
formes de la vida catalana*, written in 1944, elevates the features of "continuïtat"
'continuity,' "seny" 'judiciousness,' "mesura" 'measure,' and "ironia" 'irony' to
the status of exceptionally Catalan ways of being, the origin of which is found in
the country's mixture of Mediterranean roots and also European-ness.[21]

But one crucial formal difference exists between these former investments
in "Mediterraneanism" and Rubert de Ventós' continuation of this tradition.
While Eugeni d'Ors developed his theories for a Mediterranean Catalonia
during 17 years (from 1906 to 1921) in his column at the newspaper *La Veu de
Catalunya*, and while Vicens i Vives and Ferrater Mora wrote extensive books
to present their ideas, Rubert de Ventós compiled a brief and patchy script
made of various quotations and erratic references that do not follow a clear
narrative or chronological pattern. Despite the thematic organization of the
script in four sections ("Admiració i nostàlgia," "Joc i esport," "Foc i crítica,"
"Lletanies i poemes"), these sections and pairings appear to be rather arbitrary,
with no global narrative that justifies their presence or the absence of alternative themes. Similarly, one cannot find a dramatic justification of the difference
between the narrator, the poet, the hero, and the philosopher. They simply recite
a compendium of quotations from ancient Greek authors, German Romantics,
and modern Catalan writers. The choir is stripped of any of its classic functions
as interpreter, commentator, or judge of the dramatic action, since there is
ultimately no dramatic action.

This formal arrangement of the Empúries script is indicative of the new
context in which this Catalanist retrieval of Olympic Greece took place, namely
the world of visual media and televised spectacles. The text was conceived and
written as a television script, and its fragmented texture and brevity obey the
necessary constraints that the media impose on narratives and themes. The fact
that the text was only a part of a larger set of visual performances, the need to
adjust the text to previously assigned time frames, or the required interrup-
tions for commercials, inevitably produced a simplification and a dispersal of
the rendered topics.

But these disjointed and undeveloped narratives of Rubert de Ventós' script
involve another, deeper matter. Rubert de Ventós has affirmed that he wanted
the Empúries ceremony to contribute to the creation of a past for Catalonia.
For him, the ceremony was "treball d'estat" 'state work': the work of building

a past for a stateless nation.[22] However, the material conditions of representation of this past determined that the Empúries script resulted not in a future program for the transformation of Catalonia (like the *noucentista* program), but in a postmodern simulacrum of former attempts to configure a Mediterranean imaginary for Catalonia. Or, at least, it seems impossible to decide whether Rubert de Ventós' script constituted a new attempt to build a national past, or whether it replicated, in a characteristically postmodern way, the previous attempts. In other words, the Empúries script did not deploy a cohesive narrative to re-enact the Mediterranean imaginary. Instead, the disjointed arrangement of the text, its undeveloped narratives, and the constant quoting of past authors, suggest that, while Rubert de Ventós aimed to produce a nation-building ceremony, he delivered it by compiling and reproducing literary references, most of which belonged to former nation-building projects. The conditions of media representation explain the multiplicity and underdevelopment of narratives included in the script. Simultaneously, these characteristics of the script are a symptom of how, in the postmodern context, nation-building projects are traversed by the simulacra of television. The Empúries script necessarily had to be the way it was in order to be televisable and, consequently, its nation-building content could only be articulated as a fragmented set of allusions, desires and ideas with no general transformative program or complete narration. Even if the ultimate but ambiguous goal of the Empúries ceremony could arguably be the achievement of the independence of Catalonia (in fact, after the Olympics, Rubert de Ventós has continuously advocated self-government for the Catalans), the ceremony, because of its very formal structure, could not contain any specific set of political objectives.[23] As I have tried to show, however, the ceremony did articulate a set of ideological premises and constituted an effective visual and textual re-enactment of a Mediterranean collective imaginary. The Empúries script – by far the most intellectually sophisticated production of Barcelona's Olympic industry – is a paradigmatic example of how a *philosophe d'État*, albeit of a stateless Catalonia, must operate under the conditions of postmodern representation; the conditions that thwart and turn into a banal simulacrum the very nation-building projects that this global infrastructure of representation makes possible.

Nationalism and Europeanism

This description of the Empúries script as a banal simulacrum, however, should not be interpreted as a condemnation of the project; on the contrary, despite the ideological components and the conditions of the postmodern context, Rubert de Ventós' effort to continue the task of building Catalonia is transformative and energizing, especially to the extent that he moved away from the ideological expectations of the central state. And, indeed, the Catalanist subtext of the script made the state representatives quite nervous. As John Hargreaves describes in detail, the Empúries ceremony was another episode of a long series of conflicts between the Catalan government and the state, as well as between the different parties in Catalonia, regarding the symbolic content of the Barcelona Games. A quick perusal of the Catalan and Spanish newspapers of 1992 reveals how one of the major political battles, fought on a daily basis before the Games, involved a fundamental division between those who wanted to promote Barcelona as the capital of the Catalan nation, and those who wanted to promote it as a Spanish city. Each symbolic aspect of the Games – the national flags, the languages, the promotional advertisements, etc – stirred a battle to impose a Catalan or a Spanish marker.

One of the most significant conflicts was caused by a group of Catalanist protesters (related to separatist organizations La Crida and Acció Olímpica, and the party Esquerra Republicana de Catalunya) when they sneaked in the Empúries ceremony. The group interrupted the broadcasting of the ceremony by displaying "Freedom for Catalonia" banners and separatist flags, and by whistling at the Spanish minister of Education, Javier Solana, while he was delivering his speech. Many people had also whistled and shouted at King Juan Carlos I in 1989 at the inaugural ceremony of the Olympic stadium. This protest was probably motivated, not only by the fact that the Bourbon King represented the principal figure of long-standing Castilian power, but also because the police confiscated Catalan flags at the entrance of the stadium.[24] Another affair that generated certain commotion among state authorities took place when Jordi Pujol's government of the Generalitat launched an audacious campaign in some European and North American newspapers (*The New York Times, Financial Times, Le Monde, Le Figaro, Corriere della Sera, La Repubblica*, among others). This campaign consisted in an advertisement of two pages. On the first page, there was the map of Europe and a dot on Barcelona, and the question (in English): "In which country would you place this point?" The second page displayed the same map and Catalonia highlighted in a different color, as well as the answer to the question: "In Catalonia, of course."[25]

While these battles and campaigns produced heated, but ultimately harmless, political clashes, a more serious episode became intermingled with this ongoing confrontation between the Spanish state and the more nationalist sectors of Catalonia, including the Catalan government. This episode was known as the *Operación Garzón* and took place at the end of June of 1992, three weeks before the opening of the Games. This operation consisted in a preventive manhunt ordered by Fiscal General del Estado Baltasar Garzón, the State's Supreme Court Judge, and executed by Luis Roldán, chief of the Guardia Civil, against many Catalan independentists accused of supporting the terrorist group Terra Lliure. Before the Games, Terra Lliure began a campaign against the "Spanish Olympics," and they even set explosives in one of the Olympic offices outside Barcelona, in Banyoles. For this reason, a total of sixty people – including militants of Terra Lliure, Moviment Català d'Alliberament Nacional, Esquerra Republicana de Catalunya, Partit Comunista de Catalunya, and Alternativa Verda – were arrested. Many of them were tortured, and 30 people were sent to jail. Not surprisingly, the indiscriminate arrests and the outrageous tortures brought back the ghost of Francoist repression in many strata of Catalan society.

The majority of Catalans, however, initially perceived the operation as legitimate and convenient because of two main factors. On the one hand, even if Terra Lliure never became a major terrorist organization like ETA (since the year of its foundation, in 1978, Terra Lliure "only" set off bombs that aimed to cause "symbolic" damage), the largest part of Catalan society wished to eliminate the possibility that Catalanism could at some point be associated with terrorism. At the same time, Terra Lliure, like ETA, defined their fight in terms of national liberation, but also as a revolutionary struggle against the oppression of the working class. As they stated in their 1981 Declaration of Principles, "[Terra Lliure] lluita per la defensa de la terra, de la llengua, de la sobirania nacional, dels interessos com a treballadors i contra l'espanyolització de la societat catalana" '[Terra Lliure] fights to defend the land, the language, national sovereignty, the interests of workers, and against the Spanishization of Catalan society' (quoted in Vilaregut 47). But in the context of the 1980s, in which, as I have shown in Chapter One, previously antagonist classes engaged in a process of reconciliation, Terra Lliure's attempt to carry on class struggle seemed rather out of place. Terra Lliure had no significant social support, and the vast majority of the population explicitly refused their goals and modus operandi.

On the other hand, the significance of the Olympic event for the promotion of Barcelona, and the perception that the entire world would be looking at the Catalan capital, made everyone anxious to guarantee a safe and successful Olympics. A hypothetical terrorist attack perpetrated – either by ETA or Terra Lliure – would have tainted the Games forever, in the same way that the 1972 Olympics in Munich are remembered for the killing of Israeli athletes. This widespread concern helped Garzón and Roldán legitimize their repressive operation and gain popular support. It was only when the tortures became public – despite the fact that many media, most notably the newspaper El País, tried to cover them up – that the operation infuriated Catalonia's civil society.

The acute tensions between the Spanish state and Catalan nationalism made evident that Judge Garzón's legal procedure had political motivations. But, thanks to the process against Terra Lliure, the security forces of the government gave the impression that they could indeed prevent a terrorist attack against the Olympics. This was a dubious fact, given that it was ETA rather than Terra Lliure that had the means and infrastructure to carry out terrorist action. In hindsight, it seems clear that the terrorist threat was a mere pretext to execute a state-directed manhunt against "radical" Catalanism. After all, the 30 imprisoned people had all been freed by 1995, the year in which Terra Lliure decided to stop operating as a group.[26]

Despite these incessant political tensions, when the Games began, as Hargreaves argues, a sense of conciliation and a will to compromise prevailed (130–42). It looked as if, all of sudden, everyone had been inspired by the Olympic spirit of fraternity, even though, as Salvador Cardús brilliantly put it, everyone still had "les esgarrinxades a la pell de les calentes batalles entre el nacionalisme català i espanyol" 'their skin scratched from the fierce battles between Catalan and Spanish nationalims' (*Política* 339). The opening ceremony, as I explained in Chapter One, staged this final, albeit temporary, appeasement of political and institutional clashes. The ceremony, which combined the four official languages of the Games – Catalan, Spanish, English, and French – included traditional Catalan *sardanes* and Andalusian *flamenco*; a theatrical performance created by La Fura dels Baus honoring a mythologized Mediterranean sea; 12 human *castells* representing the 12 countries that comprised the European Economic Community; and the march of the participating countries, in which Spain occupied a privileged position.[27] To avoid the whistling of potential protesters against King Don Juan Carlos I, the Catalan national anthem, "Els Segadors," was played when the Bourbon King entered the stadium; this was a rather comical arrangement, since the anthem is a call against the subjugation of Catalonia under Castilian rule. But the calculated combination of these elements, and many others, succeeded in representing Barcelona equally connected to Catalonia, Spain, the Mediterranean, and Europe. This balanced combination contributed to create the euphoria that seemed to infuse everyone during the Barcelona Games.[28]

Together with the Mediterranean label, the embrace of Europe was another key component of the official marketing of Barcelona during the Olympics. On this point, Pasqual Maragall's local government, and Jordi Pujol's Generalitat, complemented each other, and both shared a Europeanist vocation that linked their respective agendas for Barcelona and Catalonia. Specifically, one of Pujol's defining projects was to build "L'Europa de les regions" among "Els motors d'Europa," which aimed to strengthen the political and economic ties between the regions of Lombardy, Rhône-Alpes, Baden-Württemberg, and Catalonia. Also, in 1986, Maragall, in collaboration with the city halls of Rotterdam, Birmingham, Lyon, Frankfurt, and Milan, launched the Eurocities movement, which would address common urban issues and create a lobbying voice for cities in the European Union.

This embrace of the European space had the unequivocal goal of searching for concrete economic links. As we saw, the ultimate goal of the Mediterranean label was also economic, but in that case the interests of the tourist industry were somehow disguised as a recovery of the symbolic roots with the sea and its history. In the case of Europe, by contrast, the economic component was central and explicit. The regions and cities in Pujol's and Maragall's agendas corresponded to the most prosperous areas of Europe. Their political programs were not primarily driven by the nationalist aim to link stateless nations or the project to promote urban synergies that may be running underneath nation-states. If this had been the case, the Europe of the regions and the Eurocities movement might have incorporated other national communities and non-capital cities, including, for instance, less affluent peoples such as the Corsicans or the Galicians and their capitals, Ajaccio or A Coruña. But Maragall stated very clearly the alliances that should be formed. In his programmatic *Refent Barcelona*, Maragall affirmed that he perceived himself as an "intermediari" 'intermediary' (98) between (foreign) investors and (local) entrepreneurs, and proposed that economic exchanges with the most dynamic European cities should be developed. These connections could transform Barcelona into the Northern capital of the European South. He added: "Jo crec més aviat en aquesta mena de relacions exteriors catalanes, que no pas amb una 'Internacional de Nacionalitats Oprimides' que ens equipararia amb nacionalitats europees de menys entitat que Catalunya" 'I believe in this sort of external Catalan relations rather than in an 'International of Oppressed Nationalities' that would make us equal to European nationalities of less magnitude than Catalonia' (90).

Mari Paz Balibrea rightly interprets this line as a declaration of Maragall's political positioning vis-à-vis stateless nationalisms, and specifically vis-à-vis Pujol's. She says:

> Maragall seems to be dissociating himself from what might be perceived as a form of nationalist victimization or essentialism, making clear that nationalist demands, even though at some points he invokes Catalunya and the Països Catalans in his framing of the question, are not top priority in his political agenda. ("Urbanism" 196)

Furthermore, Maragall's refusal to be associated with less powerful cities or nations reveals the central economic component of his agenda. His "local patriotism," to use Balibrea's term (197), is not as much a political project to create alternative forms of city governance beneath the nation-state as it is an attempt to establish economic ties with the most prosperous centers of the European continent.

Perhaps, despite his socialist affiliation, the economic motivations of Maragall's program are even stronger than those of Pujol's conservative nationalism. In principle, as I explained in Chapter One, a major difference between

Pujol and Maragall was the role that Catalan language played in their politics. While the former considered it the defining essence of Catalonia, Maragall's "citizen-based pragmatism," as McNeill calls it (*Urban Change* 91), put forward a non-language-oriented politics. Yet, when Maragall is questioned about whether Spanish could be a more appropriate language than Catalan to open the city to global networks, he says:

> No hem pas de ser d'una manera i semblar d'una altra, perquè ser diferents també és un atractiu. Al públic més sofisticat, a nivell universitari, artístic i cultural, al públic més culte i més curiós, li agrada la diferenciació, no té por de la diferència sinó que ve, en part, perquè sap que Barcelona és la capital d'una cultura diferent. (*Tema* 126)

> We do not need to present ourselves as something other than what we are, because difference makes us attractive. The most sophisticated, highly educated people, the audiences who are sensitive to art and culture, like differences; they are not afraid of differences. In fact, they partly come here because they know that Barcelona is the capital of a different culture.

While Pujol's nationalist politics reinforced Catalan language as the fundamental trait of Catalan identity, here Maragall is implicitly endorsing the promotion of the language, not because he wants to strengthen the innermost identity of the Catalans, but because the language can help produce a more differentiated space in the global market. Maragall even specifies that the presence of Catalan is more likely to attract sophisticated – that is: affluent and upscale – people to Barcelona and Catalonia. Therefore, although after decades of Francoist repression, the politics in support of the Catalan language constituted a well-deserved right of the Catalans and a genuine effort to democratize the Spanish state, this political project, as Maragall's words entail, had also an economic motivation: that of contributing to the differentiation of Barcelona and Catalonia in the global market.

In fact, this revitalization of the Catalan language in the context of globalization has produced a curious, dialectical effect. While Catalan has gained symbolic presence and extensive use within the public administration and the school, Castilian, and even English, have gradually become the default working languages of business and commercial interaction. We might say that Catalan has increased its exchange value as a cultural asset, but that the global market, as well as the uniformizing apparatuses of the Spanish state, have continued to relegate it and keep it, precisely, as a cultural symbol. In the post-Francoist period, it seems that the more Catalan has strengthened its public and symbolic presence, the more it has lost its effective social use.

Barcelona and Catalonia's official adherence to the Mediterranean and the European spaces has been celebrated by some of the main advocates of globalization. Manuel Castells considers Catalonia an exemplary case of the new political entities that are emerging in the network society. He writes:

> Declaring *Catalunya* at the same time European, Mediterranean, and Hispanic, Catalan nationalists, while rejecting separatism from Spain, search for a new kind of state. It would be a state of variable geometry, bringing together respect for the historically inherited Spanish state with the growing autonomy of Catalan institutions in conducing public affairs, and the integration of both Spain and *Catalunya* in a broader entity, Europe, that translates not only into the European Union, but into various networks of regional and municipal governments, as well as of civic associations, that multiply horizontal relationships throughout Europe under the tenuous shell of modern nation-states... [This model] seems to relate better than traditional notions of sovereignty to a society based on flexibility and adaptability, to a global economy, to networking of media, to the variation and interpenetration of cultures. (*Power* 50)

Similarly, Anthony Giddens considers Catalonia a model case of the new structural processes at stake in globalization:

> Globalization 'pulls away' from the nation-state in the sense that some powers nations used to possess, including those that underlay Keynesian economic management, have been weakened. However, globalization also 'pushes down' – it creates new demands and also new possibilities for regenerating local identities. The recent upsurge of Scottish nationalism in the UK shouldn't be seen as an isolated example. It is a response to the same structural processes at work elsewhere, such as those in Quebec or Catalonia. Local nationalisms aren't inevitably fragmenting. Quebec may opt out of Canada, as Scotland may out of the UK. Alternatively, each may follow the Catalan route, remaining quasi-autonomous parts of a wider national entity. (*Third Way* 31)

However, at least three main issues problematize these positive accounts of the Catalan model. First, as we have seen, this contemporary redefinition of Catalonia vis-à-vis globalization entailed a conscious and calculated selection of the alliances that should be pursued. These were exclusive alliances with the most prosperous European regions and, for this reason, Catalonia's multiple adherences not only might represent a political experiment for the flexibilization of the nation-state, but also aimed to serve the economic progress of this area. Thus, what might appear as a new political body is also the result of the establishment of regional economic ties. In late capitalism, these ties are decisive in attracting global capital to specific local spaces.

Second, in close relation to the first point, the globalization and flexibilization of Catalonia in reality involved one key change: namely, the extensive establishment of multinational companies. As I mentioned in Chapter One, the very project of the Olympic Games came from the multinational institution of the International Olympic Committee; many of the Olympic facilities were built by foreign promoters; and during these years numerous multinational companies, from McDonald's to Planet Hollywood, opened franchised businesses in

Barcelona. In the Catalan capital, the globalization of the local economy has caused what Sassen describes as the "denationalizing of urban space" in a way that raises the question, "whose city is it?" (*Globalization* XX). In this respect, is this lack of clear ownership produced by the globalization of capital not the real effect of what Castells describes as the abandonment of "traditional notions of sovereignty"? Castells presents Catalonia as a model for the flexibilization of governance, a flexibilization much needed in times of globalization. But this new "weak" sovereignty has a material side that corresponds to the diffusion of ownership and the substitution of transnational companies for the previous local businesses, with all the subsequent economic, social, and urban effects that this change entails. To put it bluntly, the loss of sovereignty has not affected nation-states or regional governments as much as the local companies that have been absorbed within the structure of subdivisions and branches of transnational corporations.

Finally, Catalonia's embrace of the transnational imaginary of Europe and the Mediterranean involved an implicit rejection of Spain, or at least a rejection of centralist Spain. Even if, as Castells says, Catalonia's links with Europe and the Mediterranean were part of the general Europeanization of Spain, we must remark that they also intended to differentiate Catalonia from the other areas of the peninsula. For this reason, Castells' inclusion of "Hispanic" as one of the defining traits of Catalonia omits the permanently difficult relations between Catalonia and Spain. Similarly, Giddens' description of the Catalan way as a conciliation between Catalonia as a "quasi-autonomous" unit, and the "wider national entity" of the state, fails to notice that the relation between the two rarely ceases to be a distrustful and contradictory one. Thus, it is not surprising that, in the midst of the apparent diffusion of power of the global world, the only political movement that has steadily grown in contemporary Catalonia is open separatism.

Gangs and Immigrants

But let us now examine a literary text that reveals some of the darker effects that these globalizing ideologies had on Barcelona's social space. Francisco Casavella's novel *El triunfo*, published in 1990, portrayed the Olympic city without the slightest presence of Europe, the Mediterranean, or even Catalans. This remarkable novel takes place in Barcelona's old quarter of El Raval during the years previous to the Olympic Games, when the city hall, as I describe in Chapter Three, began a comprehensive urban transformation of the neighborhood. *El triunfo* narrates the violent and miserable life of the dominant gang of this district full of crooks, prostitutes, heroin addicts, and street musicians – a set of characters that hardly fit in the new stylish and redesigned Barcelona.

Two main conflicts structure the plot of the novel. First, the members of the gang fight to maintain their hegemony against the newly arrived groups of Arabs and blacks, who gradually gain power and control drug dealing in the neighborhood. Second, an ex-member of the gang, El Nen, is determined to take revenge against the leader, El Gandhi, who killed his father in order to be together with his mother. This is, naturally, *Hamlet*'s plot, as indicated by the quotation from the play at the beginning of the novel: "ESPECTRO: Adiós, adiós, Hamlet, recuérdame."[29] Throughout the novel, El Nen tirelessly chases El Gandhi and two of his inseparable buddies until, at the end, in the inevitable final shooting in a deserted parking lot, El Nen kills the three men, but also gets shot by El Gandhi. This way the definitive disappearance of the gang is consummated.

None of the characters of the novel holds a proper name. They all have a nickname or gang name, such as El Gandhi, El Nen, El Tostao, el Topo, or el Palito. Their real names are rarely mentioned, thus suggesting that these characters have little personal autonomy outside the gang. Similarly, these characters are totally implanted in the streets and buildings of their neighborhood, and they never think of going beyond its boundaries. If they occasionally do, they feel unnerved and out of place: "por una fuerza mayor que nosotros, no podíamos salir del Barrio, porque a la que salíamos a una calle que no era del Barrio, caminábamos un poco y, sin decirnos nada, nos volvíamos a meter en el Barrio" 'a force larger than us kept us locked in the Barrio; when we went to a street outside the Barrio, we would walk a bit and, without saying a word, we would go back to the Barrio' (65). Even though one can easily identify this neighborhood as Barcelona's El Raval, the characters only speak of the "Barrio," written with a capital B. The text does not name any of the actual spaces of El Raval, except for a reference to Robadors Street, a quite sordid street with much prostitution (27). The Barrio maintains, throughout the novel, an indeterminate and abstract form.

In the novel, the Barrio experiences two main changes: the arrival of African immigrants and the urban renewal implemented by the city hall. These two events, which indicate that the story takes place during the 1980s, are depicted as negative and destructive forces affecting the old neighborhood. The narrator, as well as the other characters, refer to the immigrants with the highly derogatory terms "moros" and "negros," and blame them for the turmoil that is disrupting the Barrio. The main narrator states:

Antes de que llegaran los moros y los negros, al Gandhi se le llamaba don Luis y se le tenía miedo porque sí. Vamos, se le tenía miedo porque, si no le decías que sí, pringabas. Pero cuando empezaron a llegar los moros y los negros, la gente empezó a quererle un poco más.
Los moros y los negros habían venido de uno en uno y al principio hacía su gracia eso de decir hosti tú, un moro, pero ya luego se trajeron a las parientas y

a las suegras y a los ñajos y en el Barrio ya hubo más moros y más negros que cucarachas… Y como estas cosas de los moros y los negros son muy raras, los moros empezaron a mandar a los negros y, poco a poco, se fueron organizando y la cosa se puso seria. (24)

Before the moors and the blacks got here, people called Gandhi don Luis and we were all afraid of him. We were afraid because, if you didn't say yes to him, you were screwed. But when the moors and the blacks got here, people began to love him a little more.

    The moors and the blacks had arrived one at a time, and at the beginning it was fun to say, look, a moor, but then they brought their wives and mothers-in-law and kids and we had more moors and more blacks in the Barrio than cockroaches… And the moors and the blacks are very weird, so the moors began to control the blacks and, little by little, they got more organized and things got tough.

The novel alternates two narrators. On the one hand, most episodes reproduce the full declaration that El Palito makes to the police when they investigate the final killing of the gang leaders and El Nen. El Palito is a musician who belonged to El Gandhi's gang and whose real name, as he attests in his declaration, is Francisco García (127). His first-person narration, which aims to convey the authentic colloquial speech of the Barrio, tells the story between El Nen and El Gandhi that culminates in the killing of each other. On the other hand, fewer shorter chapters contain disperse autobiographical notes written by El Gandhi. In them, he recalls his years in the army, when he was sent to the last Spanish colonies in Morocco, and his return to Barcelona, where he set up the gang at the Barrio together with various ex-soldiers. These notes reveal how El Gandhi conceived his gang as an army and ruled his men as if he was a sergeant commanding his warriors:

Mis hombres se comportaban en todo como guerreros, jamás titubeaban. Les obligué a… que cuidaran su aspecto, a que bebieran y comieran con mesura, a que a todas horas no tuvieran más idea en la cabeza que la de hacerse grandes, mirar el Barrio como quien divisa, anhelante de lucha, un vasto campo campamental, vencer. Ordené que nadie perdiera el hábito en el uso de las armas. No me refería exclusivamente a su utilización, sino a esa especie de amor que con métodos tan ortodoxos como soeces nos habían inculcado en África. (82)

My men behaved like warriors, they never hung back. I forced them to… take care of their look, to drink and eat in moderation, to constantly think of becoming great, to look at the Barrio like those who, eager to fight, look out over a vast battlefield, to win. I instructed that nobody should lose their skills with the firearms. I did not refer exclusively to their use, but to that type of love that they had inculcated in us in Africa with orthodox but dirty methods.

Both narrators of *El triunfo* portray Africa and the Africans – more explicitly in the musician's declaration and less so in El Gandhi's memories – as a persistently troublesome Other for Spaniards. The text depicts the characters' racist mentality linked to a purist idea of Spain as an "anti-Arab" and "anti-African" country, an idea that naturally corresponds to the reactionary myth of Spain as the Catholic spiritual reserve of the Western world. However, by juxtaposing the two historical episodes of Spain's military conquest of North Africa in the first decades of the twentieth century, and the waves of African immigrants of the 1980s, the novel also seems to suggest that the coming of Africans to the current Barrio reciprocates Spain's previous colonial occupation of Morocco.

Spain established a protectorate in North Africa in 1913. Until 1956, when Franco finally conceded independence to Morocco, a continuous series of partisan wars (the most destructive of which was the Rif War from 1921 to 1925) were fought against Spanish colonial hegemony. Throughout the first half of the twentieth century, large numbers of Spanish soldiers were sent to Morocco to pursue the renewed "African destiny" of Spain. In fact, this "African destiny" had already begun in 1860 when General Leopoldo O'Donnell conquered Tetuan and undertook a series of Moroccan expeditions that, as Raymond Carr explains, "lay vague notions of an African mission and a new Crusade against the infidel Moors" (260). These expeditions, which constituted "a classic example of a war of honour unsupported by economic interest" (261), initiated a quite compulsive behavior pattern: in order to compensate for the loss of the American empire, Spain undertook more manageable (and unprofitable!) expeditions to North Africa so that the country could preserve its imperial self-esteem and feed the illusion that it also participated in the European colonization of the continent. The upholding of a series of infertile lands at a high cost in human lives became a clear symbol of Spain's traumatic situation as a semiperipheral country next to the European imperial powers. Unsurprisingly, the military pride of an inept army, and the imperial imaginary of an oligarchic state, were two of the key factors that led to the emergence of fascism.[30]

Given that El Gandhi conceives his gang as a prolongation of the "glorious" Spanish army, the novel ironically implies that all that remains of the former Spanish empire is a bunch of petty gangsters. Correspondingly, the struggles at the Barrio between El Gandhi and the new African groups reproduce, or maybe repeat as farce, the former wars between the Spanish army and the Moroccan insurgents. By the end of the book, when Gandhi surrenders and gives up the control of the Barrio to the Arabs, he and his buddies talk as if they were soldiers at war who had just been "aniquilado[s]" 'annihilated' (158) by the "moros." In the same way that the Moroccans gained their independence and forced Spain to withdraw in 1956, now the Arabs have also prevailed and triumphed in the Barrio.

The title *El triunfo* initially refers to a song that El Palito sings for El Gandhi to console him after his defeat. Even if the lyrics are not included in the novel, the title of the song suggests that it might be a cheering song for soldiers. Given

that the story ends with the absolute failure of the gang, the song, and by extension the novel, may function as an ironic portrait of the pathetic nature of the
Spanish imperial rhetoric. The only real triumph in *El triunfo* is the final prevalence of the Arab Other in the Barrio.

But, what is the significance of this story in relation to pre-Olympic Barcelona? The most immediate connection of the novel with this context is found
in its numerous references to the city hall's renewal of the neighborhood. As
I said, the novel does not include temporal markers, and the urban renewal
is the main indicator that the story takes place during the pre-Olympic years.
As I develop in Chapter Three, the central goal of the reformation of El Raval
was to open up public spaces, thin out the density of the neighborhood, and
improve its deficient living conditions. The sound of the tearing down of buildings reverberates throughout the novel, and the disappearance of the old spaces
produces nostalgic effects:

> Por aquellos días, al Tostao, al Topo y a mí nos gustaba ir a un parquecito nuevo
> que habían hecho los del ayuntamiento en el Barrio. A mí más que a nadie, la
> verdad, porque allí, donde estaba el parquecito, había estado el queo que tenían
> mis viejos cuando yo era chinorris. Y me gustaba sentarme en un banco de
> aquéllos y cerrar los ojos y pensar que estaba todavía en el comedor de aquella
> casa y que oía a mi padre subir las escaleras... (46)

> Those days, Tostao, Topo and I liked to go to a new park that the city hall had built
> in the Barrio. The truth is I liked it more than they did, because there, where the
> park was, was where my folks lived when I was a child. And I liked to sit down
> in one of those benches and close my eyes and think that I was still in the living
> room of that house and that I heard my dad come up the stairs...

The physical crumbling of the old Barrio epitomizes the gradual disintegration
of the gang. This downfall of the gang, in turn, functions as a symbol of the
vanishing of Spain, or at least of a certain imperial, authoritarian idea of Spain.
These series of vanishings can ultimately be read vis-à-vis the official transformation of Barcelona. In this sense, Casavella's novel shows how the city hall's
revamping and marketing of the city as a European metropolis with Mediterranean roots aimed to displace a specific collective: the collective representing
the lowest rabble of the city.

But, in an ideological move, *El triunfo* also suggests that the imaginary of
this displaced rabble was tied to traditional Spain. For the characters of the
novel, Spain is the only political and territorial entity with which they identify:
"Froilán, el Controles, que se las daba de gran conocedor de las leyes de España"
'Froilán, el Controles, who boasted that he knew well the laws of Spain' (19);
"[n]o hay en toda España un solo tío al que no le suene el Guacho" 'there is not
a single guy all over Spain who hasn't heard of el Guacho' (20); or, in the celebration of a wedding, the guests wave a flag of Spain (92). Additionally, the fact

that everyone in the novel speaks Spanish, and that the novel itself is written in Spanish, necessarily acquired political connotations in the context in which Barcelona and Catalonia launched a process of redefinition of their personality and historical inscriptions. As a symptom of this unresolved ongoing process, Casavella hesitates when he has to decide on the spelling of the few geographical markers mentioned in the text: he employs Castilian spelling in Sardañola (25), Vía Layetana (126), and Santa Coloma de Gramanet (157), but Catalan spelling in Robadors street (27) and the mountain of Montjuïc (35). In any case, *El triunfo* does not acknowledge Barcelona or Catalonia as political or territorial entities, and its characters only inhabit – physically and mentally – the two spaces of the Barrio and of Spain.

Two conclusions about the ultimate significance of the novel follow from these observations. First, *El triunfo*'s portrait of the rise and fall of El Gandhi's gang may express a deeper social anxiety about the disappearance, not only of this particular neighborhood, but also of the very sense of community that the gang epitomizes. The gang functioned as an authoritarian body that dominated the neighborhood through fear and violence, and its disappearance was not only caused by the coming of African immigrants and the urban renewal, but also by the self-destructive actions of its leader, that is, the killing of El Nen's father by El Gandhi. Despite this sequence of events, the gang brought, as El Palito's nostalgic account attests, a sense of community now forever lost. While acknowledging the pathetic and violent nature of the Barrio's characters and way of life, and by extension of Spain's own pseudo-imperial and wretched destiny, *El triunfo* undeniably articulates, despite its ironic undertones, certain nostalgia for this past.

One element seems to confirm this nostalgia, namely the conspicuous lack of allusions to Francoism throughout the novel. Given the military background of the gang's leaders, and given their authoritarian manners and Spanish nationalism, it seems that Francoism should have been an inevitable model for them. Indeed, Franco's fascism could have functioned as a much more recent model for their military pride than the colonial expeditions to Africa. El Gandhi never specifies when he and his buddies were soldiers in Morocco, but chronological vraisemblance indicates that it is likely that they went when Franco was already in power – sometime between 1939 and 1956, when Spain conceded independence to Morocco.

Thus, the absence of allusions to Francoism is all the more symptomatic. These possible allusions would have thwarted the nostalgia that the novel is articulating, since, in the still transitional early 1990s, the corpse of Francoism was still too fresh to be used as recipient for literary libidinal nostalgia. This striking absence points at one of the novel's ideological goals: that of representing a self-contained and clearly defined Spanish national community. *El triunfo* offers this representation as a compensatory device and as a literary refuge in the new globalized Barcelona, in this city in which the Catalan municipal government not only is working to erase the affiliations with Spain, but is also embracing the spaces of Europe and the Mediterranean – that is, two spaces that risk dissolving national affiliations altogether.

Alongside this reactionary nostalgia, the novel also puts forward a more critical reflection on the social dynamics of the new Barcelona. Casavella's story shows how the disintegration of "Spanish-ness" in Barcelona entailed the coming of the Arabs and the blacks. The effort to globalize and "de-Spanishize" the city (by means of embracing Europe and the Mediterranean) brought along the unsolicited influx of Third World immigration.

Even if the main waves of immigrants arrived in Barcelona after the Olympic Games, non-European immigration was already a growing phenomenon during the late 1980s, when the preparation for the Games required a massive workforce. In 1991, the official number of foreign residents in Barcelona was 23,329, which represented 1.4 % of the population. Since then, this number has substantially increased: in 2010, foreign residents amounted to 295,300, which corresponded to 18.1% of the population.[31] In Spain, in 1993, foreign residents represented 1.1% of the total population. Despite this low percentage, the 461,364 foreigners legally residing in Spain in 1994 were more than double than the 1984 figure (Mendoza, "Foreign Labour" 51). These statistics, however, do not include illegal immigrants and, as many sociologists have observed, Spain's immigration laws are particularly designed to force foreigners to remain illegal or under precarious temporary permits. As Kitty Calavita affirms,

> Spanish immigration law actively and regularly "irregularizes" people, by making it all but impossible to retain legal status over time. Indeed, it makes little sense to draw distinctions between legal and illegal immigrants... because the law ensures that legal status is temporary and subject to continuous disruptions. (531)[32]

The rationale of this legality is to sustain a constant flux of temporary workers who can provide cheap labor and also make up an industrial reserve army. In the booming industries of construction, food, and tourism of contemporary Spain, immigrants perform the temporary and least remunerated jobs, such as building, cleaning, harvesting, street vending, food supplies, domestic services, and transportation. To these services, we must add the economy of drug dealing that employs the African gangs of *El triunfo*. These gangs function as a precise metonymy for the underclass of immigrants as a whole, at least to the extent that they are marginalized by the inherent hypocrisy of the law. In addition, the fact that they are Moroccan and sub-Saharan men employed in the same sector of the economy (drug dealing) turns them into a perfect example of what Martínez Veiga has termed Spain's general "ethnic division of labour"

(107), a term that describes how each productive sector has tended to employ immigrants from the same national origin.

Given this set of conflicting forces, the phenomenon of immigration became, in the early 1990s, one of the most pressing issues in the media. In 1992, Barcelona's newspapers were very much focused on the political and urban conflicts related to the Olympic enterprise, but also included a large number of news items about immigration. Detentions and extraditions of illegal immigrants, the interception of African men risking their lives while trying to cross the Straits of Gibraltar, and the collapse of deficient housing, became part of the daily news.[33]

In this context, *El triunfo* connects these two phenomena: the gradual erasure of an old Spain from Barcelona's social space, and the unsolicited but much-needed coming of foreign immigrants. The novel seems to suggest that, to put it bluntly, in the new Barcelona Third World immigrants have replaced the Spaniards. This is the unexpected Other that has accompanied the process of globalization – and of "de-Spanishization" – of the city. Thus, *El triunfo* casts an ironic but also critical point over the city: the other forgotten triumph of Barcelona's euphoric politics is the triumph of African gangs in El Raval.

Urban Cosmopolitanism

The arrival of non-European immigrants to Olympic Barcelona, along with the simultaneous influx of mostly European, North American and Japanese tourists, materialized, and at the same time counteracted, the new cosmopolitanism that the city hall began to promote. This new cosmopolitanism, which we can call "urban cosmopolitanism," constituted another key ideological component of Barcelona's euphoric politics, together with the endorsement of the spatial imaginaries of Europe and the Mediterranean.

The most evident illustration of this third, cosmopolitan ingredient of Barcelona's municipal politics can be found in the Declaration that the city halls of Barcelona and Rio de Janeiro, taking advantage of the international publicity of the Olympic Games and the United Nations Conference on Environment and Development held in Rio, formulated and signed in 1992. "The Rio–Barcelona 1992 Declaration" consists in a partly vindicating, partly instructive manifesto that argues for a stronger political presence of cities in the contemporary world. The seven points of the Declaration deal with a wide variety of issues, but assert a major thesis: that the constitutive diversity of cities embodies and serves better than traditional nation-states the fluxes, necessities, and developments of the new globalized world. Thus, while modern states are founded on the articulation of national communities, cities are composed of individuals from multiple cultures and backgrounds. For this reason, according to the Declaration, cities have the potential to become more democratic and representative political entities than nation-states. The text claims a bigger political role for cities, and launches a concept of citizenship not founded on nationality, but simply on being an inhabitant of a city.

The first point of the Declaration endorses two classic cosmopolitan axioms: first, it expresses the commitment of cities to work for the world's peace and, second, it affirms that "[f]or us, the distinction between national and foreign is much less important than speaking of citizens of a same world."[34] Point 2 states various measures to protect the environment and promote sustainable growth. Point 3 opposes racism and xenophobia and specifies that "[t]he people who live in our cities are not nationals or foreigners. They are citizens. Diversity is our wealth and tolerance our virtue." Point 4 deals with urbanism and presents two main proposals: on the one hand, city governments must work to redistribute wealth among different neighborhoods, a task that requires common management of metropolitan areas; on the other hand, cities must fight indefinite suburban expansion and must articulate centralities and public spaces that provide signs of identity and places to gather.[35] Point 5 professes that municipal administrations, which operate in close proximity to citizens and can therefore be more attentive to people's real needs, should function as mediators between the citizens and their state or regional government. Point 6: cities must facilitate the education and economic development of young people. Finally, point 7 claims for a bigger political role of cities in the world and celebrates the creation of the International Union of Local Authorities (IULA) and the United Towns Organization (UTO) at the United Nations Conference in Rio. These two organizations, the text concludes, offer new possibilities for cooperation and exchange among cities.

Hopefully this brief summary suffices to show that the points of the Rio–Barcelona Declaration are too vague to devise an effective political project. The Declaration rejects the distinction between nationals and foreigners, but does not question at any point the boundaries implemented by nation-states. It claims for a bigger political role for cities, but there is no specific explanation on how this role can be articulated. Given that the text presents cities sometimes as independent entities, and other times as "political and social mediators" between state, national, and regional powers and the citizens, the Declaration carefully avoids potential confrontations with constituted state powers. In this sense, the text does not mention at any point the historical form of the city-state. This would seem to be an obligatory reference in this context, but taking the city-state as a model might have implied the wish for self-government and could have easily been interpreted as defiance to the sovereignty of nation-states.

What is also symptomatically absent from the Declaration is the economic role of cities in this new "world society."[36] The Declaration makes a tangential allusion to economic development when it advocates sustainable growth and better opportunities for young people, but none of the points touches on the sort of policies, let alone the type of economic system, that the city halls of Rio de Janeiro and Barcelona would endorse. However, when the Declaration states, in point 5, that cities should collaborate with central governments rather than replace them to "look after each one of [the cities'] inhabitants," it defines the role of municipal governments with a comparison: "municipal services should be as respectful of their clients as are the best private and public companies, with well-known products and services." Such a comparison constitutes a true slip of the tongue, as it contravenes the basic political frame and cosmopolitan premises of the Declaration and defines the role of city governments in explicitly economic terms. Far from being a mere equivalence to clarify the role of municipal services, this comparison is in fact key to understanding the correspondence between the Declaration's proposals and the economic role that cities play in the new global world.

Saskia Sassen has analyzed how the global economy, despite its apparent dissemination and its detachment from the constraints of place, in fact involves processes of production located in very specific sites. Given the multiple services needed for the functioning of these processes, these sites are precisely major cities, that is, a limited number of urban centers that can provide a wide variety of specialized services. As Sassen explains:

> The production process in these services benefits from proximity to other specialized services. This is the case especially in the leading and most innovative sectors of these industries. Complexity and innovation often require multiple highly specialized inputs from several industries. The production of a financial instrument, for example, requires inputs from accounting, advertising, law, economic consulting, public relations, design, and printing. The particular characteristics of production of these services... explain their pronounced concentration in major cities. (*Globalization* 207–8)

Sassen describes major cities as pieces of a global assembly line: "If one posits that besides competing they [major cities] are also the sites for transnational processes with multiple locations, then one can begin to posit the possibility of a systemic dynamic binding these cities" (212). Sassen shows how the world's major cities form an interconnected and multiple global city, which she also defines as a "function of the global grid of transactions" (213).

But, to complement her investigation with David Harvey's analysis on how spaces compete among each other to attract highly mobile capital, we must realize that major cities must work to connect themselves to the global grid of transactions, and at the same time must strive to distinguish themselves from each other in order to be more attractive to capital investments.[37] These contrary forces constitute the economic determinations of contemporary cities; as a result, cities are both allies and competitors, both collaborators and adversaries.

This dialectical logic is prevalent within capitalism in its financial or global stage. Globalization has dispersed capital as it has opened up the range of competitors to the entire planet, thereby turning competition into an omnipresent and ruthless combat. Simultaneously, however, this has required the centralization of capital in multinational companies, which can manage the big volumes of investments needed for large-scale production. This centralization, and the subsequent emergence of broad monopolies, requires the concentration of financial production in specific major cities. In this respect, the contradiction that makes global cities both allies and competitors is also part of this centralization of capital, which reduces and often eliminates the competition that the global market nonetheless needs in order to keep capital circulating.

Given this economic base, the comparison of municipal services with a private company is not a mere illustration of the new role of cities; on the contrary, it is the most exact definition of their new functions. In the globalized world, municipal governments must fulfill two main political and economic functions: first, they need to establish as many collaborative links with other world cities as possible; and, second, they must work to transform cities into unique and differentiated places that can appeal to potential global investors. Cities, again, must collaborate and compete among themselves at the same time. To follow the comparison of the Declaration, cities are companies that share interests and even merge their investments, and they simultaneously struggle to rise above the competing city-companies.

The vague political proposals of the Declaration can be effortlessly translated into concrete economic terms. The political alliances between world cities find their correspondence in the systemic binding that makes possible the transnational circulation of capital. In the same way, the overcoming of the division between nationals and foreigners can be connected to the capitalist promotion of (tax-)free circulation of laborers, customers, money, and commodities. Conceiving city dwellers simply as citizens becomes indistinguishable from conceiving them as customers. Along with this, the definition of the role of cities as "political and social mediators" between the citizens and the state seems a response to the fundamental imbalance between the global market and the states. This imbalance results from two contradictory stipulations: the necessity to make the circulation of people and commodities free and boundless, and the state regulation required for the effective control of this circulation. The proposal of cities to act as "mediators" may be a way of pointing at this imbalance. However, the proposal avoids confronting the structural contradiction that causes it, and these mediating functions turn out to be another formula to demand more political influence without questioning the structures of the nation-state and the market.

Three further points must be considered to understand the implications of this production of urban cosmopolitanism. First, Rio de Janeiro and Barcelona are neither important financial centers nor state capitals, and they have little possibilities of becoming global cities like New York, London or Tokyo, or political centers like Washington, Berlin or Paris.[38] Given these circumstances, the Declaration can be interpreted as a symptom of Barcelona's and Rio's own anxieties regarding their position in the global world. As Sassen explains, the global systemic binding concentrates production in a more and more selected number of cities. For this reason, Barcelona and Rio's pursuit of political alliances aimed at compensating their secondary position as world cities, and their Declaration sought to insert more cities into this global assembly line.

A second implication of this manufacture of urban cosmopolitanism is that it subtly opposes the Catalan nationalism represented by Jordi Pujol and his party Convergència i Unió throughout the 1980s and 1990s. The politico-commercial articulation of Barcelona as a cosmopolitan metropolis open to the world was closer to Maragall's "citizen-based pragmatism," to use McNeill's words (*Urban Change* 91), than to Pujol's conservative nationalism. While both hegemonic political programs embraced Europe and the Mediterranean, the premises of urban cosmopolitan, especially as they were presented in the Rio–Barcelona Declaration, could potentially alienate Catalans from less urban and less "cosmopolitan" areas outside Barcelona. This population comprised the majority of Pujol's voters and their common imaginary tended to be more tied to the Catalan land than to global flows of metropolitan messages. In addition, whereas Maragall promoted the autonomy of cities and their consequent detachment from their surrounding areas, Pujol pursued the opposite throughout his political career, namely to re-enact Barcelona as the capital of Catalonia. The most notorious conflict between these two positions involved the creation and subsequent elimination of the Corporació Metropolitana de Barcelona. This institution was founded in 1976 to coordinate various municipal governments of Barcelona's metropolitan area, but Pujol abolished it in 1987 in order to reduce Maragall's political influence.[39]

Finally, the Rio–Barcelona Declaration was the first prominent text of a long list of proclamations and other "cosmopolitan" documents produced in Barcelona in the post-Olympic years. For example, "The Universal Declaration of Linguistic Rights," also called "The Declaration de Barcelona," was launched in 1996 by the Catalan branch of The International PEN Club and the Centre Internacional Escarré per a les Minories Ètniques i les Nacions, with the support of Barcelona's city hall and Unesco. This document advocated the rightful protection and promotion of the world's languages. In the following years, diverse documents were also signed in Barcelona: the 1996 "Declaration of Barcelona on the Mediterranean Diet," sponsored by the city hall to promote

healthy eating habits; the 2001 "Manifest de Sant Egidi," which claimed an end
to the use of religion for violent ends; and countless declarations against the
war on Iraq in 2003.[40]

The largest output of these special types of documents, which almost constitute a distinctive politico-literary genre, came out in 2004 on the occasion of the
Fòrum Universal de les Cultures. Organized by Barcelona's city hall in collaboration with the Generalitat and the central government, the Fòrum consisted in
a five-month-long event that assembled exhibitions, conferences, and sympo-
siums to promote "cultural diversity, sustainable development and conditions for peace."[41] Among the Declarations drafted during the event, we find
the "Barcelona Commitment, or Declaration for Fair, Humane and Sustainable
Development"; the "Barcelona Development Agenda," proposing an alternative
growth path for the world; the "Agenda 21 for Culture," to contribute to the
creation of public cultural policies and the cultural development of humanity;
the "Women's Agenda," in defense of women's rights; a "Charter of Emerging
Human Rights," seeking to define human rights for the new millennium; an
"Extension of the Convention of the United Nations High Commissioner for
Refugees"; the "Fundamental Principles for a Global Convention on the Right
to Water"; the "Barcelona Manifesto," which defended the ethics of journalism
and attacked censorship and the manipulation of information; the "Barcelona
Declaration on the Role of Europe"; the "Barcelona Commitment for Coexistence," which set out the principles for the peaceful resolution of conflicts in
everyday life; the "Declaration of Barcelona. Work: Human Heritage," which
recognized work as part of human heritage; the "Manifesto Words and Future,"
in defense of the Catalan language; the "Charter on the Right of Women to the
City"; the "Barcelona Commitments on Interreligious Dialogue"; the "Manifesto
Proposal on Security in the Information Society"; the "Conclusions for a Declaration of the Rights of Indigenous People"; and the "Declaration on Tourism,
Cultural Diversity and Sustainable Development."

This specialized production of "cosmopolitan" documents is undeniably
related to Barcelona's post-Olympic industry as a major center for conventions of multinational companies. These declarations advertise Barcelona as
an open, tolerant, international meeting point in a way that directly benefits
the industry based on the organization of congresses, trade fairs, and tourist
events in general. To use Harvey's words, these documents actively produce the
"special qualities" (*Condition* 295) of cosmopolitanism and multiculturalism
that help Barcelona attract global investments in the form of visitors, conferences, fairs, etc. Along with this, this production of cosmopolitan messages, and
events like the Fòrum Universal de les Cultures, has generated a wide infrastructure of new institutions with multiple tasks, such as the Barcelona Global
Compact Center (dedicated to research and the promotion of corporate social

responsibility worldwide); the World Observatory on the State of Information; the World Secretariat for Cooperation between Broadcasting Regulators; the House of Languages, to promote policies to protect linguistic diversity; the Permanent East–West Forum; and the Digital Portal on Cultural Rights.[42] These institutions, and the exchange of people that accompany them, have also played a crucial role in the city's post-Olympic economy.

These three points (regarding the secondary positions of Barcelona and Rio in the system of world cities; the internal battles in Catalonia between Maragall's Partit dels Socialistes de Catalunya and Pujol's Convergència i Unió; and Barcelona's specialized manufacture of cosmopolitan documents) reveal how the urban cosmopolitanism of the Rio–Barcelona Declaration was less disinterested than it may have seemed at the beginning. At the same time, hindsight enables us to see that the real materialization of this urban cosmopolitanism came after 1992 in the form of tourists seduced by the city's marketing campaigns. The massive number of tourists that began to visit Barcelona after the Olympics (Rio de Janeiro was already a major tourist destination) seemed to embody well the diversity that the Rio–Barcelona Declaration embraces: "Diversity is our wealth and tolerance our virtue," as is stated in point 3. The ideology of cosmopolitanism contributed to renew the image of Barcelona, especially as a result of its self-fulfilling effects: we might say that Barcelona became cosmopolitan and diverse thanks to the very diversity of tourists who went to the city to live a cosmopolitan experience!

While international tourism represented a safe incarnation of this urban cosmopolitanism, the arrival of a new and unsolicited contingent of foreigners to Barcelona destabilized the premises of this ideology. The arrival of non-European immigrants, which to a large extent was motivated by the needs of the growing tourist industry, constituted an unexpected phenomenon that, unlike tourism, did not go well with the prospects of urban cosmopolitanism. In theory, the "diversity" of the Declaration embraced every inhabitant of the city, including undocumented immigrants. But an inevitable question arises: on what terms and conditions would these immigrants become "citizens" of the diverse city? The Declaration conceived the people who live in "our cities" neither as nationals nor as foreigners, but as citizens; but, what are the limits and what is the exact meaning of this "citizenship"?

The definition of citizen as inhabitant of a city differs from the usual concept of citizen as defined by the state laws that assign different levels of citizenship to the people residing in their territorial jurisdictions. Here, the Declaration opens up the door to an alternative concept of citizenship, a definition of citizenship beyond the nation-state, but the text does not develop it further. In reality, the Declaration remains silent regarding the obvious fact that, for somebody to be able to inhabit a city, she first needs to enter the bordered territory in which the city is located. In our present, no city and no piece of land exist outside the borders of nation-states, and citizenship and the juridical status of the population are exclusively determined by state apparatuses. Given that the Declaration avoids confronting, let alone surpassing, the structure of the state, the alternative concept of citizenship that it proposes turns out to be as attractive as it is nebulous and fruitless.

This compliance with the structure of the state indicates that the Rio–Barcelona Declaration reproduces, albeit in a simplified form, the classic Kantian conception of cosmopolitanism. In the famous essay "Perpetual Peace: A Philosophical Sketch," Kant defines the cosmopolitan right as "the right of a stranger not to be treated with hostility when he arrives on someone else's territory" (105). This right defines the conditions of universal hospitality and must be understood, not as the right of a guest, which "would require a special friendly agreement whereby he might become a member of the native household for a certain time," but as a right of resort, which entitles all human beings "to present themselves in the society of others by virtue of their right to communal possession of the earth's surface" (106).

However, despite the universal scope of these principles, Kant sketches the cosmopolitan right as part of the articles on a perpetual peace "between states" (98). Kant postulates that cosmopolitanism and hospitality ultimately depend on state jurisdictions. In fact, the very definition of them as rights assumes that cosmopolitanism and hospitality are not possible outside the law – i.e. state law. This is one of Derrida's points in *On Cosmopolitanism and Forgiveness*, where he observes that "in defining hospitality in all its rigour as law… Kant assigns to it conditions which make it dependent on state sovereignty, especially when it is a question of the right of residence" (22). Derrida analyzes further the limitations of Kantian cosmopolitanism:

> All human creatures, all finite beings endowed with reason, have received, in equal proportion, "common possession of the surface of the earth." No one can in principle, therefore, legitimately appropriate for himself the aforementioned surface (as such, as a *surface-area*) and withhold access to another man. If Kant takes great care to specify that this good or common place covers the "surface of the earth," it is doubtless so as not to exclude any point of the world or of a spherical and finite globe (globalisation), from which an infinite dispersion remains impossible; but it is above all to expel from it what is *erected, constructed, or what sets itself up* above the soil: habitat, culture, institution, State, etc. (20–1)

In other words, Kant does not propose at any point that states, institutions, cultures, or cities should be an object of communal possession; it is only the surface of the earth that belongs to everyone. This proposition has a double-edged inference: on the one hand, it commands that nobody can properly own the earth but, on the other hand, it permits people to appropriate for themselves whatever stands on the earth (states, institutions, houses, or cities).

Given these limitations, Derrida formulates the notion of a new "cosmopolitanism to come," which aims to go beyond the Kantian definition of cosmopolitan right and its dependence on state sovereignty. Derrida proposes a double articulation that negotiates between, on the one hand, the universal call for unconditional hospitality offered to everyone, to every Other, and beyond any appropriations, borders, and exclusions, and, on the other hand, the laws that must necessarily condition this hospitality, without which the universal call for hospitality would remain an empty demand. As a fruitful example of this negotiation, he endorses the experiment of the "villes-refuges," the proposal of the International Parliament of Writers to build cities of refuge for exiled, deported, and stateless people (17–18).

These ethics of hospitality came at the historical moment in which the globalization of the economy was transforming the phenomenon of immigration into a large-scale and daily experience in many territories. In Europe, immigration began in the early 1990s to pose serious challenges to state legislators and national communities. Since then, European states have had to deal with two contradictory impulses: first, they must satisfy the needs of their increasingly globalized economies (which require the constant mobility of workers and especially the influx of cheap labor), but, second, they must protect their national territories from massive invasions of foreigners. As a result of these contrary urges, immigrants are often forced to enter European land in the most dramatic ways and live in illegal and marginal conditions. As I mentioned above, in the early 1990s in Barcelona, the exciting news about the Olympic enterprise was accompanied by reports on the detention and extradition of illegal immigrants, the interception of African men and women risking their lives while trying to cross the Straits of Gibraltar, and the collapse of deficient houses for immigrants.[43]

In this context, the urban cosmopolitanism of the Rio–Barcelona Declaration appears as a mere aesthetic label and as a clever marketing strategy to promote these two cities. In fact, in Barcelona, the Declaration represented the starting point of a specialized industry devoted to formulating cosmopolitan postulates. The 1992 Declaration speaks of "a spirit of tolerance," "diversity," "integration," "exchange," and "solidarity" within the world cities, but it does not refer to any of the key implications of these concepts, such as the question of hospitality, the contradictions traversing immigration, or the spatial constraints of capitalist society. For this reason, if we want to turn urban cosmopolitanism into something more meaningful and progressive than a mere marketing strategy, we can only push these concepts toward the redefinition, or even the full implosion, of the nation-state. Illegal immigration constitutes the element which disrupts this innocuous diversity and which may open the door to a further, emancipatory understanding of urban cosmopolitanism.

The arrival of undocumented immigrants in a certain territory brings to light the current self-enclosure of cosmopolitanism inside state law. This self-enclosure manifests itself in the paradoxical circle in which undocumented immigrants fall trapped: the catch-22 situation which determines that they cannot obtain a residence permit without a job, and cannot get a job without a residence permit. And the same circle appears when one wants to obtain a work permit. In this respect, true cosmopolitanism can only take place when the existing state laws are broken and surpassed. Derrida's thinking on hospitality is a resolute attempt to push cosmopolitanism beyond state legislations. But the current dynamics of immigration perhaps compel us to rethink cosmopolitanism beyond the ethics of hospitality. In today's globalization, the movements of people have become unceasing and systemic, and they are the product of objective forces rather than subjective decisions. This turns the question of migration and residency into a primarily legal rather than ethical matter. Thus, what must guide transformative cosmopolitan politics is not so much a universal call for unconditional hospitality as a direct demand for global citizenship.

Global citizenship, however, is a contradiction in terms: for there to be citizens, there must be aliens and, therefore, in a situation in which all human beings were citizens of the same political entity, the concept of citizenship itself would become unnecessary. To put it in Carl Schmitt's terms, full global citizenship would entail the elimination of the distinction between friend and enemy, and thus no politics could be articulated. Schmitt already warned us against the frivolous wish for a global (peaceful and cosmopolitan) state:

> The political entity presupposes the real existence of an enemy and therefore coexistence with another political entity. As long as a state exists, there will thus always be in the world more than just one state. A world state which embraces the entire globe and all of humanity cannot exist... [If this state existed, what would remain] is neither politics nor state, but culture, civilization, economics, morality, law, art, entertainment, etc. (53)[44]

But the effectiveness of the demand for global citizenship is that it propels the law beyond the current restrictions of states. Despite being unrealizable and even undesirable, the legality of a global state can induce the creation of supranational jurisdictions (such as the admirable experiment of the European Union) or the establishment of transnational agreements between nation-states. These can be the effects of the cosmopolitan impulse. Global citizenship is an impossibility that can nevertheless guide (perhaps as a redemptive star rather than as a regulative idea) the cosmopolitan practices that defy the restrictions of state law.

If, as is often observed, globalization has prompted the emergence of political powers below the nation-state, then we can also imagine the possibility that political entities other than the state determine the laws of union and separa-tion of peoples. Schmitt almost always identifies political entities with the national sovereign state, but this leaves open the possibility that other entities define the rules of association and dissociation; in other words, a world without states would not have to be necessarily a world without politics: it could still be a world in which fighting collectivities of people confront other similar collec-tivities, to paraphrase Schmitt (28).

The Rio–Barcelona Declaration, despite its limitations and often trivial state-ments, points at one of these possibilities: the possibility of a sovereignty of cities. The new sovereign city, or the global version of the medieval city-state, might still be associated with larger entities like the nation-state or a coalition of states, and share with them prerogatives and apparatuses. But they would retain one autonomous power: the power to offer citizenship based not on nationality, but on being an inhabitant of the city. This power can constitute the legal expression of urban cosmopolitanism. While Derrida presented the "ville-refuges" as a positive result of the negotiation between hospitality as an ethical imperative and the laws conditioning it, this renewed form of the city-state can be a positive negotiation between unrealizable global citizenship and the necessary rules of union and separation that constitute the political.

Yet the question of urban cosmopolitanism should not only be articulated in strictly legal or political terms. In order to remain a transformative notion, urban cosmopolitanism must also confront the primary economic determina-tions that cause the contradictions between states and the market (paradig-matically exemplified by the paradoxical circle that entraps undocumented immigrants). One key fact makes it indispensable to account for the economic implications of this matter: the fact that cosmopolitanism can easily function as market ideology. Marx and Engels famously stated in *The Communist Manifesto* that "[t]he bourgeoisie has through its exploitation of the world-market given a cosmopolitan character to production and consumption in every country" (58). In fact, the cosmopolitan character of the capitalist market of the emerging bourgeois society constituted the conditions of possibility of Kant's founda-tional conception of cosmopolitanism. When Kant formulated his cosmopolitan proposals in 1795, he actually gave political content to what was already taking place in the economic sphere: the blurring of feudal and national barriers (as Marx put it in the *Grundrisse*, "capital is the endless and limitless drive to go beyond its limiting barrier" [334]), but at the same time the establishment of the new regulations of modern states. Cosmopolitanism as a political notion always carries within itself its material other, and its universal premises mesh well with the very logic of the capitalist market. For this reason, the contradiction between the expansive logic of the market and the restrictive laws of the state also finds its expression in the conflict between cosmopolitanism and state law.

These contradictions are nevertheless inherent and constitutive, and cosmopolitanism finds in them its conditions of possibility which are also its conditions of impossibility. This is the paradoxical task that a cosmopolitan politics must undertake: the task of disentangling cosmopolitanism from the market logic that inherently constitutes it and restricts it to the (non-cosmopolitan) confines of state law. Thus, the Rio–Barcelona Declaration's attempt to redefine cosmopolitanism as an urban matter – as an urban cosmopolitanism for which citizenship should not be determined by nationality – can only be meaningful if it compels us to change the new conditions of labor under globalization. The attempt to build new city-states which can provide authorized work and residency aside from nation-states must be a step in this direction. Only a politics that struggles to transform the current capitalist work conditions, and particularly the ways in which these determine and control the multiple forms of migration, can aspire to be truly cosmopolitan.

Notes

1 Hargreaves and McNeill have produced two of the most extensive sociological studies of Olympic Barcelona. But, as I describe in the Introduction, many others have also examined these "real" battles. See especially Vázquez Montalbán, *Barcelonas*; Delgado; Huertas Claveria and Andreu; Domingo i Clota and Bonet i Casas; Calavita and Ferrer; Crexell; Heeren.

2 For the main components of the conception of the modern Games, see Coubertin, especially 135–37; 163–69; 212–15; 248–55; 542–46; 580–83.

3 For an interpretation of the ideological content of this film, see Mackenzie. For general analyses of the Nazi games, see Mandell and also Krüger and Murray.

4 Even if Rubert de Ventós was undeniably the ideologue of the entire ceremony, many other people participated in its production. Suffice it to mention writer Miquel de Palol, movie director Rosa Vergés, who directed the visual staging of the televised ceremony, choreographer Cesc Gelabert, music conductor Delfí Colomer, or producers Equip Tatjer. The script of the ceremony remains unpublished. Thanks to Xavier Rubert de Ventós for lending me his original manuscript.

5 Maragall already depicted the Empordà as the land resulting from the union of the mountain and the sea in his poem "L'Empordà":

> Cap a la part del Pirineu,
> vora els serrats i a ran del mar,
> s'obre una plana riallera:
> és l'Empordà.
>
> ....
>
> A dalt de la muntanya hi ha un pastor;
> a dintre de la mar hi ha una sirena:
> ell canta al dematí que el sol hi és bo,
> ella canta a les nits de lluna plena.
>
> ....
>
> La sirena se féu un xic ençà,
> i un xic ençà el pastor de la muntanya,
> fins que es trobaren al bell mig del pla,
> i de l'amor plantaren la cabanya...

Fou l'Empordà. (178)
In a corner of the Pyrennes,
along the ridges and along the sea,
opens up a charming plain.
It is the Empordà.
....
On top of the mountain there is a shepherd,
within the sea there is a siren.
He sings at dawn the sun shines well,
she sings at full moon in the night.
....
The siren rose a little,
and a mite did the shepherd come down the mountain,
until they found themselves on the midst of the plain,
and out of love they built a little cabin...
It was the Empordà. (Prystupa 18–20)

See also Verdaguer 417–18 and 445; and Josep Pla, *El meu país*, 7–223; and *Escrits empordanesos*, especially 9–155. For a compilation of literary quotes about the Empordà, see Guillamet.

6   The poet who Maragall is referring to is, of course, his grandfather Joan Maragall. Specifically, he is quoting his article "Per l'Empordà" (1909). In a parallel article, "Als Empordanesos" (1906), Joan Maragall states that the Empordà was "la terra on més present se'm feia tot l'encís de la mare Catalunya" 'the land that best revealed the charm of Mother Catalonia' (746) and that "l'Empordà és com el cor mateix de Catalunya" 'the Empordà is like the heart of Catalonia' (747).

7   As I mentioned in Chapter One, Catalanism and Catalan culture can never be automatically identified with the bourgeoisie and their class interests. However, bourgeois Catalanism did gain hegemony within the Catalanist movements, especially from 1885 until 1917. This resulted in the production of various cultural and literary constructs, such as the synecdochical use of local spaces, which served this hegemonic position and have remained operative up to the present. We will encounter similar ideological dynamics below when we refer to *noucentisme*.

8   The quotation belongs to one of d'Ors columns, titled "Petita Oració," and published on December 11, 1909. See his *Glosari* 106–7.

9   For Prat, Catalonia should lead the way to the "federal awakening" of the Spanish peoples:
si el nacionalisme integral de Catalunya va endavant en aquesta empresa i aconsegueix de despertar amb el seu impuls i el seu exemple les forces adormides de tots els pobles espanyols, si pot inspirar a aquests pobles fe en si mateixos i en llur esdevenidor, es redreçaran de l'actual decadència, i el nacionalisme català haurà dut a compliment la seva primera acció imperialista. (118)

if Catalonia's integral nationalism carries on this enterprise and its impulse and example succeed in awakening the sleeping forces of all the Spanish peoples, if it can inspire these peoples to gain faith in themselves and their future, they will overcome the current decadence, and Catalan nationalism will have accomplished its first imperial action.

10 The political goals of bourgeois Catalanism are summarized in this declaration by Prat from his 1906 booklet "La cuestión catalana":
Contra la organización culpable de tan espantosa decadencia, contra la oligarquía política y periodística que hoy la sostiene y mangonea, contra los procedimientos de administración (!) y de gobierno (!) en esta organización arraigados y de esta oligarquía habituales, dirige sus esfuerzos el regionalismo catalán. Transformar la

> vida y constitución del Estado, sustituir la política, que tantos desastres ha engend-
> rado, por una nueva política más justa, más progresiva, más acomodada á las necesi-
> dades y corrientes de los tiempos modernos; más respetuosa de los sentimientos y
> aspiraciones de todas las regiones que integran España, tal es nuestro ideal, nuestro
> objetivo. (quoted in Colomines i Companys 33)

> Catalan regionalism directs its efforts against the organization responsible for such
> a terrible decadence, against the political and journalistic oligarchy which today
> sustains and exploits it, against the administrative (!) and governmental (!) proce-
> dures characteristic of this organization and this oligarchy. To transform the life and
> constitution of the State, to replace the politics that so many disasters have produced
> by new politics, politics that are more fair, more progressive, more adjusted to the
> needs and trends of modern times, more respectful of the sentiments and aspira-
> tions of all the regions that integrate Spain – this is our ideal, our goal.

For an analysis of the relationship between (bourgeois) Catalanism and the Spanish state from 1898 until 1917, see Colomines i Companys. For a comprehensive examination of modern Catalan imperialism, see Ucelay-Da Cal. For the link between Catalan imperial-ism and Iberian federalism, see Prat de la Riba, especially 95–118.

11 Lenin explains how imperialism as the monopoly stage of capitalism includes two central features:

> on the one hand, finance capital is the bank capital of the few big monopolist banks,
> merged with the capital of the monopolist combines of manufacturers; and, on the
> other hand, the division of the world is the transition from a colonial policy which
> has extended without hindrance to territories unoccupied by any capitalist power, to
> a colonial policy of the monopolistic possession of the territories of the world which
> have been completely divided up. (237)

12 D'Ors and the *noucentistes* were profoundly Francophile. As Murgades explains in another key article, "Ús ideològic del concepte de 'classicisime' durant el Noucentisme," *noucent-isme* was very much influenced by the turn-of-the-century classicist movement of the *École Romane* and its political expression, the Action Française, as well as by authors such as Maurice Barrès and Charles Maurras. Murgades also analyzes the class ideology of the *glosa* "Petita oració" and reveals how d'Ors' invocation to Venus may be imitating a text from 1902 by Maurras called "Invocation à Minerve" (22).

13 For further analyses of *noucentisme*, see Peran, Suàrez, and Vidal; Bilbeny (*Eugeni d'Ors and Política*); Cabré, Jufresa, and Malé; and Panyella.

14 Hughes offers a comprehensive explanation of pactism in medieval Catalonia (93–125). For a classic endorsement of pactism as a Catalan identifying trait, see Vicens i Vives.

15 Heraclitus' complete fragment says, "War is the father of all, the king of all, and he has shown some as gods, others as humans; he has made some slaves, others free." (Sweet 23).

16 See also Joan Maragall 184.

17 In Castile, in fact, these two formations – the oligarchies and the state – were often one and the same thing, as the phenomenon of *caciquismo* attests. Historian Mary Vincent explains how, given its lack of economic resources to implement policies and gain legiti-mate power, the Spanish state during the nineteenth century ceded "capacity and expense to pre-existing elites" as a pragmatic compromise. As a result, "[t]he logic of the Restora-tion system made the caciques essential to the working of the Spanish state: indeed, in many areas the caciques *were* the state..." (5). For more on *caciquismo* in Spain, see Varela Ortega.

18 In 2010, a total of 2,350,283 cruise passengers passed through Barcelona, only behind the big four Caribbean tourist ports – Miami, Port Canaveral, Port Everglades, and Mexico's Cozumel. See the 2010 corporate report of the Autoritat Portuària de Barcelona at < http://www.portdebarcelona.es>.

19 Thanks to my father, Lluís Illas, who is a big connoisseur of Mediterranean cruises, for providing me with this information.

20 In this respect, Barcelona's city hall presented the revamping of the waterfront and La Nova Icària beaches as the recovery of the city's Mediterranean essence. See Balibrea's key article "Descobrint Mediterranis: la resignificació del mar a la Barcelona postindustrial."

21 Ferrater Mora writes, for example, that the sense of concrete measure is an essentially Mediterranean trait: "La concreció que el català desitja és, doncs, la concreció ferma i angulosa de l'home mediterrani més aviat que la profunda i imprecisa substància per la qual sospira l'home hispànic." 'The concreteness desired by Catalans is the firm and sharp concreteness of the Mediterranean man rather than the profound and imprecise substance for which the Hispanic man sighs.' (76-77).

22 Rubert de Ventós, Xavier. Personal interview, 11 June 2006.

23 For Rubert de Ventós' pro-independence theses, see especially his *Catalunya: De la identitat a la independència*.

24 For a detailed account of these events, see Hargreaves 79-89, Crexell 97-119, and especially Cardús, *Política de paper* 165-95 and 291-339. Crexell provides a full chronicle of the civic group Acció Olímpica, which struggled for the Catalanization of the Games.

25 The entire text accompanying the answer was:

Barcelona is the capital of Catalonia, a country with its own culture, language and identity. A country with a population of only six million people, which has experienced a growth which has made it one of the motors of Europe. A country in which many foreign enterprises – European, North American, Japanese – have invested and are still heavily investing. A country which has understood and motivated the genius of Picasso, the force of Miró, the imagination of Dalí, the innovative approach of Tàpies, the art of Montserrat Caballé and Josep Carreras, the mastery of Pau Casals, the daring of Gaudí… A country which is visited every year by 16 million people from all over the world for its climate and its unique tourist, sports and cultural facilities. A country with the know-how to get the Olympic Games for its capital, Barcelona. Now you know where Barcelona is. In Catalonia, of course. ("Display Ad 6 – No Title")

26 On Judge Garzón's repression and Terra Lliure, see David Bassa's *L'operació Garzón: Un balanç de Barcelona '92*, which gathers horrifying descriptions of the tortures suffered by the detainees. See also Bassa, *Quan els malsons esdevenen realitat*, and Vilaregut, especially 131-58.

27 The Catalan tradition of *castellers* consists in raising human towers or "castles" by superimposing circles of people on top of one another.

28 For the complete script of the opening ceremony, see *La cerimònia d'inauguració dels Jocs Olímpics de Barcelona: Llibre de premsa*.

29 In fact, the exact words uttered by the Ghost of Hamlet's Father are: "Adieu, adieu, adieu, remember me." (*Hamlet* 1.5.91)

30 For a comprehensive historical and political analysis of the Rif War, see Balfour, *Deadly Embrace*. For studies on immigration from Morocco to Catalonia during the 1980s and 1990s, see Colectivo Ioé; King and Rodríguez-Melguizo; and Morén-Alegret, especially 74-81.

31 For statistics on Barcelona's demographics, and other data, see: <http://www.bcn.cat/estadistica/catala/dades/guiabcn/index.htm >. See also Carlota Solé and Leonardo Cavalcanti's "Las nuevas migraciones" in Degen and García, 115-29.

32 See also King and Rodríguez-Melguizo 64.

33 See, for instance, the newspapers "Avui," "La Vanguardia," or "El País" on January 13, February 7, and July 18, 1992. For a study of the more recent immigration in Spain, see Rius Sant.

34 I quote the reproduction of "The Rio-Barcelona '92 Declaration" in Castells and Borja 227-32.

35 As I explain in Chapter Three, the transformation of Barcelona during the 1980s aimed to exemplify this proposal.

36 In 1992, the word "globalization" had not yet become the ubiquitous term that it is today. The Declaration employs "world society," "one single world," and "a same world."

37 Harvey develops his classic theory in *The Condition of Postmodernity*, 293–96, as I point out in Chapter One.

38 In fact, in her seminal study *The Global City*, Sassen suggests that only these three cities, New York, London and Tokyo, qualify as leading financial centers and therefore as "global cities," a term that she originally coined.

39 These were the administrative goals of the Corporació, as stated in its initial program:

> Al amparo de las disposiciones vigentes, la Corporación Metropolitana – y los Ayuntamientos en ella integrados – creará los órganos de gestión o fundaciones públicas necesarias; constituirá, en su caso, sociedades con limitación de responsabilidad; establecerá, cuando conviniere, sociedades de economía mixta; utilizará formas indirectas de gestión – especialmente la concesión – y constituirá consorcios con entidades públicas de diferente orden o naturaleza. (Corporación 19)

> Under the current legislation, the Metropolitan Corporation – and the city halls integrated in it – will create the necessary organs of management and public foundations; will constitute societies with limited responsibilities; will establish, if needed, societies of mixed economy; will use indirect types of management – especially concession – and will constitute consortia with different public institutions.

40 See <http://www.fundacioperlapau.org/iraq/manifestos.htm>.

41 See the Fòrum's website: <http://www.barcelona2004.org>.

42 For a description of these declarations and organizations, see the Fòrum's website. For a shrewd critique of the Fòrum's ideology, see Resina, *Barcelona's Vocation* 222–34. See also Horta and Malcolm Miles' "Una olimpiada cultural: el Fórum Universal de las Culturas 2004" in Degen and García, 65–82.

43 For recent studies on immigration and the European Union, see Marc Morjé Howard; Gebrewold; Ireland; Collinson; Rogers and Tillie; Penninx et al.; and Geddes and Favell.

44 Hegel also questioned in these terms the ideal of perpetual peace, as it does not account for the dialectical relationship between states:

> Perpetual peace is often demanded as an ideal to which mankind should approximate. Thus, Kant proposed a league of sovereigns to settle disputes between states, and the Holy Alliance was meant to be an institution more or less of this kind. But the state is an individual, and negation is an essential component of individuality. Thus, even if a number of states join together as a family, this league, in its individuality, must generate opposition and create an enemy. (362, §324)

See also Hegel 368, §333.

CHAPTER THREE

The Barcelona Model of
Urban Transformation

A crucial element of Olympic Barcelona was the major urban renewal implemented by the city hall. This transformation not only illustrated or complemented these municipal politics, but essentially embodied them. The spatial
transformation of the city became the most visible component of Barcelona's
euphoric politics during the 1980s.

The urban renewal has also been the most studied and lauded aspect of
contemporary Barcelona. The general admiration that it has received in the last
20 years has generated considerable bibliography in urban and architectural
studies. Even though most studies combine a variety of approaches, this bibliography can be roughly divided into three types. First, the renewal has been
described as a unique and successful project that can represent a model for
other cities; and, indeed, as I explain in Chapter Four, many urban planners
and city halls have referred to Barcelona as their model.[1] Second, more critical
accounts have examined the transformation from urbanistic, sociological,
anthropological, or journalistic disciplines; these texts have looked at the
negative effects and darker sides of the renewal.[2] Third, a few texts analyze the
renewal in relation to capitalism and the new global order from a more theoretical standpoint.[3]

My aim here is to proceed in two directions. First, I depart from this third
critical corpus to relate Barcelona's transformation to a set of concepts and
events such as postmodernism, Critical Regionalism, the generic city, Las Vegas'
theme hotels, and Disneyworld's EPCOT. After looking over the urban history
of modern Barcelona, this chapter undertakes a close reading of the programmatic texts by municipal urban designer, Oriol Bohigas. These texts laid the
theoretical foundation of the remodeling plan, which was conceived as a set
of specific architectural interventions in the existing realities of the street, the
square, the neighborhood, and the park. What most interests me is the general
city model put forward by Bohigas, a model that promotes urban compactness,
good readability, mixture of uses, and public spaces. In this respect, the connection of this model with some general concepts and emblematic phenomena of

postmodernity can help us further explore the structural determinations that configured, sometimes openly, sometimes secretly, this historical conjuncture.

In addition, I look at Quim Monzó's fiction and its critical relationship to the new urban landscape. While most previous studies draw their critique of Barcelona's transformation from grassroots movements and activist practices, I examine the view of the transformation through the lenses of literature. I do not intend to instrumentalize Monzó's fiction and present it as a critical tool somehow equivalent to social resistances. Rather, Monzó's oblique portrait of contemporary Barcelona uncovers certain phenomena taking place underneath the radiant emergence of the Olympic city. His literature offers us the possibility of pointing at the structural determinations traversing this given social space, and it can therefore act as a powerful agent of ideological critique.

Thus, the connection of the main components of Barcelona's renewal to other contexts and to some general concepts, as well as the analysis of Monzó's intriguing portrait of the city, may hopefully provide us with a more complex and also more subversive understanding of this singular transformation.

The Urban History of Modern Barcelona

In the nineteenth century, the new Paris became an urban model for many European cities. Between 1853 and 1869, during the Second Empire of Napoleon III, Baron Haussmann, the *artiste démolisseur*, tore down many sections of the medieval city to open up the long boulevards and new public spaces characteristic of modern Paris. During this period, European cities also began to alter their medieval urban forms and create the new landscapes of industrialization. Barcelona's old city, however, was not affected by an extensive *sventramento*. There were a few exceptions that contradict this statement: streets such as Carrer Nou de la Rambla (Barcelona's first straight street, opened in 1788), Carrer Ferran (1823), Carrer Princesa (1853), or, much later, the wide Via Laietana (1908–13), are perfect examples of Haussmann-like demolitions within the old quarter. But an intricate history of political conflicts resulted in the general preservation of the medieval city.[4]

After the War of the Spanish Succession, Bourbon King Philip V imposed a series of repressive measures over Catalonia to punish the Catalans for having aligned themselves with England, Holland, Austria, and Savoy in support of the Habsburg candidate, Archduke Charles of Austria. These measures, established by the Decreto de Nueva Planta, followed from Philip V's desire to retaliate on the Catalans after the war, but they were also a consequence of the centralist structure of the new Bourbon state. Thus, in addition to abolishing Catalonia's political autonomy, imposing high taxes, and prohibiting the official use of the Catalan language, in 1716 Philip V built a Citadel in Barcelona to accommodate his army and control the rebellious city. This enormous Citadel, the construction of which entailed the demolition of most the old neighborhood of La Ribera, was built to prevent not only uprisings and riots, but also the expansion of the city itself. A royal decree prohibited Barcelona from expanding beyond its medieval walls, and, indeed, the massive Citadel, which encircled a good section of the walls, made this expansion physically impossible. As a result, Barcelona turned into the most densely populated city in Europe, with serious problems of hygiene and epidemic diseases. The medieval city remained intact, and the dawn of industrialization was not accompanied by any extensive, state-directed remodeling of its structure.

Urban renewal came later, in the middle of the nineteenth century, when popular insurgence and the demands of the emerging capitalist bourgeoisie compelled the central state to reform Barcelona. But, by then, the renewal plan did not focus on the old city; instead, it projected the demolition of the walls and the planning of the *Eixample* – literally, the expansion – beyond them. The demolition began in 1854, even though the project for the *Eixample* was not approved until 1860. The Citadel, in turn, was transformed in 1873 into Parc de la Ciutadella, designed by architect Josep Fontserè.

Engineer, urban planner and politician Ildefons Cerdà (1815–76) designed the new *Eixample*. In its definitive layout of 1863, the *Eixample* was planned as a perfect grid that would link Barcelona's medieval city with the towns of Sants, Les Corts, Sarrià, Sant Gervasi, Gràcia, Horta, Sant Andreu, and Sant Martí. The grid was composed of evenly squared blocks, and was traversed by three diagonal avenues – La Meridiana, El Paral·lel, and La Diagonal. But Cerdà did not simply design a rigid and efficient grid. Rather, his plan devised the new Barcelona as a balanced combination of wide avenues, spacious houses, green areas, inside patios, parks, and passageways, and it intended to reconcile the convenience of easy circulation with the comfort of living in a garden city.

This reconciliation of functions is one of the crucial innovations of Cerdà's theory of urbanism, which he formulated in 1867 in *Teoría general de la urbanización*. As Françoise Choay explains, Cerdà's theory articulated for the first time a multifunctional definition of urbanism. Choay writes that, for Cerdà, "urbanization resides in nothing other than the relation between rest and movement, or rather between the spaces that accommodate human repose and those that facilitate movement, that is, buildings and the network of streets" (237).

The agreement between habitation and circulation must not be interpreted as merely technical or functional. Rather, Cerdà's urbanistic work on city form attempted to have a deep social effect and cure the capitalist maladies of exploitation, inequality, and real estate speculation. His *Eixample* for Barcelona was the urban materialization of a utopian socialist politics aiming to provide equality and progress for everyone. In this respect, the spatial homogeneity of

Cerdà's grid was as significant as its multifunctionality. The square blocks and straight streets not only represented an effective layout to fulfill the needs of the modern city and accommodate a variety of urban functions; more importantly, they also constituted the urban expression of a wish for social equality. The *Eixample* aimed to eliminate, or at least reduce, social inequality by structuring the new Barcelona through the geometric uniformity of a harmonious grid.

Unsurprisingly, real estate speculation and the multiple economic interests of the fast-growing industrial city thwarted the full implementation of Cerdà's plan. During the construction of the grid throughout the second half of the nineteenth century, most gardens and other non-directly productive spaces were never built, resulting in the emergence of an *Eixample* with densely populated blocks, noisy streets, and polluting factories. Also, despite the formal uniformity of the grid, central and privileged areas inevitably appeared in opposition to more marginal ones.

One might remember here the funny, but all too real, procedure that, in Eduardo Mendoza's *La ciudad de los prodigios*, Onofre Bouvila employed to speculate with real estate during the construction of the *Eixample*. Mendoza narrates how Bouvila first would buy a cheap piece of land in a not very attractive section of the grid, where nobody wanted to live. But,

> Un día llegaron a este sitio varios carros cargados de tramos de metal; el sol al dar en el metal lanzaba unos destellos que podían ver los albañiles que levantaban las torres de la Sagrada Familia no lejos de allá. Eran vías de tranvía... Esta vez sí, se dijo la gente; no hay duda de que este sector va a más. En tres o cuatro días le habían quitado a Onofre Bouvila de las manos las parcelas por el precio que él quiso fijar. (189)

> One day, several carts appeared; sunlight gleaming on lengths of metal could be seen by the masons working on the towers of the Sagrada Familia not far from there. These were streetcar rails...
> "This time it's for real," people said. "This area is going places without a doubt."
> Within three or four days Onofre was relieved of all his lots for the price he chose to name. (Molloy 202)

However, once the lots had been sold, the workers folded back up the railway tracks and left. Bouvila had only hired them to make everybody believe that that section of the *Eixample* was about to have a streetcar or a railway station and become a thriving center. This is of course a fictitious story, but it portrays the general speculation and lucrative corruption that occurred during the expansion of the city.

Brad Epps observes how Cerdà's theory of urbanism and his project for the *Eixample*, despite their utopian socialist content, do not address class struggle nor any of the major contradictions of capitalism. In fact, according to Epps, Cerdà does the opposite: "Cerdà is concerned... with the displacement and partial undoing of class conflict through a redistribution not so much of wealth, or of the means of production, as of space" ("Modern Spaces" 154). Epps situates Cerdà somewhere in between Baron Haussmann and Marx, and explains his close connection to Utopianists Charles Fourier and Étienne Cabet. In his examination of *Teoría general de la urbanización*, Epps describes Cerdà as a Utopianist who condemned exploitation as much as revolution. The ultimate goal of his *Eixample*, like Haussmann's boulevards according to Benjamin's well-known analysis, was to provide open and wide streets to repress revolts and insurrections more efficiently. Cerdà's grid provided a perfect urban form for the implementation of state repression over social unrest.[5]

Even though the building of the *Eixample* certainly became a profitable enterprise for the bourgeoisie and facilitated the repression of class struggle, we must still ask ourselves whether Cerdà's plan contains a genuinely utopian stance that is worth retrieving. Epps observes that the rhetoric of Cerdà's *Teoría* is "strategic" (155), as he tries to persuade government officials and property owners to invest in urbanization while maintaining their status quo. Despite his own "strategic" statements against the possibility of revolution, perhaps we can still read Cerdà's plan as an attempt to transform social relations through a new spatial design. Epps concludes that Cerdà's redistribution of space aims to prevent the redistribution of wealth and the means of production. This is an accurate assessment, but we must realize that the redistribution of space can also potentially result in a relocation of wealth, as the ways in which capital spatializes itself are always an intrinsic component of capitalist production. Space is not a frame or a substratum but a material and symbolic means of social production; consequently, any transformation of it necessarily implies a rearrangement of accumulative practices.

While, as Epps rightly observes, the *Eixample* did not become a utopian and egalitarian city, Cerdà considered space to be a real means to modify social relations, and his plan tried to amend, albeit unsuccessfully, social antagonisms. Cerdà's grid neither corresponded to Haussmann's demolitions aimed at repressing class struggle, nor did it replicate the suburban "garden cities" that began to appear, especially in Britain, as the first materializations of the desire to escape from the disturbances of the city. The transformative content of Cerdà's plan can be detected in its two fundamental characteristics: on the one hand, the multifunctionality and mixture of uses aimed at fulfilling the various needs of modern urban dwellers, and, on the other hand, the ordered uniformity of the grid expressed the utopian wish for social equality. Despite its failed realization, the plan constituted an operative and simultaneously utopian articulation of the urban.

In fact, Epps, in a different version of his article (published in Catalan), also concludes that Cerdà's *Eixample* contains an authentic utopian core. He finds it in "la ruptura dels límits, la superació de les limitacions, l'obertura del clos" 'the break of limits, the overcoming of limitations, the opening of closure' of Cerdà's plan ("Els llocs d'enlloc" 117). Epps retrieves the unlimited openness of the *Eixample* against today's ghettoized and permanently surveilled global city: a very suggestive point that confirms that Cerdà's utopian urbanism continues to interpellate our present.

The grid of the *Eixample* determined the growth and shape of modern Barcelona. It epitomized the enormous economic development of the city during the second half of the nineteenth century and also the birth of political Catalanism. The *Eixample* represented the urban materialization of the political and cultural renaissance of the Catalan nation: it became, in the words of historian Jaume Vicens i Vives, the "eina d'un poble renaixent" 'tool of a reviving people' (quoted in Bohigas, *Barcelona* 129). The term "eina" accurately conveys the idea that the *Eixample* was both the cause and the effect of Barcelona's economic and political progress. The spatial transformation of the city was an essential component of this growth, as it provided an open terrain for capitalist expansion and also for the construction of symbolic buildings that embodied the new Catalanist ideology.

Two special events functioned as catalysts of this progress: the Universal Exhibition of 1888 and the International Exhibition of 1929. The Parc de la Ciutadella and its surrounding area, previously occupied by the infamous Citadel, held the first Exhibition. This event stimulated the construction of many sections of the *Eixample* and coincided with the emergence of *modernista* architecture, most notably represented by Lluís Domènech i Montaner (1850–1923), Antoni Gaudí (1852–1926), and Josep Puig i Cadafalch (1867–1956). These architects built, in the most privileged areas of the *Eixample*, private residences for the bourgeoisie that had flourished thanks to Catalonia's prosperous textile industry. The medieval and organic forms of *modernista* architecture both complemented and contrasted with the *Eixample*'s rational grid, and it is in this complementary contrast where the movement's political subtext lies. The combination of the modern, efficient structure of the grid with the historical and natural forms of *modernista* architecture perfectly embodied the twofold ambition of Catalan nationalism, namely to modernize and Europeanize Catalonia while at the same time exalting its natural territory and retrieving its past, particularly its medieval splendor, when Catalonia possessed autonomous institutions. As architect David Mackay explains,

> [*modernisme*] was much more than a local variant of Art Nouveau, because it came to be identified as a style with the overall movement of affirmation, as opposed to Spanishness, of the national character of Catalonia and its cultural independence, more in harmony with other European trends. (quoted in Busquets 164–5)

The connection of *modernisme* with these European trends, which included the French *Art Nouveau*, the German *Jugendstil*, the English *Modern Style*, and the Austrian *Sezession*, reinforced its engagement with the Catalanist project of Europeanization. Many *modernista* buildings were designed as collective symbols for the Catalan people, like Domènech i Montaner's Palau de la Música Catalana (1908) and Gaudí's Sagrada Família (1884–1926). Other buildings, even when they did not display their symbolic content as explicitly, also aimed to become landmarks of Barcelona and were key to articulating the *Eixample* as the urban expression of a reviving Catalonia. Among these mostly residential buildings, we find Domènech i Montaner's Casa Lleó Morera (1905) and Hospital de Sant Pau (1902–10); Gaudí's Casa Batlló (1905–7) and Casa Milà (1905–10); and Puig i Cadafalch's Casa Amatller (1900), Palau Macaya (1901), and Casa Terrades or Casa de les Punxes (1905).[6]

The *Eixample* was finally completed in 1929, when the International Exhibition prompted the urbanization of the area between the mountain of Montjuïc and the city. While Domènech i Montaner and Gaudí participated in the construction of the facilities of the 1888 Exhibition in Parc de la Ciutadella, in 1929 Puig i Cadafalch conceived the urban transformation that accompanied the second Exhibition. The involvement of these architects in local politics (Puig i Cadafalch even became, in 1917, the president of the Mancomunitat de Catalunya, the chief institution devoted to Catalonia's cultural renaissance), and their close ties with the ruling bourgeoisie, provided them with considerable power to intervene in the configuration of the city. This power, however, quickly diminished in 1923 when the dictatorship of Primo de Rivera took over the organization of the Exhibition and aborted, or directly tore down, the construction of Catalanist architectural symbols, such as the four columns that Puig i Cadafalch had built in Montjuïc to represent the four red stripes of the Catalan flag. Despite these restrictions, urbanization works went on and, while the 1888 Exhibition had propelled the development of the area around Parc de la Ciutadella, the second Exhibition connected Montjuïc to the *Eixample* and engendered a monumental zone around the Palau Nacional, where a long avenue accommodated the different national pavilions – among them, Mies van der Rohe's German pavilion.

Beyond its emblematic buildings, the *Eixample* presented major challenges for the new city. As Barcelona expanded and approached the surrounding towns, the municipal government needed to determine how these towns should be incorporated into the geometric grid as new districts. French architect León Jaussely won, in 1905, the competition for the *Pla d'enllaços*, the connection plan that had to address this matter. Jaussely designed an effective plan that provided urban continuity to previously disconnected areas and sutured the perimeter of the grid. Thanks to this plan, the new Barcelona became an overall compact city.

At the same time, however, the more peripheral areas of the *Eixample* accommodated the large number of immigrants from rural Catalonia and other poorer areas of the peninsula that moved to prosperous Barcelona in the first decades of the century. Rapid speculation and slow planning forced them to live in overcrowded blocks and undersupplied shanty quarters. This was the main concern addressed during the Second Republic by a group of progressive architects who aimed to revolutionize urban planning in a city that had already reached one million inhabitants. Followers of the Modern Movement, the GATCPAC (Grup d'Arquitectes i Tècnics Catalans per al Progrés de l'Arquitectura Contemporània) was founded in 1930 by Josep Lluís Sert, Josep Torres Clavé, Ricard Churruca, Germà Rodríguez Arias, Pere Armengou, and Sixt Illescas. These architects were ready to apply the principles of the Functional City to Barcelona and they devised the Macià plan, a plan commissioned by the president of the Generalitat de Catalunya, Francesc Macià. Drawn up with the close collaboration of Le Corbusier, the Macià plan opposed the suburban expansion of Barcelona and the creation of one-family homes with private gardens and backyards. The plan sought instead an operative articulation of the residential, communicative, industrial, and recreational functions of the city. Its goal was to build serialized and functional dwellings, factories, public gardens, and civic centers. To a large extent, the plan remained faithful to Cerdà's original project for the *Eixample*, even though it emphasized the efficiency that the separation of urban functions could provide and, in a characteristic modern gesture, it systematically excluded decorative ornaments. The plan aimed to recondition the city so that the basic needs of all its inhabitants, especially the most impoverished, could be fulfilled.

The growing political instability of the Republic and, above all, the outbreak of the Civil War, impeded the full execution of the Macià plan, and the GATCPAC dissolved in 1937. During the war and the immediate postwar period, construction was obviously minimal or nonexistent. But, as migrants from other parts of Spain began to arrive in the city in search of a better life, shantytowns and slums proliferated again. Speculators and builders took advantage of this situation and built large, homogeneous blocks throughout the periphery to accommodate the newcomers. Located next to highways, and disconnected from any web of services, these blocks, as one could see in many other European cities after World War II, represented the most deplorable version of the modern Functional City. The prescriptive separation of uses gave way to disjointed extensions of blocks detached from the urban fabric. In Barcelona, the construction of cheap housing in the periphery was particularly indiscriminate and unregulated. Speculators enjoyed total immunity provided by Franco and his appointed mayor in Barcelona, José María Porcioles, whose mandate lasted from 1957 to 1973. This autocratic period is known in Barcelona as *porciolisme*.

The devastating effects of these municipal policies spawned discontent among the people. During the late 1960s and early 1970s, neighborhood and grassroots movements began to organize protests and demonstrations, which were also part of a wave of heterogeneous but interlaced protests against the dictatorship, the lack of freedom, the repression of Catalan culture, and the effects of industrial reconversion over the working class.[7] *Porciolisme* finally ended in 1973 when the municipal government intended to pass a plan to construct new buildings that entailed the destruction of thousands of houses in the marginal zones of Torre Baró, Vallbona, and Trinitat. In this case, the affected neighbors protested so vehemently – they even invaded the city hall – that Franco was forced to depose Porcioles.

In 1974, the city hall, under transitional mayor Enric Massó, drew a new city plan, the *Pla general metropolità* (PGM), to order and limit the density of population and, more importantly, to reconstruct and harmonize Barcelona's urban space rather than extend it. Engineers Albert Serratosa and Joan Anton Solans revised this plan in 1976, once democracy had arrived. Despite being more regulatory than resourceful, the plan established a solid framework to limit the endless urban expansion that had torn apart Barcelona during Francoism. Without this framework, the radical transformation of the city during the Olympic years would have never been possible.

Oriol Bohigas and the Olympic City

The housing conditions and lack of public services, especially in the periphery of Barcelona, caused a high level of dissatisfaction in the last years of the dictatorship and during the transition to democracy. Popular petitions, demands from neighborhood associations, and street protests proliferated. For this reason, the improvement of living conditions in the periphery became a priority for the first elected government of the Partit del Socialistes de Catalunya. We must determine, however, whether the PSC's urban policies were part of a mere strategy to keep people content and maintain hegemony (after all, a large majority of their voters, especially the working classes who had arrived in the 1960s and 1970s, lived in the periphery), or whether they constituted a truly democratic urban politics. In other words, was the urban renewal the materialization of the city hall's postpolitics (focused on serving the everyday needs of the people and coopting popular dissension), or did the renewal contain a truly transformative drive that is worth retrieving? Or, better, did the renewal really aim to fulfill the needs of the people, or did it pursue an economic reconversion that was ultimately not transformative but repressive? To try to answer these questions, let us first examine the conceptualization and chief characteristics of this long-awaited urban renewal.

Mayor Narcís Serra appointed architect Oriol Bohigas municipal urban designer from 1980 to 1984. Bohigas launched, and personally directed, the transformation that rebuilt contemporary Barcelona. The picture of one single individual in command of the renewal of an entire city is usually associated with modernity and with figures such as Haussmann or Cerdà. In postmodernity, the endless corporatization of state apparatuses, and the predominance of commissions of technical experts, have virtually eliminated the possibility of individual ruling. In fact, mayor Serra initially appointed a commission of five members to direct the urban transformation: along with Bohigas, the members were architect Josep Anton Acebillo, planner Albert Puigdomènech, lawyer Jaume Gallofré, and vice mayor Josep Miquel Abad. But, in post-Francoist Barcelona, Bohigas played a singularly dominant and decisive role in the renewal of the city. Ole Bouman and Roemer van Toorn refer to Bohigas' "omnipotence," and write "There can be few cities that bear the stamp of the personality of their head of city planning to such an extent as Barcelona" (180). And, at the end of *La ciudad de los arquitectos*, Llàtzer Moix goes so far as to lay out the names and relations of Barcelona's architects in a family tree in which Bohigas acts as the undisputed patriarch.

Bohigas, born in 1925, actively participated in the architectural debates and cultural life that existed under the Franco regime. Most significantly, he belonged to the Grup R, founded in 1951 and composed of a group of young Catalan architects who were eager to apply new ideas to contemporary architecture. The members of the Grup R were Bohigas, Josep A. Coderch, Antoni de Moragas, Josep Partmarsó, Manuel Ribas Piera, and Josep Maria Sostres, among others. Even if these architects had little influence on the urban policies of the city hall, they designed many single brilliant buildings during the 1960s. The group embraced the functional principles of the Modern Movement, but interweaved them with a complementary care for local and regional forms. The R, as Bohigas explains, "tant servia per referir-se a reintegració, a restauració, al retrobament, com a revolució, a rebuig, a reconsideració" 'referred to reinstatement, restoration, reunion, and also to revolution, refusal, reconsideration' (*Dit o fet* 50). Their goal was to restore the Modern Movement and its revolutionary principles, but this very act of restoration implied a distance with the past and a will to recuperate something that was no longer present. The radical break with tradition proclaimed by the Modern Movement turned here into its opposite: it turned into loyalty to the "modern" past, into an allegiance to the tradition of modernity itself. By trying to remain faithful to the Modern principles, the Grup R necessarily betrayed them.

The dialectics between modernity's permanent breaking with tradition, and the fact that modernity itself turns into tradition, have constituted one of postmodernity's fundamental features. The Grup R dealt with these unsolvable dialectics by merging functionalism and regionalism. In this sense, regionalism must not be simply interpreted as a symbol of local traditions or of the past *tout court*; rather, it is a supplementary element that symptomatizes the fact that, in postmodernity, being modern can only mean being traditional, that is, being loyal to the tradition of modernity. But regionalism reveals this contradiction to the extent that it is an attempt to conceal it and displace it. Given that one can no longer be simply modern, one has to propose some supplementary regional variation, so that the new works do not seem an outmoded application of the "traditional" principles of the Modern Movement. Through the ideologemes of the regional and the local, the new works can cope with the fact that modernity is already traditional and still satisfy the imperative to be *absolument moderne*.

Bohigas became the most prolific theoretician of the Grup R, and his designs at the firm MBM, which he founded together with Josep Carbonell and David Mackay, reflected his theories of architecture and the city. However, under Franco's dictatorship he had no chances to put them into practice in any methodical and effective way (except in the design of specific residential buildings, such as those at the Roger de Flor street (1957), at Pallars street (1960), or at the Meridiana avenue (1964) – three notable examples that combine the social functions of the Modern Movement with the "aesthetic" components of regionalism).[8] It was only after democracy had arrived that Bohigas could turn his theories of functional regionalism into an extensive transformation of his home city.

When, in 1980, Bohigas had the opportunity to direct the renewal of Barcelona, he did not formulate a wide-ranging plan for the entire city. On the contrary, his ideas for the rebuilding of Barcelona opposed the comprehensiveness of systematic plans. Even though he followed the premises of the 1976 *Pla general metropolità* (PGM), and his proposals shared the same restructuring goals, he considered general plans to be the result of mere applied engineering, always too abstract and at the same time too pragmatic. He opposed the way engineers tend to approach urban change and, in Barcelona, he convinced mayor Serra to transfer many funds previously destined for Public Works to his department of Urbanism.

The problem with plans such as PGM, Bohigas argues in *Reconstrucció de Barcelona*, is their "concepte de ciutat com a sistema ideal unitari" 'concept of the city as a unitary ideal system' (9). He proposes, instead, "el concepte de ciutat com a suma conflictiva de trossos reals" 'the concept of city as a conflicting sum of real segments' (9). Bohigas justifies this dichotomy in political terms. Whereas general plans aim to dominate the city through "una mena de metafísica de la totalitat" 'a certain metaphysics of totality' (14), which is characteristic of totalitarian regimes, his democratic conception, on the contrary, focuses on the immediate realities of the street, the square, the neighborhood, and the park. His urbanism is "compromès en les definicions formals i en les decisions immediates i concretes per una millora de les condicions de vida de la gent d'avui i en una voluntat de donar significació i fins i tot expressió monumental a tota la col·lectivitat urbana" 'committed in its formal definitions and immediate and concrete decisions to improve the quality of life of today's people and willing to give meaning and even monumental expression to the entire urban collective' (23).

In his proposals, Bohigas acknowledges two main challenges: first, it is difficult to entirely avoid the abstraction of general plans if one wants to have an actual effect on the space of the city; and, second, even if democratic urbanism aims to address the real needs of the citizens, the negotiation of their demands is always difficult (185–196). He distinctly states, however, that the improvement and reconstruction of cities must be a public enterprise. Private capital is interested in constructing new buildings and developing new districts; only public administrations can bring about sensible renovation and rebuilding (13).

Bohigas argues that urban life only emerges as a result of multifunctionality and dynamic mixtures of uses. He rejects the modern urbanism of the functional or vertical city – and of Le Corbusier's paradigmatic *ville radieuse* – because it assigns separated spaces to each urban function. As one can observe in the expansion of most European cities after World War II, the separation of uses of the functional city generates suburban and segregated areas. Thus, while Bohigas shares with the Modern Movement the same commitment to change social relations through architecture, he endorses the conflicting and unclassifiable interference of urban uses. The busy street is the exemplary space in which this interference takes place. He praises "les qualitats d'interferència i de conflictivitat d'usos d'una peça urbana fonamental, que és el carrer, un espai on passa tot, on tot es relaciona, sense possibilitat de classificar-ho" 'the qualities of interference and conflict of uses in a fundamental urban piece, namely the street, a space where everything happens, where everything is related, with no possible classification' (115). For Bohigas, cars and people, houses and stores, private and public spaces, must intersect as closely as possible. Through this conception of the street, he opposes, on the one hand, "nostalgic" architects who want to transform streets, especially in old quarters, into pedestrian and monofunctional zones, and, on the other hand, technology-worshipping engineers whose plans build functional highways unaware of the effects that these have on specific urban fabrics.

To reinforce his vindication of the street, Bohigas refers to its Latin etymological root. Originally, the word "sternere" meant "to pave" and the root "str," to build. Thus, streets are essentially and at the same time a place and a path: a place to dwell and a path to circulate through. Bohigas draws the same conclusion when he brings in the Catalan and Spanish words, "carrer" and "calle," which derive from the Latin "callis," a path for the cattle. In this case, Bohigas finds the complementary meaning of street as "place" in the coincidental fact that, in Catalan, "call" means Jewish neighborhood, which he associates with the place for the community (126–7).

Leaving aside whether this genealogy is accurate or not, the retrieval of these etymologies accomplishes two things. First, the location of the origin of the street in the Roman world refutes the potential objection that Bohigas' concept only corresponds to the streets of modern metropolises. Second, this origin indicates that Bohigas' "street" is characteristic of European, and even specifically Mediterranean, cities. He devises a Graeco-Roman, and by extension European, genesis for the street as the essence of the city; correspondingly, he almost always refers to European urban forms and examples in his writings.[9] For Bohigas, the city united by its multifunctional and vibrant streets, in which private and public uses intersect, constitutes the European urban model, a model opposed to American and Asian sprawls and to Third World urbanized extensions not properly recognizable as cities.

This embrace of the European and Mediterranean city connects with the politics of Barcelona's city hall. Not only does Bohigas base his urban theory on Europe and the Mediterranean, which, as I discussed in Chapter Two, corresponded to the hegemonic imaginary spaces that sustained the euphoric politics of Barcelona, he also suggests that the reconciliation between private and public functions is the essence of the urban. That is, Bohigas' theorization of the street, in its capacity to intermingle public and private functions, complements well the plan of the city hall to establish a profitable alliance between the public administration and private companies and developers.[10]

When Bohigas applied his urban philosophy to Barcelona in the 1980s, he promoted a large variety of architectural interventions. As head of municipal urbanism, he selected numerous architects to rebuild the city. Rather than implement a comprehensive plan, his goal was to work on particular segments and suture the urban fabric in very specific zones. Bohigas proclaimed an effective slogan that summarized the task: "ens cal higienitzar el centre i monumentalitzar la perifèria" 'we must clean up the center and monumentalize the periphery' (*Reconstrucció* 65). On the one hand, his project proposed minimal but conscientious interventions that would "esponjar" the city, that is, interventions that could sponge the more densely populated areas by creating public spaces in them. No comprehensive demolition was necessary; only sensitive interventions in concrete points. On the other hand, to monumentalize the periphery referred to two specific things. First, high-speed expressways were integrated into the city so that they would no longer tear up the urban fabric and alienate entire neighborhoods. Second, new landmarks gave distinctive personality to streets and neighborhoods. Thus, public sculptures by renowned artists were placed in some of the least glamorous areas of the city. Richard

Serra, Claes Oldenburg, Roy Lichtenstein, Joan Miró, Ellsworth Kelly, Eduardo Chillida, Bryan Hunt, Jannis Kounellis, Jaume Plensa, Rebecca Horn, Frank Gehry, Fernando Botero, Antoni Tàpies, or Joan Brossa, among many others, provided works at unusually low prices because of the public and revitalizing function that they would fulfill.[11]

Bohigas' plan aimed to create new and diversified centers throughout the city. The re-equipment of strategic spaces intended to have "efectes osmòtics" 'osmotic effects' (101) and generate a process of, as philosopher Xavier Rubert de Ventós put it, "metàstasi positiva" 'positive metastasis' (quoted in Bohigas, *Dit o fet* 195). As a result, larger areas, especially disjointed districts at the periphery, could be renewed. This regeneration – based on recognizable landmarks such as sculptures, monuments, parks, or squares – should also help citizens map the city easily. The new centers would divide the city into precise, understandable sections. Most of these sections coincided with historical neighborhoods, even though these neighborhoods had often become indistinguishable because of unregulated suburban expansion during Francoism.

These were the basic parameters of the plan that had to transform Barcelona into a habitable, multifunctional, well-balanced, and, not least, beautiful metropolis. Bohigas' goal was to implement a democratic urbanism which, in principle, would return to the people the city that for decades had been in the hands of despotic speculators.

Heterogeneous Architecture in a Postmodern City

The task of returning the city to the people overlapped with the need to build the facilities to host the 1992 Olympic Games. Both projects merged in such a way that the preparation for the Games and the rebuilding of the city became synonymous with each other. Even if, in 1982, Pasqual Maragall became the new mayor, and Josep Anton Acebillo later replaced Bohigas as municipal urban designer, the city hall continued to apply Bohigas' ideas when building the facilities for the Games. This identification of the two tasks resulted in two main urbanistic decisions. First, the designation of four Olympic areas was linked to the creation of new centers. The four areas of Poblenou, Montjuïc, Vall d'Hebron, and Diagonal, situated in rather peripheral areas beyond the *Eixample*, would contain the stadiums, apartments, pavilions, swimming pools, and stores for the Games. The placing of the Olympic facilities in these four designated areas complied with Bohigas' imperative to create new centers throughout the city. Second, the city hall hired an enormous variety of architects to design specific projects for each Olympic area. There was no extensive master plan, but the same case-by-case approach that Bohigas had proclaimed for the reconstruction of the city.

It seems likely that, without the Games, the urban transformation of Barcelona would have neither attracted the same amount of investments, nor would it have generated the same level of consensus. Correspondingly, if Barcelona had not framed the hosting of the Games in a wider program of urban transformation, it might not have been elected Olympic city. Similar dynamics can be detected in Bohigas' case. Even if he criticized the Games as a futile and ephemeral event, his projects for the city evidently benefited from them; the city hall, in turn, made use of his urban philosophy to present the Olympic facilities as an essential part of the reconstruction of Barcelona.[12]

Many of the architects who participated in the renewal of Barcelona were Catalan or Spanish, but others were international figures – a fact that proved, according to Bohigas, the city's "voluntad internacionalista y cosmopolita" 'cosmopolitan and internationalist spirit' (quoted in Moix 84). Given this heterogeneity of architects, some of their urban projects fitted well into Bohigas' conceptual framework, and some of them did not. After being released from his position as urban designer in 1984, Bohigas worked from his private firm on the public projects that were assigned to him, but he always had a strong influence on mayor Maragall. This ambivalent position explains why, even if he played a central role in orchestrating the whole transformation, some of the projects agreed with his ideas, while some others, usually assigned by his successor, Josep Anton Acebillo, did not. I will briefly examine some of these works – first, those that fitted into Bohigas' plan, and then those that were energetically at odds with it.[13]

The mixed urban uses of Via Júlia. Photo by Maria Domene.

Public space and contemporary art at MACBA. Photo by Maria Domene.

Bohigas made an initial, authoritative statement in 1982 when he assigned to architects Bernardo de Sola and Josep Maria Julià the restructuring of Via Júlia at the outskirts of the city. This project, which, as Moix reveals (73), infuriated the municipal engineers, who felt that two architects were invading their terrain, produced an avenue with mixed uses for pedestrians and cars in a barely urbanized area. The project consisted in redesigning a specific space – a relatively short street – so as to generate "osmotic effects" in the surrounding area and suture a larger section of the peripheral district.

Another project that followed Bohigas' philosophy was proposed by Lluís Clotet and Òscar Tusquets in 1983 under the slogan "Del Liceu al Seminari." This project included the remodeling of some buildings in the historic center, such as the Casa de Caritat, turned by architects Helio Piñón and Albert Viaplana into the Centre de Cultura Contemporània de Barcelona (CCCB), and the creation of new ones, such as Richard Meier's 1995 Museu d'Art Contemporani de Barcelona (MACBA). These buildings for public use, located at the core of the old quarter of El Raval, aimed to revitalize a degraded area by introducing new cultural services. They provided not only new cultural facilities, but also adjacent open spaces with multiple functions.

To name a few more examples: Arata Isozaki's sports pavilion Palau Sant Jordi (1992) combined a discreetly sophisticated design with an effective functionality. The pavilion was built to hold various sport contests during the Olympics, but its multifunctionality, as well as its suggestive uniqueness, made it an ideal

The self-referential and telluric Plaça dels Països Catalans. Photo by Maria Domene.

place for all sorts of events. Manuel de Solà-Morales' Moll de la Fusta (1983–7) constituted one of the most perfect expressions of Bohigas' theories. In the area that separated the city from the port, Solà-Morales' project supplied three valuable things at the same time: a waterfront for restaurants and other leisure activities, a more rational road connection with the city belt, and the integration of the historic center to the port. This was not simply the typical conversion of an old port into a pedestrian waterfront; rather, the project accomplished the suturing of a previously disjointed fragment of the urban text.

The Plaça dels Països Catalans (1983), also by Piñón and Viaplana, was a daring design that turned a chaotic and car-ridden space in front of Sants railway station into a startling public square. This square established a clear and understandable transition between the station and its neighborhood. The previous non-place that served as an informal parking lot became an identifiable place. Despite being named "Plaça dels Països Catalans," no element in the square displayed any explicit symbolic meaning; rather, the abstract, elusive design seemed to extract its meaning from the very physical and telluric nature of the place itself. The square is paradoxical: it is simultaneously self-referential and rooted. The impossible but real effect of this self-referential design is that it prompts the emergence of that space as a rooted place.

Finally, the integration of the upper part of the city belt into the existing urban fabric was defined by some as the best urban project of Olympic Barcelona (Moix 193). The Ronda de Dalt, built by architect Bernardo de Sola and engineers Jordi Torrella and Isidoro Muñoz, in an uncommonly fruitful relation between the two disciplines, inserted a high-speed road into a variety of neighborhoods in a sensitive and well-balanced way. Unlike the vast majority of city belts, the Ronda de Dalt did not tear apart the different areas that it crossed; in fact, it tied them together in a way that facilitated both the flow of traffic and the continuity of the urban fabric.

These interventions, among many others, shared the architectural guidelines. By conceiving the city as a sum of small units, architecture could have the power to intervene in urban contexts beyond the design of single buildings. While, traditionally, architects design buildings and urban planners arrange spaces on a larger scale, Bohigas and allied architects such as Manuel de Solà-Morales or Joan Busquets blurred the boundaries of this distinction. They formulated an urbanism based on singular pieces and an architecture based on designing urban zones beyond individual buildings. "The urban project" or "the urban piece," as Busquets explains (348), became key notions to describe the intermediate zone below urban plans and above architectural projects.

But other works were less acquiescent to this hegemonic conception of the urban transformation of Barcelona. I have chosen several of these works to show four directions that diverge from Bohigas' commands. These four directions may be called rootless architecture, aestheticized architecture, pop architecture, and master planning architecture.

Ricardo Bofill's 1988 extension of Barcelona's airport was deliberately detached from its urban context. Bofill designed the terminal as a square box made of dark glass walls sustained by marble Doric columns and adorned with palm trees. Manuel Castells uses this terminal as an example of what he terms "the architecture of the end of history," which, for him, corresponds to the architecture of fluxes characteristic of the informational society. Castells describes Bofill's terminal as a nude space where everything flows: "In the middle of the cold beauty of this airport passengers have to face their terrible truth: they are alone, in the middle of the space of flows; they may lose their connection, they are suspended in the emptiness of transition" (*Rise Network* 421).

This can, of course, be said of all airports. But a few specific characteristics make Bofill's airport a particularly generic non-place. The dark glass walls of the terminal generate two effects: on the one hand, they turn the bright, Mediterranean light of the exterior into a grey, diffused dazzle that further disconnects the interior from its surrounds; on the other hand, the mirroring surfaces of these walls make the inside invisible from the outside. But the walls do not simply return the gaze to the external observer, as in a conventional mirror. Rather, they produce a third, in-between effect: their mirroring surfaces impede the vision from the outside, but their dark color makes them ultimately opaque and not reflective. The terminal emerges as a dark body whose total disconnection from the outside produces the effect of weightlessness and suspension. The marble columns and floors inside the terminal would seem to counteract this weightlessness, but their solidity is merely apparent. Despite their structural function, the classical columns look as extemporary as the palm trees disseminated throughout the terminal. (Eventually, the trees had to be removed because of the lack of light produced by the dark glass.) The solidity of the columns does not provide any sense of stability to the rapid flows of passengers and luggage around them; a situation that resembles that of those skyscrapers (by Philip Johnson, for instance) in which solid granite is an unconvincing disguise of the virtual and fictitious quality of the finance operations that take place inside them.

It is true that, for obvious reasons, airports must always be detached from the urban fabric. However, Bofill's terminal constitutes a deliberate, calculated effort to erase any identification between the airport and Barcelona, especially when compared with the old terminal from 1968. The unoriginal design of this terminal was characteristic of Barcelona's architecture during the 1960s, and the mural by Joan Miró painted at its entrance unequivocally linked the old terminal to the city and to Catalonia. The rootlessness of Bofill's design, by contrast, is categorical and complete.

In 1992, Norman Foster and Santiago Calatrava built two distinctive communication towers that clearly modified Barcelona's skyline. The innovative feature of Foster's Torre de Collserola, located on top of the mountain of Collserola, was the external display of the technological infrastructure traditionally contained inside. This variation gave the tower a unique and recognizable form. In turn, Calatrava's Torre de Telefònica, built in the Olympic ring of Montjuïc, has a twisted form. This form denotes a sophisticated but also hollow technological apparatus, which Moix has described as a "vistoso híbrido de pata de pollo y nave espacial" 'a flashy hybrid between a chicken leg and a space rocket' (216).

Moix also reveals that Foster's and Calatrava's towers were technically unnecessary (161). Barcelona already had the necessary infrastructure to broadcast the Games and transmit all the information during the event. Thus, the main purpose of the lanky towers and their high-tech innuendo was not to enhance communication but to serve as identifiable figures of Barcelona's skyline. The towers became landmarks of the city, but not with the purpose of helping citizens map out the city, as Bohigas would have wanted. They became visual landmarks serving the specular projection of Barcelona. They were aestheticized pieces in two senses: on the one hand, their function as media silhouettes was not complemented by any strictly urban use; on the other hand, the towers were in every way cut off from their urban context: even their striking white paint detached them from the brown, grey, and green colors that dominate the city and its mountains. The towers were built to function as images rather than

Remant of the industrial past at Vila Olímpica. Photo by Maria Domene

as components of the city. They were transmitters of information, but their primary goal was to transmit the image of themselves. This image circulated in two directions. Locally, the towers conveyed to the citizens of Barcelona the perception of a city connected to the global information networks; and globally, they projected – "synecdochically," as Balibrea points out ("Urbanism" 190) – the image of the whole city. They drew a new skyline that established a two-way connection between Barcelona and the global.[14]

Eduard Bru's design of the Olympic area of Vall d'Hebron represented a different type of architectural intervention. Bru, a Catalan architect from a generation younger than Bohigas', rejected the assumption that the street, the square, or the park are the departing units in the process of rebuilding cities. He argued that an area such as Vall d'Hebron, where degraded suburban residences mixed with non-urbanized hills and fields, could not be rebuilt with small compensatory interventions; instead, this area needed to be tackled through a complete rupture with its historical past. He privileged alternative urban elements such as the car, the parking lot, and rest areas, with various synthetic items. Bru made Bohigas very nervous when he installed all-colored turf grass, pavement made of gum, metal sidewalks, and folding street lamps, to create a kitsch landscape that embraced American-inspired pop architecture. In the end, however, Bru shared with Bohigas the goal of making a cohesive city for the people: he simply embraced the car instead of the street as the basic component to do it.

Last but not least, a rather unorthodox work in relation to Bohigas' theories was the Olympic village, designed by no other than Bohigas' own firm, MBM, together with Albert Puigdomènech. The design of the Olympic village constituted, not a specific project to stitch together an existing area, but a master plan that rebuilt from scratch an entire industrial neighborhood. The plan involved the removal of old factories and residences in the working class neighborhood of Poblenou, known since the nineteenth century as "the Catalan Manchester" due to its concentration of factories. In a perfect case of *tabula rasa* urbanism, the master plan erected a rejuvenated area of cleaned up beaches, new apartments, skyscrapers, stores, bars, restaurants, and a beach boardwalk.

Admittedly, the plan did contain the diversity of buildings and architects as well as the control over densities, the mixture of uses, and the overall cohesiveness that Bohigas had defended in his essays. But the Olympic village certainly did not consist in a small intervention; nor did it evolve from the previous urban text. The only vestiges of the past were a couple of unused factory chimneys, with no assigned urban function. They became aestheticized remnants that precisely symptomatized the erasure of the past.

The other reference to the proletatian times of the neighborhood was the name of the village, "La Nova Icària." This term paid homage to the group of Catalan Icarians who, following Étienne Cabet's socialist doctrines, founded a

Utopianist community, named "Icària," at the Poblenou in 1847. The reference operated as a sort of compensatory mechanism for the forgetting of the neighborhood's proletarian past. But the term had one further ideological function. "The Nova Icària" suggested that the Olympic village represented a new incarnation of Utopianist communities. Thus, the demolition of the old neighborhood would not look like a process of erasure of the past (and which served the interests of real estate developers and of the Olympic enterprise); rather, the demolition could be seen as motivated by the desire to build a new Icaria. In the same way that, in the nineteenth century, the Icarians created a new community from scratch, now the Olympic village would be built anew to embody a new utopian space. The name "La Nova Icària" accomplished the perfect crime: it erased the Utopianist past by seemingly replicating it in the Olympic village; a village that, naturally, did not represent any of the former hopes for collectivization and socialism.

But we must take a closer look at the relationship between Bohigas' precepts and the master plan of the Olympic village. To explain the transformation of Barcelona as a coherent process, Joan Busquets divides it into three groups according to the scale of the works. These groups are: 1) small interventions that pursued the revitalization of specific areas; 2) sectoral plans for the urban restructuring of road networks and the creation of new centers; and 3) other structuring keys shaping the city, such as the extension of Diagonal Avenue, the renovation of the old quarter, and the development of the seafront (354). However, despite their descriptive accuracy, these categories do not account for the fundamental internal contradiction that traversed the renewal of the city. The transformation was conceived and initiated as a sum of concrete projects that responded to specific necessities; its aim was to avoid being a systematic plan. Yet this programmed set of small interventions ultimately resulted in a total master plan. Indeed, the comprehensiveness of the transformation was both deployed and concealed by the fact that it was a sum of concrete works. A dialectical move between fragmentation and totality arbitrated the renewal of Barcelona; that is, a dialectical relationship existed between the architectural design of specific works and general urban planning.

The Olympic village, the master plan that prescribed and contained a set of heterogeneous architectural works, perhaps epitomized the whole transformation of the city. Even though it seemed to contradict Bohigas' initial theories regarding punctual interventions, this master plan actually revealed their ultimate implication: namely that the project to rebuild the city from below, and fragmentarily, aimed to reach, little by little, every corner of it, while applying the precepts of the mixture of uses, the control over densities, and general cohesiveness. The non-totalizing approach to urban change was, in the end, a way of rebuilding the totality of the city.

The Olympic village was representative of the transformation in yet another sense. The primary goal of the village was to accommodate the Olympic athletes, but its projected future uses were residential and recreational. That is, the urban uses of the new neighborhood were largely limited to these two main functions. The apartment buildings, public squares, stores, bars, restaurants, hotels, and especially the long beaches, replaced the old factories and served a new industry of leisure and tourism. The Olympic village exemplified how the urban transformation that intended to return the city to the people by regaining public spaces and neighborhood districts, also set up the infrastructure for the service and tourist industries, which have sustained much of Barcelona's economy since 1992. I will return to this key issue later.

Posterior evaluations of Barcelona's renewal have already described it as a general master plan made of heterogeneous architectural works. Even before the Games, but especially after them, the renewal became known as the Barcelona model of urban transformation. In 1990, the city was awarded the Prince of Wales Prize in Urban Design of Harvard's Department of Architecture and, in 1998, it received the Royal Gold Medal of the Royal Institute of British Architects (RIBA). In this case, it was the first time that the RIBA award went to a city and not to professionals, a fact that implied that the coherence of Barcelona's renewal was comparable to the trajectory of an individual architect. According to RIBA

> Barcelona is now more whole in every way, its fabric healed yet threaded through with new open spaces, its historic buildings refurbished yet its facilities expanded and brought up-to-the-minute. Past and present, work and play are happily intermeshed in a new totality that is more than its often splendid parts, and is better connected even to sea and mountains. (quoted in Balibrea, "Urbanism" 204)

Other evaluations also assume the transformation as a totality. Another laudatory comment comes from Pep Subirós, who writes that Barcelona has become "la primera ciutat en la qual es combina satisfactòriament un projecte de monumentalització i dignificació estètica de la ciutat amb una voluntat política més atenta als valors democràtics que no pas a la magnificació i sacralització del propi poder polític" 'the first city where a project of monumentalization and aesthetic dignification of the city is satisfactorily combined with a political will more attentive to democratic values than to the magnification and sacralization of its political power' (*Vol fletxa* 22).

Less complimentary opinions also conceive Barcelona's renewal as a cohesive whole. Some architects lament the lack of memorable single works during the 1980s and attribute it to the fact that the transformation consisted in a unified totality. Architect Alfredo Arribas argues that "cuando se construye bajo un arbitraje implícito como el conocido en estos años de gran influencia de Bohigas no se permiten excesivas singularidades. Esto tiene su contrapartida positiva: el nivel general es muy aceptable" 'when architects must build under implicit control, like Bohigas' influence during those years, excessive singularities are not allowed. This has a positive consequence: the general level is very satisfactory' (quoted in Moix 234). Along these lines, architect Ignasi de Solà-Morales affirms that "Barcelona ha generado una arquitectura refinada pero ecléctica y no experimentalista. Ha trabajado bien y deprisa. Pero desde un punto de vista intelectual, no ha alumbrado demasiadas ideas renovadoras" 'Barcelona has produced refined but eclectic and unadventurous architecture. People have worked well and fast. But from an intellectual point of view, the city has not generated many innovative ideas' (quoted in Moix 234).

Beyond these value judgments, everyone seems to assume that the singular novelty of the Barcelona model was the pursuit of a general renewal through specific projects. The urban model, based on the osmotic or positively metastatic effects of architectural works, had no precedents; or, at least, the implementation of this model to a whole city was unprecedented. There were a few previous examples of postmodern architectural interventions with urbanistic goals in mind; for instance, the renovation of Baltimore's waterfront in the early 1970s, and Renzo Piano and Richard Rogers' 1977 Centre Pompidou in Paris. But Barcelona produced a unique master plan that unfolded as a set of heterogeneous interventions that both constituted and denied the generality of the master plan itself.

A critical correlation can be established between the Olympic transformation of Barcelona and the very structural logic of postmodernism. Postmodernism is the historical system that, paradoxically and by definition, dissolves itself as a system in its constitution as a heterogeneous play of differences. As Jameson states,

> This is then the deeper paradox rehearsed by the attempt to grasp "postmodernism" in the form of periodizing or totalizing abstraction; it lies in this seeming contradiction between the attempt to unify a field and to posit the hidden identities that course through it and the logic of the very impulses of this field, which postmodernist theory itself openly characterizes as a logic of difference or differentiation. (*Postmodernism* 342)

This logic of difference originates in the logic of finance capital, which, as Harvey explains, compels spaces to differentiate themselves in order to attract capital investments (*Condition* 295). Given its mobile nature, finance capital has the liberty to decide whether to invest in a place or a company, or whether to abandon them, according to the best differential qualities and the most profitable options. Spaces, companies, and individuals must work on producing differential qualities, and must compete to attract all types of investments. Capital circulates underneath this active production of differences in more and more diffuse, untraceable ways. But, in late capitalism, what appears to be different turns out to be the same: companies that compete among each other are owned by the same corporation; places that develop differential qualities become unvaryingly generic; and individuals become ultimately interchangeable human resources. The multinational company, owned by a mixed set of companies, banks, and investors, and diversified through multiple products, localities, and subcompanies, is paradigmatic of this logic. Late capitalism or postmodernism are the names of the absent totality that constantly dissolves itself in an ever-changing field of differences on a global scale.

This global magnitude, as well as the logic of difference, are already presupposed in the concept of capital. The world market is an inherent consequence of the accumulative self-reproduction of capital, which requires the constant expansion of the sphere of circulation. As Marx states, "capital is the endless and limitless drive to go beyond its limiting barrier. Every boundary [*Grenze*] is and has to be a barrier [*Schranke*] for it" (*Grundrisse* 334). Value preserves itself, "as self-validated exchange value distinct from a use value" (270), through its constant increase. This increase is simultaneously quantitative and spatial, as the sphere of circulation must be permanently widened, regardless of "whether the sphere itself is directly expanded, or whether *more points within it are created as points of production*" (407).

The postmodern strategies of production of spatial differences must be understood along with this expansion and intensification of the capitalist market. Capitalism is the constant creation of new and different points of production and is simultaneously the global totality that produces them. In other words, capitalism unfolds as a system of differences that dissolves its very structure as a system. As Marx remarks, "capital in each of its particular phases is the negation of itself as the subject of all the various metamorphoses" (620). Postmodernity as a totality dissolved in a play of differences is ultimately another historical phase of this capitalist logic.

Going back to Barcelona, Mari Paz Balibrea has already pointed at the two-faced nature of the renewal as a master plan and as a series of unique interventions. On the one hand, she analyzes Bohigas' attacks on modern master plans as a typically postmodern claim against totality. But, on the other hand, she concludes that Barcelona's socialist government generated a process of consensus and neutralization of dissidence by using a totalizing discourse over the city. She refers to the production of "global images" and of "the totalizing image" of the city ("Urbanism" 204), and explains how "the provision of instruments that enable all citizens to *see* the city as a totality has been a highly effective way of generating consensus in Barcelona" (203).

Thus, this discontinuity between a discourse against totality and the totalizing effects of this discourse takes us to the contradictory core of the transformation of Barcelona. Even if, in hindsight, the transformation emerges as a totality, its implementation as well as its official promotion consisted in the opposite: the new city was conceived against all panopticism and as a sum of heterogeneous and multiple sites. And when a certain element did serve the production of "global" images representing Barcelona, this element functioned "synecdochically" – as Balibrea says regarding Foster's communication tower ("Urbanism" 190) – rather than panoptically. There was no central, all-encompassing plan that directly applied a totalizing strategy over the city. The figure of the panoptical is inadequate for understanding Barcelona's renewal, and also for understanding postmodern urban transformations inscribed into the logic of production of spatial differences. In Barcelona, control was implemented through agreement and cooperation. The city hall generated consensus by formulating a comprehensive urban politics, but this aimed to dissolve their comprehensiveness by focusing on specific urban projects and neighborhood demands. Consensus was generated from below, so to speak, and this made it all the more difficult for grassroots tactics or popular movements to contest these municipal politics.

Pep Subirós' celebratory account of the transformation is right in this point. Subirós recalls the example of the neighborhood associations of Ciutat Vella that, in 1987, launched a campaign called "Aquí hi ha gana" 'We are hungry here.' This campaign denounced the process of gentrification of the quarter as directed by the city hall. Subirós acknowledges the significance of this campaign, but states

> El que no hi ha, per part del moviment associatiu, són esmenes a la totalitat. Probablement perquè no hi ha models alternatius de ciutat o perquè, dit d'una altra manera, els projectes que es realitzen des de l'Ajuntament i les reivindicacions del moviment veïnal responen a un mateix model de ciutat. (*Vol fletxa* 77)

> The association movements do not formulate any motions for the rejection of the totality [of the city hall's plans]. That is probably because there are no alternative models of the city or, to put it differently, because the projects of the city hall and the demands of the neighbors correspond to the same model of the city.

This statement aims to praise the municipal urban politics, but it also shows that consensus in Barcelona was generated not only through discursive and visual harmonious designs, but especially by stressing that the city hall had the same concerns and urban model as the citizens. By means of this strategy the socialist party achieved two main political goals. First, the municipal agenda could not easily be contested by the citizens, as it was focused on, or even determined by, the demands of the neighbors. Second, potential antagonisms were reduced to necessities that had to be addressed as specific problems. Other preoccupations related to more general, structural problems had no place in the dialogue betweeen the city hall and the citizens. Thus, the socialist government gained their hegemonic position by coopting the appeal to "the real needs of the people." That is how, during the Olympic years, they succeeded in generating an exceptionally high level of consensus experienced by many Barcelonans as a feeling of collective euphoria.

Theoretical Frame: Frampton and Jacobs

Even if the Barcelona model of urban transformation was quite unique and unprecedented, we can relate it to some theories of architecture and urbanism. Moix mentions the influence on Bohigas and the Grup R of Italian architects Ernesto Rogers and Vittorio Gregotti, who publicized, in the famous magazine *Casabella*, their revision of the Modern Movement and their care for local spaces and vernacular traditions (22). Similarly, Francesc M. Muñoz observes that Aldo Rossi's 1966 *L'Architettura della cittá* was a major influence on Bohigas' theories ("Deconstrucció" 255–8).

Beyond the concrete names that influenced Bohigas, his ideas can be contextualized in a theoretical frame that illuminates their ultimate assumptions and also, perhaps, their relationship to structural conditions. Two theoreticians provide us with this fundamental frame. On the one hand, the program to create a sense of place through landmarks, restored historic buildings, and public spaces can be inscribed in what Kenneth Frampton theorized as Critical Regionalism. On the other hand, the multifunctional spaces and mixture of uses that the renewal aimed to provide may be related to Jane Jacobs' 1961 eminent proposal to save American cities from the dangers of suburbanization and monofunctional zoning.

Frampton introduced the notion of Critical Regionalism in 1980 in the last chapter of his *Modern Architecture*, and further developed it as an architectural program in his 1983 text, "Towards a Critical Regionalism: Six Points for an Architecture of Resistance" (*Labour* 76–89). To illustrate his notion, Frampton found inspiration in various examples from countries such as Italy, Finland, Portugal, Greece, Mexico, Japan, and Catalonia, and in the works of architects such as Vittorio Gregotti, Aldo Rossi, Tadao Ando, Álvaro Siza, Alvar Aalto, Luis Barragán, and, not least, Bohigas, on whose firm Frampton wrote in 1985 the booklet, *Martorell, Bohigas, Mackay: 30 años de arquitectura 1954-1984*.[15]

Frampton acknowledges the differences between these architects, but detects in them a common approach that he names Critical Regionalism: "The fundamental strategy of Critical Regionalism is to mediate the impact of universal civilization with elements derived *indirectly* from the peculiarities of a particular place" (*Labour* 82). Frampton calls for the resistance against universal civilization – his term for globalization – through the preservation of autochthonous cultures and local identities. This preservation is accomplished when architecture respects the distinctiveness of a particular site and opposes the abstract placelessness produced by technological homogenization. Thus, for instance,

> [t]he bulldozing of an irregular topography into a flat site is clearly a techno-cratic gesture which aspires to a condition of absolute *placelessness*, whereas the terracing of the same site to receive the stepped form of a building is an engage-ment in the act of 'cultivating' the site. (86)

To cultivate the site involves the retrieval of what Frampton calls, with different adjectives, the telluric, tectonic, or tactile dimension of architecture. This enigmatic notion becomes clearer if it is defined negatively. The telluric, the tectonic, and the tactile resist the "scenographic" (88); that is, they resist the subsumption of architecture under the empire of the visual image. Critical Regionalism opposes the new dominant function of architecture within the global industry of image production. Contemporary architecture is compelled to create photogenic, self-referential icons detached from all context. Thus, architectural form depends less on function or the site than on the need to project an appealing image. Critical Regionalism, in short, contests the trans-formation of architecture into advertising.

Learning from Las Vegas, the 1972 essay-manifesto by Robert Venturi, Denise Scott Brown, and Steven Izenour, was the first text that theorized the advertising functions of contemporary architecture. For these architects, in our car-ridden and high-speed society, architecture must take into account that most buildings are only seen in pictures or through the screen of the car. In today's suburbanized cities and endless sprawls, buildings must necessarily act as visually identifiable icons. Their qualities must come, not from their relation to the site or their subtle architectural features, but from their scenographic power. This is the lesson that they learned from Las Vegas' commercial billboards and casinos covered in neon lights. Venturi, Scott Brown, and Izenour realized that, if one tries to make sense of Las Vegas' buildings by examining their formal characteristics and urban arrangement, the city emerges as sheer chaos. The real landmarks organizing the space are the billboards distributed throughout Las Vegas Strip: "The graphic sign in space has become the architecture of this landscape" (13).

Las Vegas is not a deviation from the principles of architecture, nor is it a city that, somehow in accordance with its lawless economy, lacks urban structure. Las Vegas is rather an extreme manifestation, and therefore the best indicator, of the conditions of production of contemporary architecture. Thus, Venturi, Scott Brown, and Izenour show how the visual image conditions architectural form in two main ways. First, buildings are often merely functional and indis-tinguishable ("ugly and ordinary" [93] or "boring" [101]) and they express their "content" by means of a separate "decorated shed" (87). Decoration means the graphic signs, billboards, or advertising figures that announce the function of the building, such as the signs "Motel," "Casino," or "Rent-a-car." Second, in other cases the building itself is a literal, visual expression of its content, as in a hamburger stand shaped like a hamburger. Here the building, or rather "the building-becoming-sculpture" (87), is a symbol of its own commercial content. Hence, despite taking two main different forms, the visual projection of information constitutes the primary function of architecture in the suburban city.

Whereas Venturi, Scott Brown, and Izenour seem to accept this dominance of the image, Frampton defies it by alluding to another bodily sense: he emphasizes touch instead of sight. But of course he does not propose an architecture that can be literally touched rather than seen; buildings can never be invisible and, at the same time, the tactile dimension is equally inevitable in all buildings. This reformulation, however, seeks to find a way for architecture to escape from the tyranny of the image. The invisible tactile dimension hopes to resist the transformation of architecture into visual simulacra. For Frampton, this dimension of architecture can provide regional cultures the opportunity to conserve their own distinctiveness against global standardization – a point to which I will return later.

The reconstruction of Barcelona may be understood as the "cultivation" of its historical urban fabric and even of its natural landscape (as in the revamping of "La Nova Icària" beaches). The reconstruction created a differentiated and identifiable city through its public spaces and landmarks, which produced a sense of place that aimed to combat suburban uniformity. As I described above, the architectural works that fitted well into Bohigas' Critical Regionalist plan consisted in sensitive interventions that intended to bring distinctiveness to places that had become dreary and unattractive. Many of these interventions turned characterless places into peculiar sites.

Perhaps the most conspicuous transformation in this sense involved the numerous closed factories converted into public parks, such as Parc de L'Espanya Industrial (1985), Parc Pegaso (1986), Parc de l'Escorxador (1985), which replaced a slaughterhouse, or Parc de la Creueta del Coll (1987), designed by MBM and "sculpted" at the slopes of a former stone quarry. These parks opened up the closed spaces of old factories, so in a way these spaces became visible urban elements for the first time. Public parks intended to bring to light the very spaces where they were installed. In addition, these well-designed parks aimed to "illuminate" their urban surroundings by means of what Bohigas called the "osmotic effects" of architectural interventions (*Reconstrucció* 101). The designs and the placing of sculptures and other landmarks provided a distinctive personality to the parks and linked them to the historical and cultural context – for instance, by replicating an industrial landscape as in the Parc de l'Espanya Industrial, and by installing symbolic pieces such as Joan Miró's sculpture "Dona i ocell" at the Parc de l'Escorxador and Andrés Nagel's "Drac" at the Parc de l'Espanya Industrial.[16]

Restored *modernista* architecture may also be interpreted, albeit retrospectively, according to the precepts of Critical Regionalism. The preoccupation for the natural context, the reproduction of traditional and organic forms, the incorporation of historic symbols, and the use of craft techniques that characterizes the architecture of Gaudí, Domènech i Montaner, and Puig i Cadafalch, can easily be reclaimed as an autochthonous precedent of Critical Regionalism. For the Grup R, the continuation of the principles of the Modern Movement complemented a care for the local involved a direct dialogue with the masterworks of *modernista* architecture; a dialogue that culminated in the thorough restoration of these masterworks during the 1980s. Meanwhile, this link with *modernisme* also contains a Catalanist subtext. As we saw, *modernisme* constituted a prominent case of an architecture devoted to the preservation of a regional culture. In retrieving it as one of the most representative singularities of Catalonia, the Grup R sought to configure a distinctive national architectonic genealogy.

By contrast, other works – such as Norman Foster's and Santiago Calatrava's communication towers – were designed to function as emblematic icons for Barcelona's global advertising, and did not articulate any special relationship to local history or their particular sites. Similarly, MBM's Olympic village, despite being named "La Nova Icària" and having preserved a couple of factory chimneys, did not incorporate the historical memory of the industrial neighborhood of Poble Nou. This plan was not a Critical Regionalist model, but rather an example of *tabula rasa* urbanism, which reproduced historic city forms and street life in an entirely new landscape. As I mentioned, perhaps only the restored beaches of the Olympic village can be read as efforts to cultivate the site.

But, before evaluating the significance of Critical Regionalism vis-à-vis the global context, let us look at another urban theory that can help us understand further the Barcelona model.

Street life was the obsession and beloved ideal of urban theorist Jane Jacobs, whose 1961 text *The Death and Life of Great American Cities* launched the ideas that have inspired most "urban renaissance" or "new urbanism" proposals to prevent suburbanization and zonification in the last decades.[17] While Frampton aims to resist technological placelessness, Jacobs contests the separation of urban uses promoted by the Modern Movement and the suburbanization that resulted from the major modernist plans, such as Le Corbusier's *ville radieuse*, Frank Lloyd Wright's "Broadacre City," or even the previous "garden cities" of Ebenezer Howard.[18] To oppose these models, Jacobs turns to biological metaphors and conceives cities as ecosystems that function as a particular "organized complexity" (564) based on the principle of diversity. Four conditions are indispensable to generate street diversity and vital cities: multifunctional districts that ensure activities and traffic at all times of the day; short blocks and numerous streets; a mix of buildings that vary in age and condition; and a sufficiently dense concentration of people (196–7).

Even though Bohigas never makes any explicit reference to Jacobs, the coincidence of their ideas is quite complete. Both endorse urban multifunctionality and defend the diversity that this multifunctionality generates against the relentless substitution of shopping malls for local stores and suburban sprawls for compact streets.

However, in a perverse twist, Jacobs' model has been mimicked in many market places around suburbanized North America and, gradually, around the world. Jacobsian urbanism has not prompted the revitalization of downtowns and the adoption of compactness (as one can still find in North America in places like Manhattan or some districts in Boston or San Francisco). On the contrary, a simulacrum of her beloved lively downtowns has been fabricated in controlled and privatized new areas that recreate historic districts, but are enclosed in shopping malls. In a typical postmodern *détournement*, Jacobs' ideas to resist urban atomization have been neutralized and used to reinforce what she opposed. As Trevor Boddy observes, "Jacobsian urbanism has not failed, but succeeded too well – or, more accurately, a diorama of its most superficial ideas has pre-empted the public domain" (quoted in McMorrough 376).

The creation of a simulacrum of city life in shopping centers and commercial strips has not only distorted Jacobs' principles; the actual development of the shopping mall has also betrayed the principles that infused its original conception. Urban planner, Victor Gruen, invented the shopping mall shortly after World War II. Gruen built the first mall in 1954 in Northland, Detroit, and in 1956 he projected the first enclosed mall, the Southdale Center in Minneapolis. Even though Jacobs was opposed to shopping malls and the city model that they entailed, Gruen pursued, like her, the creation of civic vitality and the implementation of community-building strategies. As he stated in his texts, he intended to make shopping malls the new multipurpose town centers:

> By affording opportunities for social life and recreation in a protected pedestrian environment, by incorporating civic and educational facilities, shopping centers can fill an existing void. They can provide the needed place and opportunity for participation in modern community life that the ancient Greek Agora, the Medieval Market Place and our own Town Squares provided in the past. (*Shopping Towns USA* 24)

Gruen shares with Jacobs the assumption that multifunctional spaces are key to promoting revitalization and socialization. His ideal shopping mall also embraces the interference of multiple uses. However, as anyone can observe in any mall around the world, these spaces projected to have commercial, but also educational and civic functions, have turned out to be a mere assortment of boutiques and retail stores in the middle of suburban landscapes.[19]

Arguably, Gruen and Jacobs also coincide in another point: for them, the achievement of this interference of functions does not depend on whether spaces are public or private. Jacobs does not stipulate that public spaces are a good to be preserved, nor does Gruen seem to be promoting private malls if these must include civic uses. However, the crucial difference between the two can be found in the divergent formalization of their programs. Jacobs embraces the forms of historic urban districts and, therefore, her program relies on the presence of public streets, squares, parks, or sidewalks. On the contrary, Gruen imagines the shopping mall as a "protected pedestrian environment," which quickly invites the possibility of privatizing the social space and monitoring access. Gruen's appeal to protection conforms to the main ideological motive for suburbanization: the escape from the multiple disturbances and dangers of the city. Against this perception, Jacobs contests the idea that suburbs are safer places and demonstrates that the continuous encounter of strangers on sidewalks, and the compact cohabiting of people, keeps everybody much safer than police vigilance or segregation and seclusion (37–71).

Gruen's invention of the shopping mall shares many similarities with Walt Disney's original project for the "Experimental Prototype Community of Tomorrow" or EPCOT, conceived to be part of the Walt Disney World Resort begun in 1971. Disney envisioned EPCOT as "a planned, controlled community; a showcase for American industry and research, schools, cultural and educational opportunities. In EPCOT, there will be no slum areas because we won't let them develop. There will be no landowners and therefore no voting control" (quoted in Chung, *Guide to Shopping* 288).

Despite their appeals to multifunctionality, neither Gruen nor Disney pursue the organized complexity of Jacobs or the vibrant urban exchange of Bohigas; rather, they aim to create (characteristically suburban) self-enclosed spaces. The shopping mall and Disneyworld embody the quintessential suburban ideal of an area with no (typically urban) slum areas or "unprotected" exposure to strangers. Underneath their all too utopian, nonconflictive spaces for the community lies the desire to escape from the social altogether.

Yet, even if we grant that Gruen's and Disney's projects might have contained certain progressive contents, their actual realization eliminated all traces of these contents. In the same way that Gruen's civic malls became mere commercial sites, in 1982, after Disney's death, the board members of the Disney company decided to cancel the original, "too radical" project of EPCOT, and they turned it into a theme park with rides into future lifestyles and a sampling showcase of some world countries in miniature (Chung, *Guide to Shopping* 288). In this case, the change is not only indicative of the prevalence of economic interests when it comes to putting urban experiments into practice; the amended EPCOT park has also emerged as a highly symbolic product of the postmodern marketplace.

Its assembly of reproduced local sites and architectural symbols is an extreme manifestation of the global logic consisting in homogenizing the planet through the retrieval of local differences. Far from resisting the global, the local is one of the dominant forms through which globalization unfolds itself.

The other most conspicuous materialization of this logic can probably be found in the theme hotels in Las Vegas that reproduce the palaces of ancient Rome, the canals of Venice, the Eiffel Tower, and the skyscrapers of New York. These hotels, like EPCOT, have made an entire industry out of the transformation of local sites into scenographic icons. Venturi, Scott Brown and Izenour learned from Las Vegas that visual signification is more determining than form for contemporary architecture. They learned this lesson from the signs, billboards, and neons of Las Vegas Strip. But today, Las Vegas' architecture has experienced a further twist: the theme hotels are the dominant signs of the landscape and overshadow the billboards along the Strip; the hotels are the new photographic signs in space. Venturi, Scott Brown and Izenour's notions of the "decorated shed" and the "building-becoming-sculpture" are, of course, still valid in explaining the new scenographic hotels of Las Vegas. These megaresorts simply constitute an extension and intensification of the visual over the architectural, perhaps to the extent that the decoration and the sculptural form of the buildings collapse onto each other and become one and the same thing. The Roman columns, the Venetian canals, and the Statue of Liberty seem to be both decoration and part of the sculptural and photogenic form of the buildings.

Yet the true novelty of the theme hotels is that they symptomatize how the local itself has become a commercial sign. Unlike the billboards of the Strip, these hotels stage a scenography of the local. They might be banal and deplorable reproductions of "real" places, but, precisely because of this, they are the unambiguous sign of a structural tendency: that local spaces circulate as reproducible theme subjects and, at the same time, that a sense of the local has become a desirable component of all commodities. The themes of these megaresorts provide a sense of placeness that alleviates the anxiety produced by suburban placelessness. In them, you are not simply in another, interchangeable casino-hotel; the thematic features of the hotel are designed to make you feel that you are in a clearly identifiable place. For this reason, the most genuine thing to do in Las Vegas is no longer the driving along the Strip, but to stay inside the resorts that will gratify any imaginable desire. The theme hotels are extreme but perfect symbols of the function of the local today: the local provides a safe sense of place that conceals the intrinsic placelessness of the global market.

This takes us back to Critical Regionalism and its conditions of possibility in postmodernity. Jameson examines these conditions in relation to the same dialectics between the global and the local. In *The Seeds of Time*, Jameson refers to "the EPCOT syndrome" (205) to explain that the endorsement of local differences may ultimately reproduce the dynamic of globalization itself, as the esteem of regional products is one of the main traits of a post-Fordist economy based on giving customers as many different consumer options as possible. The production of locality, far from resisting global forces and corporations, is one of their main assets. Jameson observes that "now the 'regional' as such becomes the business of global American Disneyland-related corporations, who will redo your own native architecture for you more exactly than you can do it yourself. Is global Difference the same today as global Identity?" (205).

The differentiation of spaces in postmodernity is linked to the post-Fordist assembling of customer-oriented products. If Fordist manufacturing produced one standard model of each good (most emblematically, Ford's Model T), post-Fordism seeks to adjust products to the specific desires of customers. These desires determine the market to a much larger extent and become themselves part of the process of commodity production. "What people want" becomes the central driving force of the economy, and products must present themselves as the fulfillment of a unique, special desire (even if desires are posited and gener-ated by the products themselves). As a result, all spheres of people's lives are determined by market commodities, in an ongoing process that turns people into consumers.

In the architectural realm, Disneyworld represents, again, a perfect example of urbanism serving consumerism. Robert Venturi praises the theme park in these terms: "[Disneyworld is] nearer to what people really want than anything that architects have given them... It's symbolic of American utopia" (quoted in Chung, *Guide to Shopping* 284). Whether this is true or not, the crucial fact is that Disneyworld was built on the premise of giving people what they wanted. The park interpellates people as clients and offers them a realm of full contentment. But this realm is not utopian at all: the park is physically located in a specific area in Florida, copyrighted in 1971 as Walt Disney World Resort and reachable by plane or car. Or, rather, Disneyworld is so entirely utopian, it embodies so perfectly the – exclusively American? – utopia of a self-sustaining and classless society, that it only reproduces the current logic of consumer society, with no real utopian glimpse of a different future.

These various examples from North America – the mimicking of Jacobs' urbanism in market places, the cancellation of Critical Regionalism by the EPCOT syndrome, the theme hotels in Las Vegas, and the consumerist functions of shopping malls and Disneyworld – constitute some prominent manifesta-tions of the structure of postmodernity. Now we must see how this global structural logic also traversed Barcelona's plan of "returning the city to the people," as well as the creation of public spaces, the restoration of historical buildings, and the placing of street landmarks during the Olympic years. Thus, the plan's publicized aim to fulfill the needs of Barcelonans must be interpreted in accordance with this general transformation of citizens into consumers. The appeal to the real needs of the people effortlessly corresponds to the consumer-based paradigm of "what people want." In this sense, the city hall acted as a service provider, and the participation of citizens in city affairs overlapped with the conventional relation between customers and companies.

Since the Olympic Games, Barcelona has become one of the most attractive and fashionable tourist destinations in Europe. Luxurious hotels, haute cuisine restaurants, global franchises, and all sorts of boutiques have appeared in the city to satisfy the "needs" of the crowds who visit the renewed avenues, the restored *modernista* architecture, the public parks, and the sunny beaches of the city.[20] But this touristification of Barcelona is not only a – fortunate or disastrous – consequence of the Olympic Games. Rather, it reveals the ultimate meaning of the urban transformation, or, better, it points at the structural conditions under which this transformation became possible. The tourist exploitation of the city was not a secondary aspect, but a primary cause of the urban renewal, as it nourished two of the most profitable new industries of the city: services and construction. In the last ten years, these industries have increased their productivity by two and, according to the last available data, they represent, respectively, 86.8% and 4.3% of the city's economy.[21] Ironically, or perhaps tragically, the renewal that intended to bring the city back to the people also attracted crowds of tourists that began to occupy the new public spaces and therefore took the city away from the people. Like Jacobsian urbanism, the problem with the "Barcelona model" of urban transformation may be that it has succeeded too well. Its new public spaces have attracted so many people that they have finally been emptied out of all publicness. Its success has been the cause of its own failure.

Writer Quim Monzó, in his work as reporter, has attentively portrayed the post-Olympic touristification of Barcelona. In 2004, he published a selection of newspaper articles in which he described the tourists' stereotypical interaction with Barcelona. As he joins a guided tour around the city, he writes:

> Quan arribem davant de la Pedrera succeeix una cosa curiosa. Cap dels turistes no para cap mena d'atenció a l'edifici fins que la guia explica que és "la Pedrera, by Antoni Gaudí". Llavors sí: tots la metrallen amb les càmeres. Tots menys un, que no encerta a identificar-la.
> –Which one is it? – pregunta.
> –That one over there – li diu el del costat.
> I aleshores sí: apreta el botonet i la grava, per veure-la amb calma assegut al sofà de casa seva a Milwaukee, per exemple. (*Catorze ciutats* 71)

> When we arrive at the Pedrera a remarkable thing happens. None of the tourists pays attention to the building until the guide explains that it is "la Pedrera, by Antoni Gaudí." Then everybody starts to fire at it with the camera – everybody except for one person, who cannot identify it.

–Which one is it?, he asks.

–That one over there, says the person next to him.

And then he pushes the button and starts recording it. This way he will be able to watch it calmly sitting on the couch of his house in Milwaukee, for example.

Two aspects of the narration are especially symptomatic. First, the text says, not that the tourists take pictures of Gaudí's building, but that they "metrallen" 'fire at' it. This word emphasizes the violence inflicted on the building by the presence of the tourists, thus suggesting that the tourists are (symbolically) killing the building with their cameras. Second, Monzó's text shows how he, as a Barcelonan, had to mix with a group of tourists to access the most emblematic buildings of his city. His example reveals how the relation of the natives to their city has also become mediated by tourism.

This touristification of Barcelona denotes that the city has succeeded in projecting herself as a differentiated space and an attractive set of emblematic images. Historic and new architecture, and the creation of other urban landmarks, were key components of this marketing. However, as Harvey and Jameson have shown, the successful differentiation of spaces indicates their assimilation into global sameness. Along these lines, architect Rem Koolhaas has coined the term "Generic City" to refer to this homogenization of spaces in contemporary cities. According to him, the restoration of historical buildings and the production of city identity are two of the main agents of the homogenizing Generic, as it is precisely through "the relentless conversion of utilitarian space into 'public' space, pedestrianization, the creation of new parks, planting, bridging, exposing, the systematic restoring of historic mediocrity, [that] all authenticity is relentlessly evacuated" (*Small* 1249). Remarkably, Koolhaas mentions Barcelona as an exemplary case of this process: "Sometimes an old, singular city, like Barcelona, by oversimplifying its identity, turns Generic. It becomes transparent, like a logo. The reverse never happens... at least not yet" (1250).[22]

Thus, the "Barcelona model" of urban transformation emerges as an adjustment of the city's fabric and architectural heritage to the new marketing needs. Again, the touristification, museification, or Disneylandization that the city has experienced as a result of the Olympic event is not an unexpected consequence of the urban renewal, but it is rather the manifestation of its inner driving force. For this reason, we must not only see EPCOT or Las Vegas as fake reproductions of European cities or ancient cultures; the key point is that now, historic cities happen to be the real imitators of North American theme parks. Barcelona is a visible sign that European cities have become the real imitation of their imitation.

Quim Monzó's Dystopian Counter-Image

Quim Monzó's fiction constitutes a relevant portrait of the transformation of Barcelona into a postmodern simulacrum. Monzó became, during the pre- and post-Olympic years, one of the most successful and representative Catalan authors, and his collections of short stories have remained bestsellers since their publication in the 1980s and 1990s.

A striking feature of Monzó's short stories is that they seldom refer to Barcelona. Monzó depicts Barcelona as a dehistoricized city made up of a series of standard and anonymous settings. His Barcelona is a spectral city with atemporal places where citizens are identifiable only as grammatical traces, clothing brands, and social stereotypes. Only a few arbitrary signs allow the reader to identify Monzó's urban landscape. *L'illa de Maians* is the enigmatic title of a 1985 collection of short stories that refers to an island that, up until the fifteenth century, existed as a barrier between the city and the Mediterranean. Later, layers of sedimentation incorporated the island into the current extension of the old quarter, and the island of Maians became a spectral reference to a forgotten past. Also, this collection is divided into three parts titled, with oblique allusions to Barcelona: "Carrer dels dies feiners," an extinct popular designation of a Barcelona street; "A handkerchief or neckerchief of soft twilled silk," which is one of the meanings of the word "Barcelona" according to the Oxford English Dictionary; and "La Casa de la Estilográfica," a reference to a disappeared office supplies store.[23]

The 30 stories of another collection from 1992, *El perquè de tot plegat*, do not contain any location mark except for one: a "cafeteria a la Diagonal" – a cafeteria in one of the avenues of Barcelona's *Eixample*, where two characters have a drink. Finally, there is not a single reference to Barcelona in the last collection of short stories that I will examine. The title of this collection from 1996, *Guadalajara*, although inspired by the well-known *Mariachi* song, even enigmatically alludes to two other cities, the homonymous cities in Castilla la Mancha and Mexico.

In Monzó's stories, spaces are simply designated as a generic apartment, a hotel room, a bar, a street, a highway, or a hospital. In the few cases in which spaces are described, the specifications consist of a plain list of the – serialized – objects contained in them. For example, a hotel room: "Els donen una habitació amb dos llits individuals, dues tauletes de nit, una taula per escriure (hi ha sobres i paper de carta amb la capçalera de l'hotel, en una carpeta), una cadira i un minibar amb un televisor al damunt" 'They give them a room with two twin beds, two bedside tables, a desk (there are envelopes and sheets with the hotel letterheads, in a folder), a chair, and a minibar with a TV on top' (*Perquè* 21). This hotel is located in an unnamed "ciutat llunyana" 'far-away city' (21).

And, although we find occasional references to real cities, regions, and states, there are no detailed descriptions of them, nor is there a clear reason why these cities are mentioned.[24]

In another story, a man is in a woman's apartment, the location of which is never specified. The man even acknowledges the difficulty of describing the place: "Eren a ca la noia, i si li haguessin demanat de descriure-la, no hauria sabut com fer-ho. De cua d'ull va mirar el llarg moble de fusta clara, envernissat; va veure-hi un plat de ceràmica brillant, un tambó marroquí, un tub d'aspirines, tres llibres i una pipa blanca holandesa" 'They were at her house, and if he had been asked to describe it, he would not have known how to do it. He looked obliquely at the light-colored, varnished large piece of furniture; on it he could see a shiny pottery plate, a Moroccan drum, an aspirin tube, three books, and a white Dutch pipe' (*L'illa* 12).

Characters are also designated by generic labels. In most cases they are simply a man, a woman, a boy, or a girl. Further specifications consist of a color, such as "l'home blau" 'the blue man' and "l'home magenta" 'the magenta man' (*Perquè* 55); an adjective, as in "la dona fatal" 'the femme fatale' and "l'home irresistible" 'the irresistible man' (*Perquè* 49); or an unutterable, agrammatical name, such as "Grmpf" and "Pti" (*Perquè* 27). These labels depict the characters as empty stereotypes lacking what is conventionally known as personality or inner self. They visibly embody the three features that Jameson finds in postmodern cultural artifacts: flatness or depthlessness, a deathly quality, and the waning of affect (*Postmodernism* 9–11). These characters are both superficial and unfathomable, with no access to any individual inside or to any supposedly "personal feelings."[25]

This disidentification with any particular location or historical context contrasts with an obvious feature of Monzó's stories, namely the fact that they are written in Catalan.

As a minority language, Catalan is immediately associated with an actual region, a distinct community, and even with Catalan nationalism. The Catalan language does not circulate as a global language and it can hardly be detached from its specific territory and political history. Thus, this inherent tension between the unidentified characters and spaces, and the highly particularizing language of the stories, may be interpreted as an attempt to imagine Barcelona and Catalonia as fully globalized places that still maintain their vernacular language. Monzó's standard, easily universalizable characters, and urban spaces, denote an eagerness to avoid provincialism and the association of Catalan culture with tradition, folklore, or the countryside. Monzó deals with the anxiety about the gradual erasure of minority languages under globalization by portraying the homogenizing global forces in Catalan. This way he demonstrates that Catalan can function in this new context as well. Caragh

Wells, who has already pointed at the contrast between generic spaces and local language in Monzó, puts it in suggestive terms: "Monzó's achievement is to link the rhythms of the local and the global together, and present them in mutual interrogation, thereby representing the phenomenon of cultural hybridity... in contemporary Barcelona" (92). Yet, given that the notion of cultural hybridity implies a certain form of accomplishment, perhaps we should employ a more hypothetical tone and say that an underlying hope traverses Monzó's short stories: the hope that reconciliation between globalization and his minor culture may be possible.

Monzó's stories can also be inscribed in the context of transitional Spain. From this viewpoint, his stereotypical and unidentified spaces and characters aim to create a literary representation compliant with the official *pacto del olvido*, that is, the tacit collective pact to forget Spain's Francoist years and move toward the definitive abandonment of its semiperipheral condition. In this context, Monzó's stories offered an appealing and timely imaginary to Catalans and Spaniards, as it allowed them to perceive themselves as fully modern and perceive their territory as global and homogenized. The provision of this imaginary certainly played a part in the widespread success of the stories.

But there is one fundamental component of the stories that must be understood in relation to the new urban reality of Barcelona. This component is the circular plots, the claustrophobic spaces, and the Moebius strips from which the characters of the stories cannot escape. In Monzó's fiction, circular enclosures are omnipresent at all levels. For instance, in "L'amor," an archivist treats with disdain and coldness the soccer player she is dating. He is madly in love with her and keeps insisting that she should not be afraid of expressing her true feelings for him. When, after months of treating him cruelly, she finally gives herself over to him and proposes that they move in together, he cannot help reacting with coldness and disdain (*Perquè* 17–20). In "Halitosi," a man's breath is so bad-smelling that he has to isolate himself from society until nobody is able to tell him that his breath has just stopped smelling bad (*L'illa* 105–9). And the Kafkian "Gregor" is the story of a bug that wakes up one morning transformed into a human being whose first human act is to smash three disgusting bugs that he finds in the closet (*Guadalajara* 49–57).

These characters are trapped in worlds, and specifically in urban worlds, that are oppressively closed, but also painlessly flat. Monzó's world is tragic, but does not produce any romantic wreckages; it is hopeless, but without any modernist seclusions; it is absurd, but with no existentialist Sisyphean chains. In this respect, the stories' verbs in the present tense must be understood as the temporal correspondence of these spatial enclosures. This predominant present tense suggests that the characters inhabit a perpetual present with no sense of the past or the future, with neither unsettled traumas nor secret longings.

At the beginning of the story "La força centrípeta," a man is unable to leave his apartment because, when he opens the door, he encounters the same hall where he is. Two firemen go to rescue him, but they get stuck in the same circle. At this point, the man can successfully leave the apartment. The firemen can also leave the apartment but not the building, as the stairs begin to reproduce themselves endlessly. Meanwhile, a neighbor is killed and, after scenes of panic and screams, the other neighbors in the building attribute the crime to the firemen, who cannot offer a plausible alibi in their defense. The story ends with the hearse that carries the coffin with the dead neighbor driving around the city in circles and unable to find the cemetery. The city is totally unrecognizable: "Són en una zona de la ciutat plena de magatzems. Són illes i illes de cases amb naus industrials i camions (enormes) aparcats. Els carrers tenen noms desconeguts per la majoria de ciutadants, ells inclosos" 'They are in an area of the city full of warehouses. There are blocks and blocks of houses with industrial plants and (enormous) trucks parked. The names of the streets are unknown to most citizens, including them' (*Guadalajara* 124). In the end, the hearse driver admits that he does not know where they are and tries to go back to their starting point,

> [p]erò no hi ha manera d'arribar-hi i es troben, de cop, en una plaça quadrada. És una plaça que du el nom d'un general de fa un parell de segles, amb un gran arbre de tronc retorçat al bell mig, al damunt del qual dos nens juguen a fer caure l'altre, i on no va a parar cap carrer tret d'aquell del qual vénen. (127)

> [b]ut there is no way of getting there and they suddenly find themselves in a square. It is a square that bears the name of a general from a couple of centuries ago, with a big, twisted tree in its center, on top of which two kids are playing to make the other fall, and where no street ends except for the one from which they came.

In this claustrophobic metropolis, houses, streets, and neighborhoods are totally unidentified. Most citizens do not recognize street names; and the name of the square referring to an unnamed historic general does not help the characters locate themselves either.

The same urban traits can be found in the story "Casa amb jardí," set in a claustrophobic and homogeneous residential suburb. In this story, a man leaves work and returns to his home, a two-storey, single-family house in a suburban villa. A dog and a woman welcome him; he licks his hand, she kisses his lips. Then he sits on the couch to work on a crossword while she begins to watch TV. All of a sudden, he realizes that the woman sitting next to him is not his wife, that he has never owned a pet, and that this is not his house. Astounded, he wonders how he could possibly miss these changes and why the strange woman is acting as if she was his wife. He knows that he is not suffering amnesia because he can perfectly remember his real wife. He notices that the house is identical to his, like each one in that villa. He looks out the window and sees the same landscape he would see from his house. He knows he could leave, or at least check, the house number, but "fer-ho li fa por: ignora per què, però no sent cap desig de comprovar què passa" 'he is afraid of doing it: he does not know why, but he does not feel like checking out what is going on' (*L'illa* 19). In the end, he imagines the moment when he and the woman will go to bed together, and "[a]quest pensament li produeix, de forma immediata, una erecció" '[t]his thought produces in him an immediate erection' (21).

This relatively happy ending provides a twist that opens up the possibility of escaping this dystopia: the possibility of enjoying the very indeterminacy and interchangeability of this urban landscape. Sexual excitement represents here the acceptance of the current hopeless circumstances, but also points at the beginning of a potential journey of discovery and new exchanges. Sex, a ubiquitous theme in Monzó's stories, seems to provide one of the few ways to cope with the inexorability of this dystopian situation.

However, a later story cancels out even this possibility. In "La gelosia," a man enjoys how a woman is praising, touching, and licking his penis. But she does it so insistently and obsessively that the situation begins to distress him. He finally asks her whether his penis is the only thing in which she is interested, and suddenly her devotion turns into anger. She calls him crazy, gets dressed and leaves, while he "s'asseu al llit, es posa la mà dreta sota el membre, flàccid, l'alça una mica i el contempla, entre furiós i encuriosit" 'sits on the bed, puts his right hand under his flaccid penis, lifts it, and contemplates it with fury and curiosity' (*Perquè* 61).[26] Thus, while in "Casa amb jardí" the final erection opened the possibility of living new experiences, here the flaccid member, despite awakening curiosity to his possessor, becomes a mere remainder of a thwarted relationship, a burdensome piece that objectifies the subject holding it. The penis stands as an impediment to establish any subjective – let alone collective – connection.

In his study of Barcelona's cultural production of the 1980s and 1990s, *La ciutat interrompuda*, Julià Guillamon remarks that Monzó's fiction paradigmatically portrays Barcelona as an "interrupted city," that is, as a city with an erased sense of the past and with no historical memory. In relation to Monzó's short stories, however, this suggestive concept of the "interrupted city" must be expanded and unfolded in at least two ways. On the one hand, Monzó's depiction of an "interrupted" Barcelona – or of what remains of Barcelona in the scattered and oblique location marks contained in his stories – contrasts with the official transformation of the city during the 1980s, which involved a comprehensive and unprecedented restoration of its historical and architectural heritage. Monzó's dehistoricized Barcelona coincides with the period when the city began to be most aware and most fond of its past. On the other hand, in Monzó, this temporal interruption comes with a spatial counterpart: the presence of an uninterrupted city, a city that has spread everywhere leaving no space for any – rural, natural, non-urban – outside.

Such a representation of Barcelona as an uninterrupted and disidentified city contrasts with the official reimagining of it as an idiosyncratic and highly appealing place. But if, following David Harvey again, the production of city identity is part of the strategies to attract investments from transnational capital, in the form of headquarters, tourists, manufacturers, conventions, or services that can potentially be placed anywhere, then doesn't Monzó's uninterrupted and dystopian city embody the flows of global capital that determine territorial transformations in late capitalism? Monzó's standardized city reveals the material reality underneath Barcelona's acclaimed renewal; he portrays, in other words, the production of global sameness that is masked as configuration of special places.

Another important story is titled "Barcelona." Except for the title, the story does not contain further elements that link it to the real city. In the story, a man and a woman talk. She complains that he does not listen to her. She says that during the two nights they have spent together he has only talked about himself and has not been interested in her. He has not asked about who she is or what she does. After a moment of perplexity, he reacts and apologizes. He says that he had never realized how self-centered he could be and that he cannot stand egotistic people. He says that he needs her to help him find out why and when he behaves this way. In the end, he says: "voldria saber què, o quin seguit de coses han fet de mi un egotista... m'agradaria deixar de ser així amb tu... Perquè m'interesses molt. Per això necessito que m'ajudis a descobrir en quines ocasions em comporto així... I perquè ho faig. M'agradaria que en parléssim" 'I'd like to know what or what sort of things have made me an egotistic person... I would like to stop being this way with you... Because I'm interested in you. That's why I need you to help me find out when I behave this way, and why I do it. I would like to talk about it with you' (*L'illa* 14).

The fact that Monzó titled this story "Barcelona" can be simply interpreted as a *boutade* about the typical egotism of Barcelonans – the same that is often said about New Yorkers or Parisians. But there is also another possibility, namely that Barcelona is an egotistic city talking all the time about itself. If the "active production of places with special qualities," as Harvey puts it (*Condition* 295), involves the fabrication and advertising of the characteristics that make places peculiar, does this egotistic character not symptomatize Barcelona's new investment in its own self-absorbed differentiation as an identifiable place? That is, Monzó's character reveals how the competition among cities to attract global capital produces the effect that, like the man of the story, cities "are always talking about themselves." The official promotion of cities as cosmopolitan and receptive places – and Barcelona has intensely used these labels – does not imply a will to open them to others, but a marketing strategy to attract global capital, in the same way that the man is interested in the woman only to continue being wrapped up with himself.

This is the truth that Monzó's short stories reveal about Barcelona: its renovation and the rehabilitation of its historical past has standardized the city, rather than produce a sense of place. All that remains of Barcelona in these stories are some scattered location markers. Monzó's unrecognizable urban landscapes can thus be interpreted as the dystopian counter-image of the charming images of the new Barcelona. These uninterrupted, but also self-enclosed, landscapes unveil the ongoing process of commodification of spaces and territories, which, in turn, interpellate the people who inhabit them as equally generic individuals. These commodified urban spaces incorporate people as serialized stereotypes, and they ultimately commodify them as well.

Another story, "La inestabilitat," shows the destabilizing effects of the expansion of commodification on individual lives. Tired of having his car radio stolen, a man decides to take the radio with him every time he parks. Then he gets a call from a television contest; they want to ask him a couple of questions for the show. He answers them correctly and he is awarded a beach apartment, where he meets a neighbor whose husband suddenly dies. Then he marries her, they have two children, and the story ends enigmatically one morning while he gets in his car: "Encaixa la ràdio a lloc, l'engega, sintonitza una emisora, es cobreix la cara amb les dues mans i, amb totes les forces de què és capaç, intenta plorar, però no se'n surt mai' 'He returns the radio to its place, turns it on, tunes into a station, covers his face with his hands and, with every bit of his strength, he tries to cry, but he never can do it' (*Perquè* 76). This fast-paced story, also set in a series of standardized urban spaces, describes the life of a contemporary man ruled by an unpredictable game of chance: is this game not a perfect symbol of the constantly changing world dominated by mobile capital and infinite commodity exchange?

Yet, despite full commodification, in the end this postmodern man struggles against the waning of his affect by attempting to cry. Even if he cannot do it, his attempt indicates a moment of recognition of the real conditions of his situation. That is, even if the possibility of expressing affect turns out to be impossible, or precisely because of this, this final act reveals the totally commodified space that surrounds and also constitutes him. His dry tears, like the flaccid penis of "La gelosia," are remnants that attest the impossibility of a non-commodified existence or a non-objectified exchange. But, in their very constitution as residues, they set, if not an outside, at least an internal limit to commodification, which consequently uncovers it as a historical – and not inexorable – process.

But there is still another limit to commodification. By portraying it as a thorough and unmitigated phenomenon, Monzó's stories raise the question of whether they are themselves a commodified product, in the function of, for instance, a cultural representation serving in some way the marketing of Barcelona, or whether they escape, however minimally, the inescapability of their context and their content. But these two options entail a paradox. On the one hand, if the stories are commodified artifacts, then they cannot be accurate and comprehensive accounts of full commodification; they would be merely reproducing the systemic logic, with no possibility of disrupting it. On the other hand, if these narratives remain outside commodification, then they are also inaccurate accounts, as they constitute the proof that commodification is not absolute. Yet, what really escapes the foreclosure of full commodification is this paradox, that is, the unspoken oscillation between the two possibilities. This undecidability asserts the impossibility of escaping commodification, but also posits an internal and contradictory limit to it represented by the very existence of the stories. Their existence subverts the inexorability of the process that they describe. Their depiction of the city as a hermetically enclosed space, with no past, no future, and no outside, undermines the very unavoidability of this dystopian but all too real state. This, logically, opens up the possibility of a different historical situation: the possibility of a non-commodified space beyond the current conditions of production. Monzó's portrait of Barcelona as an unrecognizable city, subsumed under a global homogenizing logic of production, paradoxically offers us a glimpse of the possibility of a different, undetermined future.[27]

These stories point at what Rem Koolhaas observes about Barcelona, namely that the oversimplification of its identity has turned it into a Generic City. Koolhaas adds that the reverse transformation of a generic or commodified space into a singular one "never happens… at least not yet" (*Small* 1250). Let us hope that the detection of the hidden structural logics of the new Barcelona, and the search for an internal limit to their commodifying effects, as found in Monzó's fiction, constitutes a first step to help future singularity occur.

Notes

1 We find this viewpoint in Joan Busquets and in Pep Subirós. Given that Busquets worked as Coordinator of Urbanism for the city hall during the Olympic years and that Subirós was Advisor on Cultural Affairs to mayor Pasqual Maragall, it is not surprising that their books are positive accounts of the renewal. For a complete bibliography in English on Barcelona's urbanism, see Marshall 251–55. For bibliography in Catalan and Spanish, see Busquets 461–63.

2 See Introduction, n. 4.

3 As I explain in the Introduction, Roca i Albert, Balibrea, and Resina have written the more theoretical studies on contemporary Barcelona.

4 For an excellent study of Barcelona's urban history, see Busquets; for descriptions of these initial modern projects, see especially pages 78–121.

5 In "Paris, the Capital of the Nineteenth Century," Benjamin writes:
> The true goal of Haussmann's projects was to secure the city against civil war. He wanted to make the erection of barricades in Paris impossible for all time... Widening the streets is designed to make the erection of barricades impossible, and new streets are to furnish the shortest route between the barracks and the worker's districts. (12)

6 For an ideological analysis of Gaudí, see Lahuerta. For the political writings and architectural theories of Domènech i Montaner and Puig i Cadafalch, see Domènech i Montaner and Barral i Altet, respectively.

7 For a full explanation of the various struggles in the neighborhoods during the 1960s and 1970s, see McNeill, *Urban Change* 118–25. See also Molinero and Ysàs; Huertas Claveria and Andreu; Domingo i Clota and Bonet i Casas; Calavita and Ferrer; and McDonough, who analyzes the conflicts at El Raval district.

8 See Piñón for a detailed analysis of the evolution of Catalan architecture (and particularly of MBM) from the Grup R to the 1970s.

9 With two exceptions: Bohigas has written two articles on the "urban cancers" of American shopping malls (*El present* 213–26) and one article on Tokyo and Hong Kong (*Dit o fet* 45–47), in which he condemns the disproportionate levels of real estate speculation in Asian cities.

10 I examine the relation between Barcelona and non-European city models in Chapter Four.

11 For a full list of the artists and sculptors and their works, see Subirós, *Vol fletxa* 128–31. See also catalogs by Fundació Joan Miró and Moldoveanu, Capó, and Casasús.

12 Bohigas later declared:
> I was totally against the Games and I think it was an absolute disaster for the culture of Barcelona. I think it was a mistake of the first order to try and give Barcelona which is a monoculture a place among the great powers. We behave as though culture is flourishing in Barcelona but the opposite is the case. I think that in the long term the city will benefit far more from an easily accessible museum with an unrivalled collection, than it does from short-lasting spectacles. Events like that don't lead to anything that lasts unless you have the cultural conditions in the form of schools, theatres and cultural centers to guarantee a good aftermath. I am not against spectacles as such, but before you know it it's all over and you're back to square one. (quoted in Bouman and van Toorn 184)

In this harsh criticism of the Olympics, Bohigas omits the fact that the Games provided many new architectural works and prompted the transformation of Barcelona. Two things can be said here. On the one hand, his focus on culture and the long-term benefits for the city reveals how he conceives architecture not as spectacle that exhausts itself, but as an art that should always have cultural and civil functions. On the other hand, however, his omission of architecture might be an attempt to dissociate the urban transformation from the Games, even though they were part of the same enterprise throughout the 1980s.

13 For a complete list of urban interventions in Barcelona from 1981 to 1992, see Subirós, *Vol fletxa* 122–7.

14 A group of 58 local architects, among them Bohigas, signed a public letter to protest against the incongruity of Calatrava's design. See Moix 214–16.

15 Frampton has also written a laudatory article on contemporary Catalan architecture; see "1977–1996. Excerpts from a Golden Age."

16 The "drac" or dragon is a highly symbolic figure of Catalan folklore. The legend explains that Sant Jordi, Catalonia's patron, fought against a fire-spitting dragon and finally killed it.

17 I refer to "Urban Renaissance" and "New Urbanism" in Chapter Four.

18 See Le Corbusier; Lloyd Wright; and Howard, *To-morrow*. For selected excerpts and bibliography, see LeGates and Stout 321–29 and 336–49.

19 For a detailed and entertaining chronicle of Gruen's life and work, see Hardwick. For Gruen's own texts, see his *Shopping Towns USA* and *The Heart of Our Cities*. But the most interesting work on Gruen's urban projects is Alex Wall's *Victor Gruen: From Urban Shop to the New City*.

20 For various statistics regarding the growth of Barcelona's tourist industry, see the Barcelona Data Sheet 2011 in <http://www.bcn.es/negocis/en/>.

21 See the Barcelona Data Sheet 2011.

22 Koolhaas has often referred to the conspicuous commercialization of contemporary Barcelona. In "Junkspace," where he looks at the different forms through which spaces have become commodified and serialized, he mentions the city: "Through Junkspace old aura is transfused with new luster to spawn sudden commercial viability: Barcelona amalgamated with the Olympics..." (416). Or, in "Miestakes," he refers to the reconstruction in 1985–7 of Mies' Barcelona Pavilion, directed by architects Ignasi de Solà-Morales, Cristian Cirici, and Fernando Ramos, as an example of modernism commodified by urban marketing. Similarly, Brad Epps observes how Mies' Pavilion seems to ask for the solitary, modern *promeneur* as its ideal visitor – an experience that is no longer possible in a building and a city fully devoted to tourism. ("Modern Spaces" 176–77)

23 Julià Guillamon has deciphered these oblique allusions in *La ciutat interrompuda*, 188–9.

24 Some of the mentioned cities are, among others, the Italian Castagnaro, Casteggio, Voguera, Alessandria, Piacenza (*L'illa* 48); Bergamo, Marseille, Milano, Bordeaux, Lyon, Bilbao, Toulouse, Strasbourg (*L'illa* 53); Aberdeen (*Perquè* 30); Florence, Pisa (*Perquè* 43); and Birmingham (*Guadalajara* 165). Perhaps the fact that all these cities are, like Barcelona, European and not state capitals is not arbitrary. But we can also find Brussels (*L'illa* 53), Rome (*Perquè* 56), Paris (*Guadalajara* 161), and Berlin (*Guadalajara* 169); the regions of New Scotland (*Perquè* 49), Mallorca (*Perquè* 87), the Aegean Islands (*Guadalajara* 167), and Hawaii (*Guadalajara* 168); and the states Laos, Cambodia, Thailand (*Guadalajara* 163); Chile, and Japan (*Guadalajara* 168).

25 An extreme and amusing example of the depiction of characters as sterotypes is the series of random traits used to describe a man in the story "L'eufòria dels troians" (*Perquè* 83–97). Throughout the story, he is characterized as "L'home que durant la infantesa havia tingut una certa fe religiosa"; "l'home que a la infantesa s'havia interessat per la matemàtica"; "l'home que a la infantesa havia tingut problemes d'inadaptació"; "l'home que va tenir de noi una caçadora de pell de la qual encara es recorda"; "l'home que de noi va anar a Mallorca de viatge de fi de curs l'últim any de batxillerat"; "l'home que d'adolescent s'emprovava davant del mirall de l'armari els sostenidors de sa mare"; "l'home que va tenir la primera nòvia als quinze anys"; etc. 'The man who had some religious faith during his childhood'; 'the man who was interested in mathematics as a child'; 'the man who had adaptation problems as a child'; 'the man who as a teenager owned a leather jacket that he still remembers'; 'the man who traveled to Mallorca in his last year of high school'; 'the man who as a teenager would try on his mother's bra in front of the mirror'; 'the man who had his first girlfriend when he was fifteen'; etc). The evident effect is that his whole biography consists of a succession of random stereotypical features.

26 Erections have a nuclear function in much of Monzó's fiction. His 1989 novel *La magnitud de la tragèdia* narrates the story of a man who suffers a deadly disease that gives him a permanent erection. For a gender studies critique of Monzó's representation of men, see Josep-Anton Fernàndez, "My Tragedy is Bigger Than Yours: Masculinity in Trouble and the Crisis of Male Authorship in Quim Monzó's Novels."

27 Here I follow Alberto Moreiras' reading of the story "La lotería en Babilonia," by Jorge Luis Borges, to whom Monzó's fiction has been connected by many literary reviewers. "La lotería en Babilonia," published in 1941, narrates how a lottery system determines every event and the destiny of every individual in Babilonia. This lottery is controlled by "la Compañía," whose "funcionamiento silencioso [es] comparable al de Dios" 'silent functioning [is] comparable to that of God' (*Ficciones* 79). Moreiras reads this story as an allegory of the Keynesian state and also as an anticipation of the subsequent neoliberal society of control. For him, the crucial point of the story is that it is undecidable whether the narration is an external account of how the lottery works, in which case the story would maintain the difference between experiential consciousness and knowledge – that is, between the fact that Babilonians live without knowing that their lives are determined by the lottery and the narrative account of this fact – or whether the same text is a product of the absolute "Compañía," which "means to opt for the reification of history and to collapse knowledge into experience" (178). For Moreiras, the oscillation between the two possibilities opens up an outside to the all-encompassing state: "By showing that everything depends on either affirming or negating the subsumption of life under the domination of capital allegorized as state power, Borges opens up the possibility of an alternative history: a history of the radical negation of ideological universality, or of its revelation as false consciousness" (183).

Similarly, Monzó's portrait of an absolutely commodified urban space brings up the question about whether his narrative accounts are, or are not part of, this space. What matters is not the answer but the positing of the question, which opens up the possibility of escaping this enclosed space.

CHAPTER FOUR

Learning from Barcelona

Perhaps in contradiction with the previous analysis of the urban renewal of Barcelona and its correlation with postmodern phenomena such as the shopping mall, Disneyworld, or Las Vegas' theme hotels, this chapter explores whether Barcelona can represent an exemplary model for contemporary cities, and even for the city of the future. My main question is: Does this urban model contain any transformative contents worth retrieving? If so, can this model be applied to other cities? To what extent was this transformation an irreproducible case determined by specific historical circumstances; and to what extent is it transposable and exemplary? In short, what are the model components (if there are any) of the Barcelona model?

The renewal of Barcelona soon became internationally praised. As I mentioned in the previous chapter, in 1990 the city was awarded the Prince of Wales Prize in Urban Design of Harvard's Department of Architecture and, in 1998, the city hall received the Royal Gold Medal of the Royal Institute of British Architects (RIBA). As sociologist Patrick Le Galès asserts, Barcelona unquestionably became a model for European cities: "The example of Barcelona has been used innumerable times by Europe's entire stock of urban elites and consultants. The joint activity of urban restructuring and organizing of the 1992 Olympic Games has led to a view of the city as a model of success to be copied and envied" (210).

Also, Barcelona plays an exemplary role in the collective proposal *Towards an Urban Renaissance*, in which the architectural team Urban Task Force discusses various guidelines for the regeneration of British cities. In the introduction to the book, after a foreword written by mayor Pasqual Maragall, Richard Rogers, chairman of the group, states that "[i]n the quality of our urban design and strategic planning, we are probably 20 years behind places like Amsterdam and Barcelona" (7). Or, to mention one last example, Charles Landry's *The Art of City-Making* also praises Barcelona's renewal and presents it as an exemplary model (361–8).

It seems evident that the values of the Barcelona model–urban compactness, good readability, mixture of uses, and the promotion of public spaces

– can effortlessly be embraced by other European cities, which share similar urban structures and face similar challenges regarding their new functions as global cities. But other questions emerge: How do these values interact with the so-called American or Asian megalopolises? Do they interpellate in any way the American and Asian "urban Leviathans," to use Diane E. Davis' definition of Mexico City? While in Chapter Three I tried to show how suburban North America (the shopping mall, Disneyworld, Las Vegas' hotels) might have transformed Barcelona, can Barcelona in turn transform the model of the suburban city?

The examination of Barcelona vis-à-vis divergent city forms should help us better understand the historical significance of its urban politics during the Olympic years. However, I do not intend to make a comparison between Barcelona and other international metropolises, nor do I want to focus on the supposed cultural differences between various urban models. My aim is simpler and at the same time more speculative. The relation of Barcelona to other models aims to shed light on the conditions of possibility of the city in our contemporary times. Thus, this chapter operates at two levels. On the one hand, it hopes to extract architectural lessons from Barcelona's urbanistic forms and proposals: "Learning from Barcelona" naturally follows the path of Venturi, Scott Brown and Izenour and their architectural treatise *Learning from Las Vegas*. On the other hand, the chapter aims to depart from the strictly architectural sphere and engage in a more general reflection on the nature of the city by analyzing two of its essential components: master plans and public spaces. Through this double procedure, perhaps the potential transformative content of Barcelona will not elude us.

Contesting the Barcelona Model

Before exploring this transformative content, let us look at internal critiques of the Barcelona model. As we have already observed, the collective euphoria generated by the Olympic Games not only silenced opposing voices but, presumably, also left them with no plausible arguments against the event. A large number of social antagonisms seemed to be overcome at last, and the Games appeared as the solution to the many deficiencies that had affected Barcelona for decades. One of the few critical publications, the magazine *Dissidència: Butlletí antiolímpic*, which remained marginal, but was pioneering in portraying the 1992 Games as a spectacle serving multinational capitalism, observed, with exasperation, how Catalan society was characterized by a "silenci esclatant," "[un] tant-se-me'n-fotisme mesell," and "[una] somnolència social en la qual vivim ensopits els catalans" 'striking silence,' 'a stubborn indifference,' and 'a social lethargy in which Catalans live' (*Dissidència*). After the Games, another underground

magazine, *A/parte. Publicación contrainformativa*, admitted that there had been
no real opposition to the Olympics. In an anonymous article from 1993, they
attributed this absence to the collective euphoria generated by shrewd politicians, but also quickly embraced by complacent citizens. This euphoria left no
space for dissent:

> Según se fué acercando el 92, la ilusión colectiva que generaron los JJOO fue
> cerrando todo espacio para el antagonismo. Una vez finalizadas las obras (con
> menos fallos de los que nosotros deseábamos) se produjo el mayor fenómeno de
> creación de identidad de los últimos años. La participación ciudadana fué masiva.
> El entusiasmo, delirante. !Por fín Barcelona en el centro del mundo! Ni siquiera
> la presencia del Rey provocó las iras catalanistas. Todo quedó atado y bién atado
> gracias a la hábil gestión de los políticos. (sic)[1]

> As 92 approached, the collective delusion generated by the Olympic Games shut
> down all spaces for antagonism. Once the works had been finished (with less
> errors than we wished), the biggest phenomenon of identity formation in years
> was produced. People's participation was massive; their enthusiasm was delir-
> ious. At last Barcelona was the center of the world! Not even the presence of the
> King generated Catalanist rage. The astute management of the politicians left no
> loose ends.

Another critique of this deactivation of dissidence can be found in the 1989
song "Terra-Billy" by Els Pets, a Catalan pop band whose lyrics mix juvenile
topics with political themes. "Terra-Billy" begins by stating that, whereas under
Francoism people sung together protest songs (of the *nova cançó*) and longed
for a different, democratic world, now everybody is content watching TV and
nobody believes in political utopias of any sort. Then the song attacks Barcelona's Olympic project:

> I ara Barcelona
> pels Jocs la netejaran,
> i tot el que no sona
> aquí baix ho portaran.
> *Manguis* i *xoriços*
> fora de la capital.
> I aquí en quatre pisos
> fotran aquest personal.
> Putes, putes Olimpíades!
> Bombes, *petardos* al 92!
> Barna s'endú les medalles
> i aquí les escorrialles.
> Oh, trist racó d'aquest Mediterrani mort!
> Oh, trist racó d'aquest Mediterrani mort!
> Desperta't, espavila't,
> que ara és el teu torn! (Els Pets)

And now for the Games
they will clean up Barcelona,
and they will bring down here
all the things with no value.
Muggers and crooks
out of the city.
They will put these people
in apartments around here.
Fuck, fuck the Olympics!
Bombs, petards on 92!
Barcelona will get the medals,
we will get the trash.
Oh, sad corner of a dead Mediterranean!
Oh, sad corner of a dead Mediterranean!
Wake up, move on,
now it's your turn!

The rage of these lyrics against the Olympics and the hygienization of Barcelona seems proportional to the inability to oppose this process in any effective way. The total violence against the Olympic project advocated by the song appears as a symptom of the seeming impossibility of articulating a tactics of resistance. The song is as angry at the Olympics as it is at the people for not going up against them. The song exhorts people to "wake up" and "move on," but it remains unclear what it is exactly that they should do. The anger of the lyrics seems to result from the fact that no real ways of contesting the Games could be envisioned.

Yet, intense social conflicts emerged on at least two occasions during the Olympic transformation. On the one hand, several Catalan nationalist organizations campaigned against the Spanishization of the Games and used the event to claim independence for Catalonia. As I explained in Chapter Two, these campaigns triggered the repressive measures of state judge Baltasar Garzón against radical Catalanists. His preventive manhunt against Catalan independentists accused of supporting terrorist group Terra Lliure resulted in the incarceration and torture of 60 people. The so-called *Operación Garzón* brought back the ghost of Francoist repression in many strata of Catalan society and caused some political turmoil in the weeks before the opening of the Games.

On the other hand, many urban projects in Barcelona raised protests and gathered people in demonstrations in the affected neighborhoods. Two urban conflicts in particular became symptoms of a latent anxiety about the Olympic transformation: the anxiety about the price that more marginal areas of the city would have to pay for the global promotion of Barcelona. First, neighbors of the peripheral area of Cobasa at Sant Adrià del Besòs initiated a furious battle against the city hall in 1990 to stop the building of residences for the poor and disadvantaged inhabitants of the nearby neighborhood of La Mina. The protesters claimed that they were not against the people of La Mina; instead, they opposed the municipal refunctionalization and privatization of an area that was intended for public facilities. While this was likely the final goal of the project, the fact that the new inhabitants would come from the most underprivileged area of the city undeniably played a role in this vehement clash. Finally, after a week-long state of siege between neighbors and the police, the city hall cancelled the project.[2]

Second, on November 11, 1990, a building at the peripheral area of Turó de la Peira collapsed because of aluminosis, an "architectural disease" caused by the disintegration of certain low-quality types of concrete. After this case, official inspections detected aluminosis in thousands of apartments in peripheral neighborhoods. The city hall, focused on building the new Olympic areas, dealt with this issue slowly and indecisively. At the same time, given that the affected buildings were built during the Francoist years of *desarrollismo*, the municipal authorities could easily shirk the blame for the incident. Also, the constructor of the collapsed building at Turó de la Peira, Román Sanahuja, was by that time developing many other buildings in Barcelona (among them the shopping center of L'Illa Diagonal, designed by Rafael Moneo and Manuel de Solà-Morales) and, therefore, the public powers had little interest in confronting him.[3]

During the Olympic years, critical voices in newspapers and street bulletins began to speak of the rising costs of living, as well as the devious and unscrupulous expropriations required to carry out the renewal. However, only underground movements such as the *okupa*, the collective of squatters that occupy abandoned properties to protest against real estate speculation, rejected the Olympic urban transformation as a whole.[4]

Social antagonisms re-emerged more visibly as the long-term effects of the Olympics, especially touristification and gentrification, became evident. In the post-Olympic years, when the fame of Barcelona as a cosmopolitan city with cultural centers and sunny beaches, with a rich architectural heritage and a cool nightlife, conquered all corners of the world, more and more local organizations and movements appeared, this time not to oppose a specific remodeling project or demand a facility, but to contest the Barcelona model as a whole.

As I mentioned in the Introduction and in Chapter Three, a considerable number of books and articles have come out to critique the effects of Barcelona's transformation.[5] But let me focus here on one of the best articulated theorizations of this new opposition. The volume *Tour-ismes: La derrota de la dissensió* contains the texts of an exhibition held in Barcelona in 2004 which analyzed the symbolic and material effects of the tourist industry over the city. Despite the variety of articles, one basic concern traverses the texts: the concern for the disappearance of the heterogeneous and "real" city underneath the touristified city. The articles of the volume present the opposition between, on the one hand, predetermined maps, planned circuits and commodifying tourism and, on the other hand, the city of the people whose movements and lives are irreducibly singular. This fundamental dichotomy lies at the core of these articles and their effort to regain a sense of the real city. New dissidences can be formulated in this real city, despite the fact that, as the title of the volume states, tourism has neutralized and even eliminated dissent.

This dichotomy between the city dominated by tourism and the world of the people relies on Michel de Certeau's well-known division between the ruling eyes of panoptical powers and the heterogeneity of street pedestrians. As he explains in the famous essay "Walking in the City," the untraceable itineraries of pedestrians embody the heterogeneous street realm that eludes the disciplinary watch of power. For Certeau, these itineraries, in a similar way to the Situationists' *dérives*, contain a model of urban tactics and dissidence.[6] Correspondingly, the underlying assumption of the *Tour-ismes* volume is that tourism must be unmasked as a sort of panoptical power that controls the city through its creation of predetermined itineraries and its prepackaging of city highlights and "places of interest."

Three articles of the catalogue, written by Xavier Antich, Manuel Delgado, and Joan Roca i Albert, respectively, express this point from different angles.[7] They share the same anxiety about the emergence of mass tourism and the subsequent commodification of urban spaces, and they search for the unstable, non-sanitized areas in which one can experience the "real" city. Antich denounces the excessive planning and cultural despotism that has characterized the intelligentsia associated with the city hall (and composed, among others, of Oriol Bohigas, Xavier Rubert de Ventós, Pep Subirós, Eugenio Trías, and mayor Pasqual Maragall). Delgado recommends walking the city at night, when the empty city becomes phantasmagorical and surprisingly more public. Finally, Roca i Albert explains the educational and also allegorical value of the city itineraries that he assigns to his high school students. He encourages them to walk through multiple areas of the city so that they can see the different historical layers and class divisions contained in it.

These three suggestive articles are representative of the most frequent critique of the Barcelona model. According to this critique, the model consists in the municipal master plan that has been imposed over a heterogeneous city to serve the interests of the tourist industry. Thus, the municipal politics branded as the Barcelona model have constituted a panoptical device that works to control and eventually eradicate the multiplicity of the real citizens, as well as their social and historical living space. This process of eradication has even been categorically defined as a case of "fascismo postmoderno" 'postmodern fascism.'[8]

However, if we look back at the original premises of the Barcelona model, are the values of heterogeneity and the needs of the real citizens not the same values that sustained the politics of the Olympic transformation? Did not the municipal politics focus on creating public spaces, making streets multifunctional, retrieving the historic past, and promoting the so-called "city of the people"? After having devised a series of itineraries through the city, Roca i Albert affirms that his goal is to instill urban citizenship into his students, since Barcelona must "retrobar-se" 'recover itself' and assume its "continuïtat amb el passat industrial, fer el paper de capital política de Catalunya, i convertir-se en metròpoli amb aspiracions globals" 'continuity with its industrial past, function as the political capital of Catalonia, and become a metropolis with global aspirations' (*Tour-ismes* 112). But, are the terms and goals of this task not exactly the same as those proposed by mayor Pasqual Maragall, whose 1991 book *La ciutat retrobada* even contains the same adjective to describe his political agenda for the city?

Unlike most critics, Mari Paz Balibrea has begun to evaluate the Barcelona model in more positive terms and has opened a more productive critical path. While she had criticized the model as an attempt to enclose the city under a "totalizing image" ("Urbanism" 204), more recently she has argued that the model as conceived in the 1980s can be opposed to the sheer commodification of the 1990s. In "Barcelona: del modelo a la marca," she acknowledges that the urban transformations of the Barcelona model carried "el sello de una visión modernizadora y progresista muy coherente, derivada de la ideología de los actores sociales que las lleva[ro]n a cabo" 'the imprint of a modernizing, progressive, and very coherent view based on the ideology of the social actors that realized them' (7). After the Olympic Games, Balibrea continues, Barcelona has become an increasingly touristified and undemocratic city that serves the interests of global companies and visitors, rather than the needs of local citizens. She names this newer city "the Barcelona trademark" and, while admitting that the notions of "the Barcelona model" and "the Barcelona trademark" overlap in many ways, Balibrea calls for a re-enactment of the "transformaciones urbanas sociales positivas" 'positive urban social transformations' (10) characteristic of the Barcelona model of the 1980s. In the end, she writes:

> si recuperamos el concepto del modelo como una particular forma de entender la relación con el espacio urbano que consiste en afirmar el derecho de todos los ciudadanos a la ciudad, que es posible materializar en concreto, con la participación de muchos, en transformaciones urbanas sociales positivas, su validez [del modelo Barcelona] persiste y es actualizable en el ahora y en el mañana. (10)

> if we retrieve the concept of the model as a particular way of understanding the relation with urban space, by which we can affirm the right of all citizens to the city, and which can result, with the participation of many people, in positive

urban social transformations, its value [of the Barcelona model] persists and can
be enacted today and tomorrow.

Thus, in comparison to most critiques of the Barcelona model, Balibrea takes
a step further and acknowledges that the values and practices that can oppose
the touristified city – public space, heterogeneity, the city of the "real people,"
etc – coincide with the very principles of the model. But, what are the exact
principles to be endorsed and re-enacted? We must recall that, as I tried to show
in Chapter Three, the reduction of the model to a trademark, or, in other words,
the Disneyfication of the new "city of the people," was not an unfortunate deviation from the original plan; given the structural conditions of late capitalism, it
was rather its necessary outcome. For this reason, the possible continuation of
the principles of the Barcelona model must take effect within, and at the same
time against, the structural conditions of the market.

There is one fundamental characteristic of the Barcelona model that interpellates our present. The model consisted in an urban master plan over the entire
city implemented through specific architectural projects that would provide
public spaces, new centers, and landmarks in previously disjointed areas. If this
model is to be retrieved, then its constitution as a totalizing master plan is an
essential aspect that cannot be overlooked. In fact, master planning is a vital
tool to control the unremitting forces of private interests. Even if the model
failed in Barcelona, and contributed to converting the city into a trademark,
its potential as a civic and democratizing tool could only derive from being
a municipal master plan that would limit the spaces of the private economic
agents in the city. This leads us to a tentative conclusion: the Barcelona model
failed – not because it imposed a totalizing, panoptical pattern on the city, but,
on the contrary, because it could not impose it in a full and effective way. I will
return to this point later.

Another assumption of the critiques in *Tour-ismes* must be questioned,
namely the division between the "real" and the "fake" and touristified parts
of the city. I already referred to some of the contradictions that traverse this
division in the Introduction a propos Manuel Delgado's *La ciudad mentirosa*; a
division that has constituted a common base of most critiques of the Barcelona model and also of economic assessments such as Miren Etxezarreta, Albert
Recio, and Lourdes Viladomiu's article "Barcelona, an Extraverted City." After
analyzing, with great precision, the commodification of contemporary Barcelona, Etxezarreta, Recio, and Viladomiu affirm that the city should find a real
economic base that replaces the volatile tourist industry. They address a rhetor-
ical question to the city's political leaders:

> When will they realize that the "domestic" life of a city is a permanent and stable
> source of economic activity and that urban planning designed to improve the
> quality of life of the city's inhabitants is the best basis for development? Only

then will it be possible to take advantage of, and profit from, Barcelona's attraction as a drawing card for people from other places. (251)

Yet this conceptual division between domestic life and ephemeral tourism is problematic for at least three reasons. First, the experience of the "real" city of local residents finds its dialectical counterpart in the very experience of the tourist. That is, the "real" city of the citizens coincides with what the archetypal tourist looks for: direct contact with the real thing. In principle, tourism does not intend to touristify the city but aims to provide experiences of authentic places, cultures, and cities. The consequence of this fact is not only that tourism instantly commodifies the reality to which it claims to provide access; more seriously, tourism also makes the distinction between real city and touristified city collapse. Where are the exact limits of the two? How can we distinguish between them, if what the tourist wants coincides with what the local citizen embodies? The experience of this real city can simultaneously represent the moment of appearance of the citizen and the defining spirit of the tourist, and this coincidence irrevocably problematizes the separation between the two.

Second, the categories of the citizen and the visitor constantly intersect in the everyday dynamics of our contemporary world. The global mobility of capital compels people – from executives to students, from athletes to actors – to spend long periods in other cities and, therefore, a clear-cut division between inhabitants and visitors can no longer be established. The attempt to maintain such division implies a certain nostalgia for a past in which people lived their lives in the same place, knew their neighbors, and shopped at the same stores. At the same time, the portrait of the tourist as a detrimental figure versus the favorable category of the citizen resembles the separation between foreigners and local natives, if not between illegal immigrants and legal citizens. This close similarity makes one wonder if this distinction may also secretly contain a proprietorial drive and the desire for safer, less mobile human communities.

The notions of real city and real people contain a third problematic aspect. These notions assume that the citizens' accumulation of experience has produced a certain city identity, an identity that, as Roca i Albert and Maragall might say, needs to be "recovered." But if, as Harvey has shown, city identities are the product of, or at least are immediately subsumed under, the strategies of differentiation of spaces in postmodernity, the retrieval of the real identity of a city cannot constitute a critical step. It becomes difficult to distinguish between the real identity and the manufactured identity of cities. In this respect, would it not be more effective to renounce the "real city" as a critical notion altogether? If one really wants to set the conditions for heterogeneity to appear, then an identity based on a tacit conception of real citizens, even if this notion embraces the widest diversity, would constrain, rather than open out, urban heterogeneity. As I will try to show later, future urban tactics should have the courage to renounce what Rem Koolhaas, in an attack to the production of distinctive and identifying city centers, calls "the straitjacket of identity" (*Small* 1250).

To renounce the "real city" brings a surprising consequence. Tourism has a subversive effect that can be useful to the same critical positions that denounce its mystifying content. The experience of the tourist (or the immigrant, albeit she constitutes an entirely different social figure) represents a form of non-belonging and a case of intrusion and expropriation. Crowds of tourists in city centers produce visible expropriations of these spaces. For this reason, tourists and visitors implicitly question the proprietorial – or "prioprietorial," to use Derrida's term, that suggests property and priority ("Marx & Sons" 222) – relation that natives have with "their" city or territory. Even if the tourist constitutes a commodified figure by definition, her condition as outsider unbalances the relation between territory and natives and weakens the identification between the two. Or perhaps, we should say that the unique relation between territory and natives becomes possible only through the vanishing mediation of tourism, as if this relation could only exist through the eye of the other.

In this context, a radicalization of the principles of the Barcelona model might be critically more effective than the dismissal of the model as a whole. The goals of building the city of the people and providing public space ultimately point to the opening of the city to everyone, local or foreigner, citizen or tourist, native or immigrant. Even if these goals have been constantly interrupted by economic and political determinations, the last horizon of these urban politics can help us see not only how the Barcelona model interpellates other city models, but also how its principles have been disregarded in post-Olympic Barcelona.

The Antimodel of Barcelona: The Suburban Megalopolis

In today's ongoing process of urbanization of the entire planet, industrial European metropolises tend to look old and outdated. In the public imaginary, the most common image of a contemporary globalized city consists in a downtown with glass-covered skyscrapers and surrounded by an endless extension of suburban neighborhoods connected by permanently congested highways. Traditional European cities, with their pedestrian-friendly neighborhoods and human-scaled dimensions, seem to be too small and too restrictive for our highly mobile and ever-changing society. The assumed form of global cities, which corresponds to most North American cities – although it has also become hegemonic throughout Asia, South America, and even Africa – combines two main elements: on the one hand, a downtown, where skyscrapers give material expression to the power of corporations, and, on the other hand, endless suburban extensions where individuals and families have their much-dreamed-of homes. The progress of corporations, and the sacred space of individuals and the nuclear family, are the ideological postulates sustaining this city model, a model based on concentrated vertical growth in downtowns and unlimited horizontal expansion in suburbs.

While the European city model traditionally comprises cohesiveness, compactness, and the presence of numerous public spaces, global cities are associated with car-ridden and disconnected areas, the absence of public space, and ghettoization. To analyze recent paradigms in urbanism, the Project on the City group (directed by Rem Koolhaas) has studied the so-called new Asian city in its manifestation at the Pearl River Delta, which comprises the cities of Guangzhou, Shenzhen, Zhuhai, Macao, and Hong Kong. These cities embody one of the most extreme examples of present globalization, and help us detect the structural tendencies of today's urbanism: they are, in other words, the cities that come closer to what the future city might look like. According to Koolhaas et al., they represent "nothing more or less than the coexistence of a number of apparently unconnected buildings which, by the simple fact of sharing a certain proximity, form an urban condition" (*Mutations* 310). Koolhaas lists some of the fundamental traits of these cities: the disappearance of historical referents produced by the so-called *tabula rasa* urbanism; a territory become entirely artificial; urban and architectural instability caused by continuous, high-speed construction; a mechanical, infinitely reproducible architecture; and speculation and corruption as the chief forms of planning.[9]

The characteristics of the Pearl River Delta cities point at the dominant tendencies shaping urban forms throughout the world. A series of sociological terms have tried to define this hegemonic model. Each term stresses a different feature of the model, but they all coincide in acknowledging the unprecedented dispersion urban fabrics. Thus, Jean Gottmann's "megalopolis" emphasizes population growth and the physical expansion of cities; Manuel Castells' "informational city" accounts for the management and transmission of flows of information; François Ascher's "metapolis" conveys the spatial heterogeneity of contemporary cities;[10] Robert Fishman's "technoburb" or "techno-city" focuses on the emergence of peripheral, self-sufficient zones structured around highway corridors; Thomas Sieverts' "*Zwischenstadt*," or "in-between city," describes the new urban formation that has resulted from the dissolution of the city from below (due to the appearance of disconnected living spaces) and from above (due to the connection with the global system); and Allen J. Scott and Edward W. Soja's "exopolis," which takes Orange County as a paradigmatic example, is "literally the 'city without' in the double sense of the expanding Outer (vs. Inner) City as well as the city that no longer is, the ex-city" (435).[11]

These concepts are precise and seemingly objective descriptions of contemporary city forms. Underneath this sociological impartiality, however, one might detect a contradictory feature. On the one hand, these concepts aim to present the dispersion and unlimitedness of contemporary cities as a sign of our times, that is, as the urban materialization of the mobility and diversity of our society. The implication here is that more traditional, compact cities do not correspond to the social changes and new developments of our contemporary world. The conception of cities as spaces of flows and polynuclear places, even if it in principle only describes a palpable reality, implicitly celebrates this reality as liberation from the limiting compactness of the classic European city. And yet, on the other hand, these notions seem to contain a concealed nostalgia for this absent compact city, for this entity that could be simply called "city" without having to add any further prefixes or adjectives. The "city" or the polis operate as haunting concepts that no longer serve to understand the present but that, contradictorily, still determine the perception and judgment of contemporary cities.[12]

Furthermore, in presenting the informational city or the metapolis as the embodiment of the multiplicity of a globalized world, these sociological approaches imply that the European city model belongs to previous historical periods. The European city is associated, by default, with the capitals of modern nation-states, the industrial city, and the metropolitan centers of imperial powers. That is, while these concepts are evidently very useful in understanding today's hegemonic urban forms, they produce an ideological effect by which the compactness and orderliness of European cities appear as forms of the past and are associated with national (and also imperial, colonial, even totalitarian) states. Through this series of tacit equivalences, it looks as if, in the present context, European "good city forms," to use Kevin Lynch's term, would repress the emerging, spontaneous, and heterogeneous flows characteristic of our global times. European traditional models appear as closed totalities that are imposed from above on heterogeneous realities, and the values of visibility, legibility, cohesion, and center-periphery hierarchy rapidly sound Eurocentric.[13]

In this sense, the notion of "dual city," used by many urban geographers to describe Third World cities, presupposes the duality between, on the one hand, the areas built by colonial powers and characterized by their regular plans and, on the other hand, the chaotic areas of indigenous communities. This is, according to Anthony O'Connor's *The African City*, the underlying trait of African cities. O'Connor refers to Africa's economic dependency to explain the identifying components of its cities, which "include large-scale 'formal' and small-scale 'informal' sectors of the economy, one originally largely under alien control, and the other almost entirely indigenous; and areas of high-quality, low-density housing juxtaposed with areas of densely-packed, shanty dwellings" (310–1).

Yet while, during colonialism, the European urban model justifiably stood as a symbol of imperial oppression vis-à-vis indigenous slums, today, when colonialism has transfigured into globalization and the flows of finance capital and the techniques of subcontracting, outsourcing, and direct investment have replaced physical exploitation and control, European colonial centers can no longer be seen as the urban representative of governing metropolises. In fact, we might even encounter the opposite: what if the shanty towns and suburban agglomerations are not only a place of spontaneous heterogeneity and indigenous diversity, but also the true materialization of the global economy ruled by decentered corporations and hectic financial power? The very places of urban diversity may be uncannily mirroring the new agents of oppression. But, before coming to conclusions, let us examine more features of the gigantic megalopolises.[14]

Another illustrative example of the view of European models as outdated city forms can be found in Barrie Shelton's *Learning from the Japanese City*, in which he argues that the Japanese, and by extension Eastern, city offers a chaotic, fragmented, and horizontal layout opposed to the linear, cohesive, and vertical model of the Western city. Shelton asserts that, while Western cities have focused on their physical pattern and aesthetic composition, Eastern cities have put greater emphasis on their content and information, as shown by the profusion of signs, neon lights, advertisements, and electronic screens that famously cover up many buildings and streets in Japan. In his effort to differentiate the Japanese city, Shelton exclusively attributes this profusion to the continuing national tradition of enlivening urban spaces. Thus, current signs and lights simply replace the former "wind-generated flappings, inflations and gyrations of cotton and bamboo" (IX). But Shelton never mentions the possibility that this phenomenon might also have some connection with the exuberant display of commercial lights in city centers all over the world (and which replicates Times Square or Piccadilly Circus). His main concern is to portray Western city models as too restrictive and hierarchical for the new multifaceted global reality and to show that the Japanese city provides a more adequate model for it. As its title implies, the book is directed toward Western audiences who must learn from the Japanese examples to live in the new global megacities.

Despite the enormous variety of forms, non-European megalopolises are simultaneously depicted as monstrous phenomena – "urban Leviathans," to use Diane E. Davis' term for Mexico City – and as places of boundless and exciting multiplicities. One can notice this double perception in the omnipresent and constantly updated statistics that count population growth in big cities. The abundance of this kind of statistics signals an anxiety about the immensity of megacities, an anxiety that mixes fear and excitement: how much bigger can cities grow? Which cities will reach the top 10 positions this year? Will there ever be a geographic or demographic limit to growth? This anxiousness is even more palpable in the predictions that estimate, based on current growth rates, the nightmarish dimensions of future cities.

The apparently objective approach of these statistics entails another ideological assumption, namely that growth ultimately means, to a greater or lesser extent, progress and emancipation. But, strictly speaking, can this progress be ever measured? The eagerness to account for the unprecedented level of urbanization in the twentieth century and the beginning of the twenty first century – statistically, 10% of the world population lived in cities in 1900, whereas now the number has raised to at least 50% – has caused us to forget the more crucial question: To what extent can we say that everyone who occupies an urbanized territory lives in a "city"?[15] In other words, what makes a city a city in our global times? These questions seem impossible to answer, but they are nevertheless dramatically relevant, especially in the largest world megalopolises, as one wonders what kind of "city air" the millions of people who live in slums, ghettos, peripheries, shanty towns, and *favelas* breathe.

Statistical information and sociological accounts of urban growth are insufficient to bring answers to these questions, even though their descriptive accuracy is fundamental to analyzing the living conditions of the world population. To begin the difficult task of answering these questions, and see how the Barcelona model relates to them, we must first recall two of the most influential sociological studies of today's cities: Manuel Castells' work on the "informational city" and Saskia Sassen's work on the "global city." The interaction of these two analyses will shed light on the relationship between the dominant representation of today's urban world and its real conditions of production.

Castells conceives globalization as a network society and as a post-industrial web of channels of information that interconnects subjects on a global scale. This model finds its spatial correspondence in the diffuse megalopolis, and Castells also presents as a paradigmatic example the urban agglomeration of the Pearl River Delta (*Rise Network* 406–9). The city of the network society is "the informational city," which

> is not a place, but a process. A process by which centers of production and consumption of advanced services, and their ancillary local societies, are connected in a global network, while simultaneously downplaying the linkages with their hinterlands, on the basis of information flows. (386)

These flows can be flows of information, but also of capital, technology, organizational interactions, images, sounds, or symbols. The definition of flows in Castells is formal and spatial, as they consist in the "sequences of exchange and interaction between physically disjointed positions held by social actors in the economic, political, and symbolic structures of society" (412). Thus, cities are centers of command and control of these flows.

The problem with this description is not that it is wrong. Intuitively, it seems an accurate account of the most noticeable features of today's cities. However, the question is whether the informational city and the network society epitomize a new historical period, as Castells argues, or whether they represent a mere expansion of the technological and communicative functions of industrial metropolises. That is, wasn't the modern metropolis already a space of flows of information, capital, technology, and signs? Weren't the modern streets, squares, or newspapers channels of information like today's highways, malls, airports, or the internet? Differences of scale and magnitude certainly exist between the modern world and the network society. But is there an essential and epochal difference? Castells' description, which is dominant in the socio-logical field and the mass media, seems to overcome the model of the modern metropolis, but, in fact, it may only be ratifying the – undoubtedly complex – extension of its main characteristics.

By claiming that the change from the modern metropolis to the informa-tional city is a truly historical one, Castells makes an ideological move. The consequence of presenting the technologies of information and the informa-tional city as the most defining characteristics of the contemporary world is the abandonment of the Marxist framework of the mode of production. Peter Marcuse shows how Castells' notion of the network society entails a reifying move toward depoliticization:

> [In Castells], [c]apitalism is conflated with globalization, but in an ambiguous and ahistorical fashion; technology, the media, demographic changes, the state appear as homogeneous, autonomous entities, actors themselves, behind whom actual actors are not to be seen. It is a classic case of reification, making the relations among human beings appear as a relationship among things, the relationships of social and economic positions appear as relationships to or against technology, to or against the ascendance of "information." (137)

Thus, Castells' agentless network society reifies social relations by presenting them as primarily determined by the technologies of communication. His analysis retains a structuralist basis, but he has replaced the semantic meaning of the structure: the structure no longer corresponds to the economic mode of production, but consists instead in a technological network. Or, rather, as Althusser taught us (see the Introduction), while for Marxism the structure is the concealed economic form that makes possible the contents of the social, Castells' network society is structure turned into "content;" that is, the struc-ture has been converted into an engine that runs and accommodates the flows of information. Despite its appearance as mere form and space, this machinery ultimately determines the contents of the social and the political in techno-logical terms.

Against the accusation of depoliticization, Castells might say, in his own defense, that the network society and its flexible and widespread channels, far from depoliticizing the world, open up new possibilities for all kinds of collec-tives to carry out their political struggles. This is certainly true. However, by substituting technology for the mode of production, what he cancels out – and this is the root of depoliticization – is the possibility of a systemic transformation of society. In this scheme, revolutionary practices can no longer be countersystemic; that is, within the conception of the world as technological network, the final horizon of the struggles taking place in it can only be the further development and improvement of technology itself.

As a concluding observation, Marcuse says: "What needs analysis, for political evaluation, is the extent to which those who use the "space of flows," the dominant groups in the global society, are or are not free of locational bounds" (146).

This is what, implicitly opposing Castells, Sassen famously analyzed in *The Global City*, which focused on the world's three most global cities: New York, London, and Tokyo. Instead of regarding global cities as centers of an informational, post-industrial, and even postproductive system, Sassen (as I already mentioned in Chapter Two) examines the actual process of production of financial services. Sassen comes to the unexpected conclusion that, in contrast to the prevalent view of globalization as full diffusion of means, assets, and capital, the world economy needs more centralized control and management.

This central control takes place in very specific global cities. Sassen argues that, even though these cities might have already been centers for trade and banking, they have intensified their functions in four new ways: they act as command points in the organization of the world economy; as locations for finance and specialized service firms; as sites of production and innovations; and as markets for these products and innovations (3–4). Global cities are the sites of production of those specialized services needed by complex organizations to run a dispersed network of factories, offices, and service outlets. Services and financial goods are manufactured in these cities, which become the places from which effective control over the global assembly line of production is exercised.

Sassen also observes that the economic functions of the global city generate an ever-increasing social polarization. Leading industries such as banking, advertising, accounting, legal practices, and architectural firms, need the services of low-paying jobs – from cleaners to waiters, from babysitters to clerks. The low salaries are nonetheless attractive for job-seeking migrants, who are compelled to live in unaffordable cities that concentrate high levels of wealth. The evident result of this polarization is the growing urban poverty in global cities: people having more than one job, structural unemployment, undersupplied districts, the homeless rabble, etc. The severe tensions produced by social polarization indicate that the network society is founded on a material base that is much less fluid and multidirectional than Castells' "spaces of flows" seem to suggest.

In terms of urban form, the discrepancy between the representation of global cities as centers of the network society and the material reality of their production processes becomes visible in one main feature of the megalopolis. As I said, the most basic format of today's city consists in the vertical downtown (with industries that produce financial goods) surrounded by an endless extension of suburban buildings. But this format has also a third element: the web of permanently jam-packed highways and roads traversing the city. Are these congested highways not the perfect expression of the contradiction between the dissemination of goods, people and information in the global network, and the centralizing forces required to regulate and finance this network? Thus, the congested highways of car-ridden megalopolises may be read as a return of the repressed materiality of the network society. These spaces of massive traffic are the negative counter-image of the spaces of flows: they are the spaces in which the city does not flow anymore, so to speak. The discord between the streams of cars and the traffic jams is a precise materialization of the contradiction between the expansive and the centralizing forces of capitalism. At the same time, however, the problem of traffic is only a tolerable side effect of the treatment against the dangers of social polarization. Traffic is the lesser evil: it is a burdensome but supportable consequence of the suburbanization that has fragmented and ghettoized the city so that the antagonisms caused by social inequality can be contained.

The Role of Architecture

The social and economic polarization of today's cities finds its architectural equivalent in the growing distance between the few outstanding buildings designed by star architects, and the vast majority of banal apartment complexes, industrial sites, and office buildings that intensify the unstructured formlessness of suburban sprawls. This is one of the points of Oriol Bohigas' 2004 book *Contra la incontinència urbana*. Once again, Bohigas proposes that we combat suburban sprawling, which he names urban incontinence, and implement an urbanism ruled by the principles of legibility, compactness, mixture of uses, and public space. Regarding the role of architecture, Bohigas claims that, despite the intrinsic quality of today's most celebrated designs, star architects – and he mentions Bernard Tschumi, Frank O. Gehry, Rem Koolhaas, Zaha Hadid, Daniel Libeskind, and Coop Himmelblau (35) – tend to focus only on the artistic originality of their designs and dismiss the moral obligation to create architectural models. Great architecture has forgotten this central principle of the Modern Movement: that models must be envisioned so that more modest architecture can apply them. Bohigas writes:

Només vull subratllar que moltes d'aquestes obres han oblidat l'altre atribut de l'arquitectura: ser directament servicial -sense ser servil- o seguir un camí experimental que no s'exhaureixi en la mateixa exhibició, sinó que ofereixi resultats a l'arquitectura corrent i modesta, aquella que es troba lluny de les línies experimentals – per incapacitat o per circumstàncies impositives – i que acaba sent la que s'encarrega de servir uns programes quotidians sense rebel·lies innovadores, i, per tant, necessitada de models clars i llegibles. Vull dir, doncs, que a aquestes obres genials els manca l'exigència de ser models interpretables. (56)

I only want to stress that many of these works have forgotten the other attribute of architecture: to be directly serviceable – albeit not servile – or to pursue an experimental path that is not exhausted in its exhibition but that offers results to modest, average architecture. This architecture, due to incapacity or to imposed circumstances, is far from experimental: it serves everyday programs with no innovative rebellions and it therefore needs clear and legible models. What I mean is that these superb works lack the exigency of being explicable models.

According to Bohigas, architecture no longer provides applicable models because it has been transformed into material for visual consumption. He denounces the subsumption of architecture under photography and, by extension, its prevalent function as a market logo. He also observes that star architects no longer design residential buildings (198). Is this a symptom, he asks, that architects are no longer concerned with urban and social well-being?

Here we could mention notable exceptions to this statement: for instance, Gehry's apartment complexes in Dusseldorf, or Jean Nouvel's 1985–7 project of Nemasus Housing in Nîmes, a project of social housing aimed to readapt Le Corbusier's "machines for living in." But Bohigas himself refers to some contemporary projects that have maintained the double role of architecture as an artistic creation and a serviceable practice. He cites Renzo Piano and Richard Rogers' Centre Pompidou, Enric Miralles and Carme Pinós' cementery in Igualada, at the outskirts of Barcelona, Rafael Moneo's Kursaal in Donostia, and Álvaro Siza's Department of Architecture in Porto, among others (56). Bohigas stresses that, not coincidentally, public institutions have commissioned and financed these works. He therefore concludes that architecture can only experiment with new forms, and at the same time be useful to the collective if it is public, even though the reality is that this "responsabilitat del sector públic s'ha esfumat amb la desaparició de les polítiques socialistes" 'responsibility of the public sector has faded away with the disappearance of socialist politics' (46).

Yet, if we consider today's architectural masterworks in their relation to the global city, we can see how they fulfill one of Bohigas' crucial demands, namely to set identifiable landmarks in the city. Despite their subsumption under photography, but precisely thanks to their visual attractiveness, original designs can become landmarks that contribute to the desired readability of the city. If a particular building must act as an architectural landmark, does it not need to be especially irreproducible and inexplicable as a model? A contradiction thus arises when architecture is expected to become an applicable model and a landmark for the city.

At the same time, many of the most celebrated buildings designed by star architects are public: Gehry's 1997 Guggenheim Museum in Bilbao or the 2004 Walt Disney Auditorium in Los Angeles; Koolhaas' 2004 Public Library in Seattle or the Casa da Musica in Porto, also completed in 2004; Hadid's 2003 Rosenthal Center for Contemporary Art in Cincinnati; Libeskind's 1999 Jewish Museum in Berlin; or Tschumi's 1998 Parc de la Villete in Paris, to limit the list to architects already mentioned by Bohigas. These designs make evident that the integration of the building into the urban fabric is an increasingly positive value, and sometimes an indispensable prerequisite, of architectural projects. Even if Bohigas is right in denouncing the subsumption of architecture under photography, this subsumption does not fully explain the meaning and role of these buildings. These buildings show that unique designs can function as cohesive landmarks that promote urban continuity and provide public space.

It thus seems difficult to decide whether a building constitutes an urban landmark, or whether it is mere material for photographic consumption. But another contradiction follows from this relation between singular buildings and the city. On the one hand, a building can become a landmark (and a photograph) when it stands out in the urban context, that is, when it risks fracturing and disrupting this context. But, on the other hand, this disruption is also necessary if the building must function as a unifying element of its urban context. This is a contradictory role for architecture in the global city: buildings must detach themselves from the urban fabric in order to function as potential catalysts of it.

One more dialectical reflection. The need to attract global tourists and offer interesting sites has generated a positive effect on cities. This effect is the construction of a series of architectural masterworks that, besides providing raw material for the tourists' cameras, potentially have a unifying function in specific areas of the city. Precisely because they need to be open and accessible to be photographed, these landmarks avoid the typical self-enclosure of postmodern architecture, of those "cities within the city" represented by the paradigmatic case of John Portman's 1977 Westin Bonaventure Hotel in Los Angeles, or by the contemporary skyscraper that repels the city around it with its mirror glass, as Jameson has shown us.[16] While Portman's hotels, and most skyscrapers, refuse to integrate their private spaces into the urban fabric outside, the public architecture of tourism aims to open itself to the city, even if it is only to be consumed by tourists. As a result of this public openness, creations such as those by Gehry, Koolhaas, Hadid, Libeskind, or Tschumi implicitly oppose urban atomization and its privatizing pattern. In suburbanized megacities, the attempt to contest atomization often remains isolated and ineffective. However, whether these works actually succeed in unifying larger urban areas or not, the point is that their architectural uniqueness, in reality, entails an urbanistic role: their individuality always sets up a landmark that can potentially stitch the urban fabric that surrounds them.

Jameson observes that the mirror glass skin of Portman's Bonaventure Hotel not only repels the city outside it, "a repulsion for which we have analogies in those reflector sunglasses which make it impossible for your interlocutor to see your own eyes and thereby achieve a certain aggressivity toward and power over the Other," but also makes the hotel virtually placeless and invisible, since "when you seek to look at the hotel's outer walls you cannot see the hotel itself, but only the distorted images of everything that surrounds it" (*Postmodernism* 42). In contrast to this paradigmatic building of the postmodern hyperspace, the distinctive masterpieces produced for today's city marketing seem to pursue the opposite: they request permanent visual attention and aesthetic contemplation. They immediately become icons that identify the city, and they aim to remain present in everyone's mind, or at least in everyone's photographs, at all times. These sophisticated architectural masterpieces function not only as photographic material (or as sculptural work, as Bohigas observes [*Incontinència* 78]), but also as new true landmarks for the city. They act as perfect urban pieces, which provide public space and help individuals map out the city. The problem they often encounter, however, is that the city that should be surrounding them has simply disappeared.

Master Plans and Public Space

Barcelona may teach us something about how to make the city appear again. Two components of the Barcelona model are notoriously absent in today's megalopolises: master plans and public spaces. In fact, these two components are necessarily incompatible with the structure of megalopolises. On the one hand, the constant growth of megacities is only possible because of lack of master planning. Against the common perception that urban growth is a spontaneous phenomenon that cannot be contained nor controlled, the reality is that the vast accumulation of suburbs, slums, and shanty towns results from the lack of master plans that reorganize and maximize the use of urban space.

On the other hand, the absence of public spaces must be attributed not only to the privatization and commodification of space, but to the very form (or formlessness) of megalopolises. The endless extension of megacities reduces the opportunities for public gatherings, so that, ironically, the more cities expand, the less space they can offer to the collective. Privatization of the city is not only enforced by way of erecting gates, restricting access, building highways that tear up the urban continuity of old neighborhoods, and keeping under surveillance enclosed shopping malls. The reduction of public space in megalopolises is also caused by their formal arrangement, which involves constant car use, insufficient density, waste of space, segregation, and unequal distribution of services. Privatization and social atomization are thus inherent to suburban sprawls. This correlation already preoccupied the first theorist of the megalopolis, Jean Gottmann, who asked "How Big Can Cities Grow?" In addition to recommending a fairer distribution and regulation of urban functions, Gottman responded "[as much as] life in them remains pleasant" (160). The vagueness of this response symptomatizes an anxiety about the disruptive effects of the growth of megalopolises.

The Barcelona model, based on a series of architectural projects that, as we saw in Chapter Three, were interwoven in a comprehensive city plan, fought against suburbanization by creating new centers and implementing urban values. In order to achieve its goals, the plan implicitly had to limit the extension of its action. The different projects determined areas of intervention so that they could generate the desired urban continuity. To facilitate this, the city hall created a new administrative distribution of ten well-defined districts. Urban renewal enforced a limit to the city's expansion, although in Barcelona this limit was, to a large extent, already imposed by the natural barriers of the Mediterranean and the mountains of Collserola. One of the keys to the success of the Barcelona model was that it included the restrictions of a general city plan. As James Steele writes in *Architecture Today*, "[m]any of the remaining buildings… are less impressive than the scope of the framework they delineate and this example of incremental or implied planning is the real model for the future that Barcelona represents" (476).

Along these lines, Bohigas, who (as we saw in Chapter Three) refused systematic master plans in the 1980s, has later observed that, not coincidentally, the most attractive cities are those that cannot expand: his examples are Manhattan, Venice, and Barcelona. He has even brought up the idea that medieval walls must be built again in order to limit urban growth.[17] Even if this seems an eccentric proposal, medieval walls have an equivalent in the contemporary context: urban master plans.

But how can we devise master plans for megalopolises that are seemingly uncontrollable and unmanageable? Is this really a viable course of urban transformation in our contemporary context? No clear and categorical response exists for these questions. Whether master planning is a viable possibility or not remains to be seen. What is clear, however, is that master plans constitute the only tool available to contest the disruptive effects of endless suburban expansion. The simple binary opposition between master planning and unrestrained growth lies at the core of any understanding of the urban today.

This is the underlying opposition that some critiques of the Barcelona model have missed. Most notably, geographer Francesc M. Muñoz has questioned the Barcelona model as conceived by Bohigas for not having addressed what he calls the "ciutat multiplicada" 'multiplied city.' This term describes how contemporary cities have turned into multiple concentrations of spaces for consumption that interpellate people as consumers rather than as citizens ("Deconstrucció" 268). The "multiplied city" is thus another term in the sequence of words coined by sociologists to represent megacities ("metapolis," "in-between city," "exopolis," etc). Muñoz's critique of the Barcelona model rightly points at the reality of suburbanization and sprawling that has accompanied this model. Yet, this reality should not be interpreted as an unaccounted-for limit of Bohigas' theories; on the contrary, diffused urbanization is precisely the point of departure and also the target of the Barcelona model. If this model fell short, or even failed in substantial aspects, it was not because it did not acknowledge the reality of the multiplied city, but because this type of city, which urban geographers tend to present as an inevitable reality, prevailed in many areas of metropolitan Barcelona.

In another article, "La ciutat multiplicada," Muñoz writes "qualsevol política que intenti aconseguir més grau de *compactació* del territori metropolità, i així contradir les tendències territorials vers la difusió, no pot obviar la realitat difusa que s'ha conformat durant els últims quinze o vint anys" 'any politics attempting to achieve a higher degree of compactness of the metropolitan territory, and thus contradict the territorial tendencies toward diffusion, cannot ignore the diffuse reality that has arisen in the last 15 or 20 years' (80).

This is an accurate remark that, in fact, defines the goal of urban politics that seeks territorial compactness. The goal is to acknowledge and oppose the tendencies toward diffusion, and for this reason it is necessary to analyze the specific social conditions of production of these "territorial tendencies." Muñoz also claims that the square, the street, or the park, are outdated urban forms no longer suitable for our diffused cities. Indeed, our contemporary reality confirms his point: today, squares, streets, and parks are increasingly touristified, controlled, monitored, or simply empty and disused. Muñoz compels us to accept alternative spaces as the new places of interaction – spaces such as gas stations, parking lots, movie theaters, gardens, or grocery stores.[18] Yet, when considering these places as potential compacting tools of the suburban city, are we not ultimately trying to transform them into new versions of the square, the street, or the park? In other words, are the square, the street, or the park not the archetypal organizational forms that can compact a city, if they can indeed articulate places of density and diversity? Despite their infinite variations and shapes, these forms perhaps remain the essential, insurmountable components of the city.

Master plans, which in today's context are often dismissed as despotic or at least obsolete impositions over cities, constitute tools to limit the capitalist logic of suburban expansion. Against the view that the city should grow freely and spontaneously, master plans can oppose at a formal level the disruptive effects of suburbanization. Their panoptical and totalizing frame over the suburban city, instead of enforcing more control and repressing urban hetero-geneity, as Certeauian positions might argue, can contest the suburban atomi-zation that thwarts heterogeneous exchanges. As can be deduced from the Barcelona model, master plans can provide the density and formal containment that promote distinctively urban interactions.

In the last 25 years, New Urbanism and Urban Renaissance movements have proposed the control of urban expansion through master plans. A well-known example is the Downtown Strategic Plan for Los Angeles designed by the New Urbanists, whose 1987 manifesto (signed by Andres Duany, Eliza-beth Plater-Zyberg, Stefanos Polyzoides, Elizabeth Moule, Daniel Solomon, and Peter Calthorpe) proclaimed the necessity to revitalize cities by promoting the same elements endorsed by Bohigas: mixed uses, high density, human-scaled and pedestrian zones, public space, etc. Their assumption was also that these elements could be obtained by means of comprehensive master plans.[19]

Master plans are also indispensable if specific architectural interventions must reform larger areas. Without the structure of master plans, single build-ings remain isolated landmarks and cannot function as catalysts of urban continuity. As we observed, this is the problem that many architectural master-pieces encounter today: their potential as suturing elements of the urban fabric remains ineffective because they are not inscribed in larger plans. Take, for instance, the case of Dallas, Texas, which in recent years has gathered a series of public masterpieces that built an arts district in downtown. Buildings such as I. M. Pei's 1989 Morton H. Meyerson Symphony Center, Renzo Piano's 2003 Nasher Sculpture Center, Rem Koolhaas and Joshua Prince-Ramus' 2009 Dee and Charles Wyly Theater, or Norman Foster's 2009 Margot and Bill Winspear Opera House, are graceful and inspired works. Yet, given Dallas' lack of compactness, they are unable to form the cohesive arts district that civic leaders envisioned. Extensive highways and parking lots keep these buildings from having an urban impact beyond their boundaries; as a result, the potential effect of their public openness is deactivated.

Without a comprehensive vision, even big urban projects fail to fulfill their revitalizing goals. Take, for instance, the example of the Centennial Olympic Park built in downtown Atlanta for the 1996 Olympic Games. This park, designed by Barbara Faga's firm EDAW (curiously, the same firm that designed the area of Diagonal Mar in Barcelona, which became the first evident case of large-scale privatization of open space in post-Olympic Barcelona), remained surrounded by highways, parking lots, and buildings connected by elevated bridges that left the streets virtually deserted. Symptomatically, one of these buildings is John Portman's Westin Peachtree Center, which presents the same self-enclosure of his Bonaventure Hotel in Los Angeles. In this context, Centennial Park appears as a disconnected island, as a space open to nothing but its own urban isolation.

Perhaps as a hopeful sign that things begin to change and that it has become evident that architecture and urbanism without master planning have little transformative effects, today a new form of master plans has appeared, a form that takes the Barcelona model a step further. While this model consisted in a series of architectural interventions articulated through an implicit general plan, today's emerging form is that of the master plan conceived and designed as an architectural piece in itself. This type of master plan undertakes the planning of an entire area as if it was a single building, so that engineering and urbanism become subordinated to the mandates of architectural form. These new master plans turn the conventional process around: if, traditionally, architecture had to operate within the framework of plans, here plans are part of the totality of an architectural design.

Two of the best avant-garde architects, Rem Koolhaas and Zaha Hadid, have, in recent years, designed a good amount of master plan projects. Koolhaas and his Office for Metropolitan Architecture (OMA) have been commissioned a master plan for the London district of the White City; a master plan for the former coal refinery Zeche Zollverein in Essen, Germany, which aims to transform this industrial landscape into a multifunctional center; the redesign of the city of Lille in France, which has become a key center between Paris, London, and Brussels; and the master plan S-Project in Seoul, in which they "initiate a strategy for the creation of an identity comparable with the Manhattan grid, Vienna Ringstrasse or Barcelona City."[20] Koolhaas embraces the design of master plans as a task to transform cities radically, a task that many people would consider impossible. Referring to Lille, Koolhaas writes: "[p]aradoxically, at the end of the twentieth century, the frank admission of the Promethean ambition – like, for example, to change the destiny of an entire city, is taboo."[21] The comprehensive and all-encompassing scope of master plans turn them into truly transformative instruments. Master plans have the power to do the seemingly impossible thing of remaking a whole city.

One could argue that these master plans can effectively work in European cities like London, Essen, or Lille, but not in suburban megalopolises, the gigantic scale of which is beyond the reach of even the most ambitious master plans. This potential critique is contested by Zaha Hadid and Patrik Schumacher's projected One-North master plan for Singapore. This city is one of the Asian Tiger cities precisely described by Koolhaas et al. as a product of "nothing more or less than the coexistence of a number of apparently unconnected buildings"

(*Mutations* 310). Hadid, who has also projected the Zorrozaurre master plan in Bilbao and the Kartal Pendik master plan in Istanbul, among many others, has applied her sinuous, computer-generated, Suprematist spatial language to a whole urban area of Singapore. The plan unfolds as a disfigured and asymmetrical grid that provides a flexible but unified and readable urban structure. This structure fuses the uniqueness of the architectural design of a building and the extensive scope of an urban plan. The planning of a city and the design of a building become, so to speak, one and the same thing.

The key aspect of Hadid and Schumacher's master plan is that the fluctuating and bewildering shapes of the design incorporate the traditional values of the city, namely mixture of uses, readability, and compactness. The plan devises centers as catalysts of urban intensification; parks, plazas, and public spaces that can articulate city life; a clear and well-defined district division; and the multifunctionality of residences, companies, stores, and spaces for leisure. Although the area is expected to be occupied by high-tech, finance, and research industries, the plan aims to generate an actual and heterogeneous urban form in an effort to create an alternative model to the isolated, mono-dimensional research zones so common in North America (such as the Research Triangle Park in North Carolina).

Hadid's plan even contests the *tabula rasa* urbanism characteristic of the new Asian city by creating "heritage areas" that promote a "built environment of distinctive character and a clear sense of local identity" (Papadakis 125). Whether this production of locality is really achieved, or whether it develops a simulacrum of it, does not matter as much as the implicit recognition of the sense of place as an urban value. In other words, whether Hadid and Schumacher's master plan fulfills its aspirations or not, the plan proves that the seemingly uncontainable growth of megalopolises can be contested with imaginative and far-reaching projects. This master plan, like all of Hadid's works, cannot be applied as a formal model – as Bohigas, following the imperatives of the Modern Movement, would demand. But what is exemplary in this architectural plan is its reformative and programmatic ambition: it is by attempting to radically transform city space that the plan revives the Modern impulse.

Hadid has never stopped exploring the paths opened by the Modern Movement. She already stated at the beginning of her career in 1983, in an implicit attack against postmodern architecture devoted to the ironic and playful reproduction of the past, that

> there is only one way and that is to go forward along the path paved by the experiments of the early Modernists. Their efforts have been aborted and their projects untested. Our task is not to resurrect them but to develop them further. This task of fulfilling the proper role of architecture, not only aesthetically but programmatically, will unveil new territories. (2)

Or, Kenneth Frampton summarizes in one statement Hadid's relationship to Modernism: "For her, the modern project is not only incomplete; it has hardly even begun" (in Hadid 4).

Hadid's determination to reform an entire city, like Koolhaas' admission of the Promethean ambition, is the real model offered by these master plans. But this reformative force does not originate in the mere experimental search for new and multiple urban forms. On the contrary, the ultimate goal of this search for new forms is to apply in contemporary cities the classic, or perhaps just essential, conditions of the urban. Master plans are thus the means to put these conditions into effect.

Master plans can only become tools capable of containing the atomizing logic of capital and its concomitant suburbanization if they are accompanied by another major component of the Barcelona model: the creation of public space. As we saw above, the extensive growth of megalopolises hinders the development of public spaces. Megalopolises certainly have public spaces, but their own scattering logic dismantles the urban continuity based on squares, sidewalks, or lively parks. Furthermore, the absence of communal spaces is an intended effect of the dispersion of single-family residences and isolated buildings, a dispersion that aims to offer individuals an escape from the heterogeneities of the social.

Yet, as we saw in Chapter Three, the promotion of public space in compact cities may be linked not to collective and democratic uses, but rather to the industry of image-building. One of the central functions of today's public spaces is to supply "spatial entertainment" to tourists and citizens. In this sense, Ole Bouman and Roemer van Toorn are highly critical of some of Barcelona's public sites. According to them, these sites were so beautifully designed that they discourage people from using them. These spaces do not seem to provide a place for collective gatherings or for the expression of social conflicts; on the contrary, their stylish structures tend to conceal and even suppress these. In their article "Beth Galí. España Invertebrada Revisited," Bouman and van Toorn specifically focus on architect Beth Galí (who is also Bohigas' wife) and her remodeling of the Fossar de la Pedrera cemetery in 1986 and the Parc del Migdia in 1992. They argue that the tactile beauty of Galí's work masks the real conflicts that are taking place outside these public islands. In her, the tactile does not embody the resistance that Frampton theorized as Critical Regionalism. Instead, they write

> [f]orm... acts as a distraction from the failure to solve social discords. ... The outward tactility no longer has anything to do with that resistance that some [i.e. Frampton] hoped to see in it, in their search for an answer to cultural globalisation. This is not an architecture of dissension but of diversion. (160)

Yet, the beautiful designs of these spaces can be interpreted as a depoliticizing gesture, as Bouman and van Toorn do, or, on the contrary, they can be read as an unreserved challenge to social reality. The aesthetic quality of these spaces, which we should not forget are public, can result in the creation of alternative, pleasant places; places that transmit to the citizens a sense of harmony and peace lacking in the surrounding areas. As a result of this experience, the rest of the city can suddenly become unbearably chaotic, decaying, or simply "ugly." Is it too far-fetched to believe that this perception can potentially bring a consciousness for change? Even if these public spaces mainly function as places for leisure activities, their aesthetico-political potential is not exhausted by these functions. Urban beautiful forms can operate both ways: as alienating masks of troubling realities or as paradigms of what the city should ideally look like. What is hastily dismissed as fastidious design or urban beautification may sometimes contain transformative directives rather than regressive models. At the same time, we must bear in mind that what ultimately makes possible this progressive dimension of stylish spaces and designs is their public nature. The publicness of Galí's works and of so many others in Barcelona – an aspect that Bouman and van Toorn completely overlook – constitutes the most valuable contribution of the Barcelona model.

Due to touristification and Disneylandization, Barcelona's new public spaces acquired many not-so-public functions. But let us examine the most essential question: What would be the truly public functions of a public space? In principle, public spaces are spaces that belong to everybody or, rather, that should not belong to anybody. But two main determinant factors, one legal and one economic, make this non-belonging impossible; or, at least, they drastically reduce the potential openness of public spaces. On the one hand, common public spaces such as squares, parks, streets, stations, libraries, or airports, belong to city halls, regional governments, and states. This ownership is not merely nominal, as it resolves that these spaces are only open to legal citizens, residents, or visitors of the city. This basic condition, implemented by nation-states, establishes who can and who cannot dwell in public spaces, and the task of legal forces is to verify that all dwellers have legal documents to occupy them. On the other hand, public spaces are also defined by the urban functions of commerce, work, leisure, circulation, and communication. These economic activities, although they cannot be characterized as properly public, are also constitutive of public space.

For these reasons, is it not strictly impossible to find a specific urban activity that can be conceived as purely public, with no further functional purpose or economic interest? What kind of experiences could embody the publicness of public space without participating in some degree in the functions of leisure, work, communication, or commerce? In this respect, it is revealing that Bohigas' texts define the essential components of the city, namely the streets, the park, and the square, indistinctly as public spaces (or "espais col·lectius" 'collective spaces' [*Incontinència* 156]) and as the space for the conflictive mixture of commercial, communicative, and other social functions. The publicness of public spaces is always constrained by two elements: the specific social exchanges taking place in them, and the legal restrictions that establish which individuals will be allowed to find communitarian and political recognition in these spaces and which ones will be denied access to them.

Leaving aside the different nature of these constrains, what becomes clear is that public space emerges as an impossibility and as a paradox that corresponds, in turn, to the constitutive essence of the city. The impossibility of public space is twofold: on the one hand, common space stands for the city's fundamental openness to virtually everyone; but, on the other hand, what takes place in the city as a result of this openness materializes in the commercial, social, collective, or political functions of the city, and these functions precisely restrict the city to a limited number of agents and individuals (those who can afford to live in it, those who are legal citizens, etc). Public space makes possible the taking place of everything that takes place in the city; in fact, it *is* the city. But, as soon as these functions have effect, the city stops being public. In other words, public space opens the city to everyone and to every possible event, but it simultaneously constitutes the city through the specific – economic, proprietorial, determinant, identitarian, divisive, calculative – exchanges that take place in it. Public space and the city cannot have a specific function, but they must make possible all potential urban functions. Public space is the structural and constitutive impossibility of the city; and, while the actual public streets, squares, or parks point toward this absolute openness of the city, they remain the traces or failed embodiments of this openness. Public space promises an openness that it cannot fulfill, as it cannot exist outside economic instances and urban functions. At the same time, however, public space never stops promising this radical openness.

The essential publicness of the city is revealed only negatively as a disavowal of the appropriations of the public itself. The fact that there is no "proper" use of public space, since all uses enclose private interests or have restrictive effects, indicates that public space emerges not as a positive realization of the urban but, on the contrary, as the critique of all appropriations of the urban. Paradoxically, the publicness of public space reveals itself through the impossibility of finding a purely public use of this space; therefore, it only takes form in the uncovering of the necessarily "false" public uses of it. Public space must be conceived negatively as the task to interrupt and dismantle any interested appropriations of the public and the city.

Critiques of the privatization, atomization, or touristification of the city must depart from this essential publicness that cannot be appropriated and that must remain absolutely and unconditionally open to everyone. This means that, strictly speaking, cities cannot even belong to their "citizens" or to their "real people." Thus, as we saw in the criticism of the touristification of Barcelona in the *Tour-ismes* volume, a common assumption in urban studies is that political activism and urban dissension must rely on the experience of the "real" city of the citizens. From this viewpoint, the main function of public space consists in representing and accommodating the (infinite and ultimately unrepresentable) heterogeneity of people that live in the city. However, a critique that is solely based on the figure of the citizen and her actions cannot account for the negative essence of public space.

Public space must not only be conceived as the place in which citizens carry out, as Balibrea puts it, "transformaciones urbanas sociales positivas" 'positive urban social transformations' ("Barcelona" 10). This positive definition must be complemented with the negative definition of public space, so that we do not assume the identification of public space with certain groups of citizens, even if these groups are defined with all-encompassing categories such as the people, the locals, or the citizens. A defense of the city and of urban citizenship that does not account for the indeterminate constitution of public space – this space that always remains withdrawn, that only emerges as a critique of the appropriations of itself, that offers a primordial openness to others – runs the risk of being a mere retrieval of street heterogeneity. If this heterogeneity is not founded on, and at the same time dismantled by, the (non-)essence of public space, it might after all mesh too well with the multicultural logic of late capitalism, which promotes urban diversity and local vibrancy.

Finally, we must comment on two complementary claims against the essence of public space. One line of reasoning draws on the European origin of public space and another argument insists on the irrelevance of this type of space in today's cities. Under the pretext of historicizing public space, these arguments aim to attack it as a Eurocentric category and ultimately as an obsolete typology.

The Greek agora constituted the first historical manifestation of public space. Yet, this historical case is not an ideal that cities must follow; nor does it stipulate a specific typology or urban figure. Given precisely the historicity and contingency of the diverse public spaces in the world's countless cities, public space must be conceived as the unrepresentable, non-cultural conditions of possibility of the city. Although these conditions emerged historically at the Greek polis, public space cannot be comprehended or exhausted as a Eurocentric concept. The very constituent openness of public space dissolves its own genealogical determination as Greek or European. But let me return to this point later a propos Heidegger's thinking on the polis.

On the other hand, it is often said that, in the era of communication networks, virtual interactive webs fulfill the functions of public space. According to this view, there is no need to worry about public urban forms because the network system has replaced the street and the square and is now the main "site" for all types of social exchanges. Three things can be said against this objection. First, it is true that the technologies of communication have opened up new forms of public exchange; yet, they have not substituted the old ones: they just complement them. Urban public spaces and communication networks simply coexist. In fact, have they not always coexisted, as communicative technologies, whether rudimentary or advanced, have always been an elemental part of human settlements?

Second, the modern development of the network society has neither dissolved the urban nor has it been indifferent to it. On the contrary, this development has been accompanied by an unprecedented expansion of cities and urbanization. Not only networks have not replaced metropolises, but, as Sassen has shown, the new assembly lines of globalization have concentrated the production of financial, managerial, and administrative services in cities. Urban settlements continue to be a very present phenomenon indeed.

Finally, one could turn this objection against itself and say that, precisely because of the disappearance of public space caused by the technological networks, urban public spaces are more relevant than ever. The proclamation that public spaces have become outdated or wasteful reinforces their significance, as public space must, by definition, be useless and undetermined. The more geographers and urban sociologists certify the inadequacy and obsolescence of public space in contemporary cities, the more public space symbolizes the vanishing essence of the urban. The empty and apparently incongruous common spaces in car-ridden megalopolises are the clearest manifestation of this lack in today's cities: the lack of the urban itself.

In this respect, and going back to our study case, Barcelona's politics of creation of public space have the potential to challenge the configuration of today's megalopolises. These new spaces immediately served Barcelona's image-building industry, they provided visual and spatial goods to tourists, and they permitted the PSC and the city hall to implement a politics of consensus, which instigated, in turn, the euphoria of the Olympic project. Nevertheless, the urban transformation, and especially Bohigas' elaborate theorization of it, pointed toward the constitutive essence of the city. Public space, in the fundamental forms of streets, squares, and parks, is the only essential urban ground, as it embodies the taking place of the city itself.

The Barcelona model, beyond its concrete – successful or failed – application, calls for the unifying articulation of cities through public space and the implementation of cohesive master plans. This call should not be identified with a mere nostalgia for the European city, a nostalgia that drives tourists to experience simulacra of city life in Europe's old centers, EPCOT, or Las Vegas' hotels. Rather, the endorsement of the street, the square, or the park aims to oppose the context of today's megalopolises, in which these urban forms have been mutilated and disfigured. The ghost of the old, master-planned, public city is already haunting megalopolises. In Barcelona itself, in the touristified and increasingly polarized post-Olympic city, the ghost of "the Barcelona model" is haunting "the Barcelona trademark," as Balibrea's 2004 article "Barcelona: del modelo a la marca" exemplifies. Will this haunting ghost change one day the destiny of megalopolises, or will these keep growing infinitely until the whole globe becomes one single global mega-/ex-/meta-/Ur-/techno-/multi-/Über-/non-/omni-city?

Urban Public Spaces

After examining how master plans can challenge the capitalist logic of suburban expansion, let us try to explore further the potential of the other main (universalizable) component of the Barcelona model: the vindication of public space. To do so, we should begin by relating the question of public space back to Frampton's Critical Regionalism. As I explained in Chapter Three, Frampton endorses the types of architecture that resist global homogenization through the care of local places, and his project can be effortlessly connected to Bohigas' ideas for the reconstruction of the city. The effectiveness of Frampton's project is uncertain, since, as Jameson has demonstrated, Critical Regionalism runs the risk of collapsing into the same global logic that it is trying to oppose: the logic of late capitalism which promotes the production of local difference.[22] However, one component of Critical Regionalism can help us examine the ultimate implications of a call for public space. This component, slipped in by Frampton to substantiate his theories, is Heidegger's conception of space.

In his well-known 1951 essay "Building Dwelling Thinking," Heidegger argues that the phenomenological essence of space only appears in the act of dwelling in a certain definite place. But the boundaries of this place are not what a merely technical and calculative view would claim: that is, they are not limits where something stops and something else starts. On the contrary,

> as the Greeks recognized, the boundary is that from which something *begins its essential unfolding*. ... Space is in essence that for which room has been made, that which is let into its bounds. That for which room is made is always granted and hence is joined, that is, gathered, by virtue of a locale... *Accordingly, spaces receive their essential being from locales and not from "space."* (356)

For Heidegger, space must not be understood as the Roman endless continuum, the Cartesian *extensio*, or the technological modern placelessness: three genealogical precedents of today's capitalist globalization. Space is the place-bound bringing forth of Being, the gathering that makes something appear in its essence. Space is the taking-place of Being as *aletheia* or unconcealment, that is, as the bringing forth of beings by way of what unfolds from concealment and becomes present in its coming alongside in unconcealment. Heidegger analyzes various forms of obliteration of the essence of Being as they resulted from the transition from Greece to the Roman imperial world. The translation of *aletheia* as *veritas*, of *Hypokeimenon* as *subiectum*, or of *Energeia* as *actualitas*, established the fundamental basis on which the Western world is installed.[23]

One central element defines this basis: the conception of truth as the correspondence between *intellectus* and *rei*, that is, between the subject's mind and the real things. This correspondence, in turn, involves the resultant perception of the subject, as the being who knows, vis-à-vis the world, conceived as the objective reality to be known. This conceptual frame institutes an imperial logic – the Roman, and by extension Western, imperial logic – that pursues the domination of the world space. The initial gesture of this domination is the very conception of the world as a thing that can be delimited and sectioned in measurable parts. This fundamental conception uproots the world and flattens it in order to exert imperial, technological, and also simply subjective domination on it.[24]

Frampton appropriates Heidegger's thinking on space for his architecture of resistance, but first he passes it through the filter of Hannah Arendt. In the connection of Critical Regionalism with Heidegger's reflection on "locales," Frampton inserts one of Arendt's humanist assumptions: the fusion of placeness and human collectivity. Thus, he affirms that "[t]he bounded place-form, in its public mode, is also essential to what Hannah Arendt has termed 'the space of human appearance'" (*Labour* 85). In this respect, Frampton subscribes to Arendt's understanding of the political essence of the Greek polis in terms of urban density. Arendt writes in *The Human Condition*:

> The only indispensable material factor in the generation of power is the living together of people. Only where men live so close together that the potentialities for action are always present will power remain with them and the foundation of cities, which as city states have remained paradigmatic for all Western political organization, is therefore the most important material prerequisite for power. (quoted in Frampton, *Labour* 85)

Frampton retrieves the compact polis as an urban model to be opposed to the placelessness of contemporary megalopolises. Accordingly, he establishes the correspondences between, on the one hand, the polis, urban density, sense of place, humanity and democracy, and, on the other hand, the megalopolis, urban sprawl, placelessness, the inhuman and undemocratic politics.

Frampton turns to Arendt's humanism to ensure that the retrieval of Heidegger does not include a potential endorsement of the rootedness in the soil and the provincialism associated with his thinking on space. In this sense, Heidegger never entirely frees his thinking of this association and of the ambiguity of his examples. These examples can be interpreted as mere illustrations of his thinking on the forgetting of the essence of Being, but they also indicate a predilection for rural, regional, and provincial spaces. The references to the rural world intend to contest modern and technological placelessness, since, for Heidegger, the modern metropolis is the culmination of the process of forgetting of the essence of Being initiated by the Roman empire. However, these references also potentially foreclose his thinking and turn it into an idealization of the countryside, if not into subtle nationalist ideology.

In "Building Dwelling Thinking," Heidegger exemplifies the essence of place with the deep-rooted dwelling of peasants in a farmhouse in the Black Forest. After having presented this example as a model of essential building, he ascertains that this is a mere example from the past, not a future program in any sense: "Our reference to the Black Forest farm in no way means that we should or could go back to building such houses; rather, it illustrates by a dwelling that *has been* how it was able to build" (362). Similarly, in his 1934 article "Why do I stay in the provinces?," Heidegger admits that his work is related to the rootedness of the peasants: "The inner relationship of my own work to the Black Forest and its people comes from a centuries-long and irreplaceable rootedness in the Alemannian–Swabian soil" (28). But he then rejects the rhetoric of the rootedness in the soil and attributes it to a typically urban and inauthentic relationship to the provinces:

> The world of the city runs the risk of falling into a destructive error. A very loud and very active and very fashionable obtrusiveness often passes itself off as concern for the world and existence of the peasant. But this goes exactly contrary to the one and only thing that now needs to be done, namely, to keep one's distance from the life of the peasant, to leave their existence more than ever to its own law, to keep hands off lest it be dragged into the literati's dishonest chatter about "folk-character" and "rootedness in the soil." (29)

It thus seems clear that Heidegger aims to go beyond nationalist appropriations of the German soil or urban idealizations of the countryside. The ambiguity, however, still remains, and it never becomes clear whether Heidegger's "stay in the provinces" really overcomes these foreclosures or whether it simply radicalizes them and secretly pursues an even purer and more *völkisch* ideal of the rural.[25]

Heidegger's thinking on the Greek polis is not untouched by the same ambiguity. In *Parmenides*, Heidegger explains that the essence of the polis cannot be identified with the Roman *res publica*, which represents the subordination of the people to imperial law, nor with the city or the modern state, as misinterpreted by the translation of Plato's dialogue on the polis as "the Republic." The polis, says Heidegger, is the pole as the place around which all beings turn and precisely in such a way that in the domain of this place beings show their turning and their condition. The pole, as this place, lets beings appear in their Being and show the totality of their condition. The pole does not produce and does not create beings in their Being, but as pole it is the abode of the unconcealedness of beings as a whole. The [polis] is the essence of the place [*Ort*], or, as we say, it is the settlement [*Ort-schaft*] of the historical dwelling of Greek humanity. (89–90)

The polis thus correlates with the notion of place or topos:

The essence of the place consists in holding gathered, as the present "where," the circumference of what is in its nexus, what pertains to it and is "of" it, of the place. The place is the originally gathering holding of what belongs together and is thus for the most part a manifold of places reciprocally related by belonging together, which we call a settlement or a district [*Ortschaft*]. (117)

Throughout the text, Heidegger translates topos as *Ortschaft*, which refers to place or locality in general, but also to the specific urban form of the village or the small town. Here we find the same ambiguity between the meditation on the essence of place and the endorsement of the provincial town as the embodiment of this essence. Moreover, Heidegger deliberately uses *Ortschaft* against the common understanding of the polis as *Stadt* or city, and, by extension, against the mistaken translation of Plato's *Politeia* as *Platons Staat*. Heidegger thus contests the misuse of the Greek polis as the genealogical foundation of the city and the modern state. Against this common perception, he implies that democracy does not constitute the most defining essence of the polis; instead, the polis is the place where Being unfolds in the very constitution of the place. The destabilizing effects of this new assumption for modern democracy, the city and the state are, naturally, incalculable.

Charles Bambach, in *Heidegger's Roots*, explains how this stance must not be understood as anti-political, but as

[a] new politics of the anti-political: an originary politics of the *arche* that dispenses with, extinguishes, and deracinates the aggressively nationalist dimension from the old politics of the earth, the homeland, the soil, and the fatherland. ... Heidegger will now assert [in *Parmenides* 91] that "the essence of power is foreign to the *polis*." (187)

Therefore, Heidegger's polis cannot constitute a place for political programs that identify, as Arendt does, politics with the generation of power. It cannot contain any struggle defined in positive terms and it cannot even accommodate the potential of constituent power either. The polis as the spatial foundation of democracy is completely redefined: the *demos* can no longer be understood in humanist terms as the people or the citizens, let alone the community or the *Volk*; and politics cannot correspond to the negotiation and distribution of power. Power is always necessarily an imperial substance, and it entails the forgetting of the essence of Being and of place. For this reason, the polis, as the place which "lets beings appear in their Being," demands the permanent confrontation and ultimate dismantling of all forms of political power.

Frampton eliminates these destabilizing effects and the underlying ambiguity of Heidegger's thinking on the place by fusing it with Arendt's humanist polis, that is, with the polis conceived as the place where people live together and generate power. After Heidegger, Arendt's polis, urgently set against the danger of totalitarianism, takes a step back in search of a safer and nonconflictive origin for the enlightened and democratic city. The polis conceived as the space of human appearance assures that there is no possible, dangerous ambiguity regarding the essence of place; it assures that the place of the political is founded on the coexistence of human beings. But, at the same time, this humanist polis eliminates the radical openness – beyond power, beyond the home, beyond all rooting – of Heidegger's politics of the anti-political.

Given this dilemma, a series of questions emerge: Can we maintain the oppositional force of Heidegger's thinking on the place without necessarily rejecting the form of the city and without retrieving rural landscapes? Can we dismantle the modern (imperial, placeless) structure of the political without getting rid of democracy itself? Can this essence of the place be at least glimpsed in today's cities? Can architecture and architectural interventions in cities retain in any way the essence of their etymological root *arche*, which Heidegger translates as the beginning and the ruling origin of being (Bambach 193)? Can we recover a sense of place without falling either into nationalist ideology or into the humanist ideology that establishes the human body and the physical nearness of human beings as conditions for democracy?

Urban public spaces, even if only in an oblique and tangential way, can point toward a constructive answer to these questions. Their urban condition cancels the possibility of translating the essence of the polis into antimodern rural villages and settlements, which, like Heidegger's famous "ski hut," mesh too well with *völkisch* ideology. But the open indeterminacy of public spaces, augmented by the fact that the megalopolis has condemned them to be outmoded and often empty spaces, also cancels the possibility of defining them as the place of the living together of people. This in-between stance, by which public spaces still constitute the essence of the urban, but at the same time do not function primordially as places for human physical gathering, may contain a potential realm for political tactics and locational democracy. In other words, the indeterminacy of public spaces that has resulted from the dismantling of the modern metropolis has brought two unexpected possibilities: first, the possibility of overcoming the humanist premise that conceives public spaces as places for local and national communities and, second, the possibility of unleashing the emancipatory potential offered by the evacuated places given their very indeterminate emptiness.

Urban public spaces provide a sense of place that can never be properly defined in positive, constituent terms. This sense of place does not result from the institution of an origin or the supply of signs for a common identity; instead, it can only manifest itself as emancipatory politics, that is, as politics that aim at liberating the public from the inevitable foreclosures and determinations of the public itself.

Derrida's rereading of Plato's word *khōra* as found in the *Timaeus* provides us with a parallel notion that can help us further define the meaning of urban public space. In *On the Name*, Derrida writes that *khōra* is the "irreplaceable and unplaceable place" (111) that gives place to every being. But *khōra* is neither *eidos* nor image, it is neither an idea nor a thing, neither *logos* nor *mythos*; rather, it is the irreducible difference between them, the spacing that makes them possible in their very difference and determined constitution. "*Khōra* receives, so as to give place to them, all the determinations, but she/it does not possess any of them as her/its own" (99). *Khōra* is essentially unnameable and, for this reason, when the word is translated as "'place,' 'location,' 'region,' [or] 'country'" (93), the word inevitably falls prey to a particular set of assumptions and interpretations.[26]

Public space is also this unnameable notion that receives and gives place to all the determinations of the city without possessing any of them. But, in the same way that *khōra* can never be translated without introducing a sequence of ideological postulations, public space can never appear without the actual carrying out of specific urban functions, uses, and appropriations.

To follow on this question, we must point at the fact that, while Derrida does not translate *khōra*, he speaks of it in spatial terms. Or, better, what must be remarked is that Derrida decided to speak of a spatial term such as *khōra* to begin with. This selection may be indicative of a historical determination, namely that, in postmodernity, the preoccupation with space has become predominant in describing our historical and ontological situation, and the language of space has become especially insightful in revisiting the concepts of metaphysics. Isn't this predominance of space, and the subsequent abandonment of the dimensions of time or progress, a symptom of one defining characteristic of our times, namely that there is apparently no possibility of imagining real historical change? The prevalence of spatial terminology in Derrida not only might tell us something about the historicity and equivocality of his own texts, but it especially shows us how space is a crucial element to think the current conditions of possibility for the task of politics. Politics understood as the permanent confrontation with all forms of existing power – a confrontation that reactualizes the promise of radical historical change – entails a spatial expression that has become more and more central. It is, for this reason, that urban public spaces can bring forth a fundamental enunciation of this task.

Now, returning to the contingencies of Barcelona, we must realize that the post-Olympic city has not only undergone massive touristification and gentrification, but has also witnessed a large profusion of political movements. Anti-corporate globalization activists, *okupes* or squatters against private property, anarchists protesting speculation, antiwar demonstrators, and Catalanist groups yelling against the Spanish state, have recurrently taken over the streets.[27] Public space has played a crucial role in the emergence of these urban demonstrations. We should not go so far as to say that political activity has augmented thanks to the creation of public spaces; rather, contemporary protests connect with a long tradition of Catalan dissent, and Barcelona has been known throughout modernity as a particularly rebellious and red city.[28] Yet, political actions are certainly more visible and potentially more effective in compact cities in which public spaces accommodate and offer exposure to collective gatherings. The irony is that the creation of public spaces during the Olympic years may have intensified the political activity of the city in many cases against the municipal government that promoted these spaces.

In post-Olympic Barcelona, urban public spaces have given place to another major social phenomenon: the arrival of large numbers of immigrants. Many of the undocumented, non-European immigrants who arrived in the city in the last decade have been forced to dwell in public squares and parks, trapped in a catch-22 situation for not being allowed to get a job without a work permit, and not being allowed to get a work permit without a job. Public spaces have given visibility to the exclusions affecting this collective. Similarly, another widespread phenomenon linked to public space in Barcelona is homelessness, as Bohigas himself observes with regard to the renovation of the Plaça Reial, which the city hall assigned to Federico Correa and Alfonso Milà in 1982:

> We also thought we were doing a good thing by making a genuine living room in the city with the use of concentric benches. Now, listen to this! The square as a living room has become such an enormous success that it is mainly used by marginals. Every day they do things there we'd rather not have to see. (quoted in Bouman and van Toorn 188)

Despite the antagonisms and suffering that these various collectives represent, do they not embody, better than anyone, the publicness of Barcelona's public spaces? That is, have the public spaces of the Barcelona model not contributed in one way or another to the emergence of these oppositional movements and these marginal, but, nevertheless, truly urban figures? In these cases, public space has appeared as a host, as an open place for the articulation of subversive tactics or the dwelling of individual and collective subjects. All these movements deploy specific ideological contents, and some of them probably use public space only to gain visibility in the media. In the same way, the dwelling of illegal immigrants and homeless people in public space is evidently a deplorable fact related to many social and political deficiencies. However, their political claims, and their very presence, are a sign of the living openness of public spaces. This openness makes possible the appearance of new urban beings and social phenomena, but at the same time prevents them from establishing authentic, subjective, or communal forms of belonging. The essence of public space is thus revealed as spatial assistance for the taking place of all events, and also as vindication of the same publicness of the place. Strictly speaking, public space makes us all homeless, and turns us into hosts of the place. The public place intrinsically commands the imperative to be "good hosts," that is, to be critical of the attempts to appropriate, by means of ideological foreclosures, the places open to all.

Notes

1 "Adiós al noventa y dos," *A/parte. Publicación contrainformativa* 5 (1993), 4.

2 For a full analysis of the Besòs conflict, see Institut d'Estudis Metropolitans, *Análisis de un conflicto urbano: El caso de Sant Adrià del Besòs*.

3 For a full account of the buildings affected by aluminosis, see Federació d'Associacions de Veïns de Barcelona (FAVB).

4 See *A/parte* 2 (1992) and 5 (1993). Another pioneering but isolated critique of the social disruptions caused by Barcelona's Olympic enterprise was Pere López's article "1992, objectiu de tots? Ciutat-empresa i dualitat social a la Barcelona olímpica." See also Vázquez Montalbán's *Barcelonas*.

5 See Balibrea; McNeill; Delgado; Degen; Heeren; Muñoz; Capel; Montaner; Monclús; Borja; Marshall; Degen and García; Unió Temporal d'Escribes; and Espai en blanc.

6 See Certeau 91–110.

7 In *Tour-ismes*, see Manuel Delgado, "Ciutats de mentida. El turisme cultural com a estratègia de desactivació urbana," 54–66; Xavier Antich, "On són les ferides? Post-imatges i ficcions de la rosa de foc," 78–85; Joan Roca i Albert, "L'itinerari com a forma artística. La ciutat i la ciutadania," 101–13.

8 See <http://www.espaienblanc.net>.

9 See Koolhaas, *Mutations*, 209-335. See Chung et al., *Great Leap Forward*, for the complete essays on the Pearl River Delta's project.

10 Ascher defines "metapolis" as
    une métapole est l'ensemble des espaces dont tout ou partie des habitants, des activités économiques ou des territoires sont intégrés dans le fonctionnement quotidien (ordinaire) d'une métropole. Une métapole constitue généralement un seul bassin d'emploi, d'habitat et d'activités. Les espaces qui composent une métapole sont profondément hétérogènes et pas nécessairement contigus... [Les métapoles] sont mono ou polynucléaires, plus ou moins agglomérées ou éclatées, hétérogènes, polarisées ou segmentées, denses ou étales; elles suivent des dynamiques de croissance radio-concentriques, en doigts de gants, linéaires, en grappes, ou encore "métastasiques." (34)
    a metapolis is a set of spaces in which all or part of its inhabitants, economic activies, or territories are integrated into the normal (ordinary) functioning of a metropolis. A metapolis generally constitutes a single basin of employment, housing, and activities. The spaces that compose a metapolis are profoundly heterogeneous and

not necessarily contiguous… [Metapolises] are mono or polinuclear, more or less compressed or splintered, heterogeneous, polarized or fragmented, dense or sprawled; they conform to patterns of growth that can be concentric, like fingers in a glove, lineal, in clusters, or even "metastatic."

11 See Gottmann; Castells, *The Informational City*; Ascher; Fishman; Sieverts; and Scott and Soja.

12 Among these geographers, Edward W. Soja has already pointed at these contradictions. His studies analyze the contemporary city, not in any celebratory manner, but with the aim of confronting and changing it in radical ways. See his classic *Postmodern Geographies*, or, for an excellent map of the main discourses on today's cities, see "Six Discourses on the Postmetropolis." "Postmetropolis" is yet another term to describe the contemporary city. This article lists other terms coined by geographers and sociologists. This list is almost as endless as the cities that they describe: "edge city," "post-suburbia," "metroplex," "technopoles," "technoburbs," "urban villages," "county-cities," "regional cities," "the 100-mile city," etc. (193)

13 For comprehensive studies of – European – normative theories of city form, see Lynch and Choay.

14 For recent studies on African cities, see Simone; and Falola and Salm. Interestingly, Achille Mbembe and Sarah Nuttall have revived the term "metropolis" for an issue of *Public Culture* on "Johannesburg – The Elusive Metropolis." As they explain in the introduction, "metropolis" is a term that, given the theorizations by Benjamin, Simmel, or Weber, and regardless of its European origin, alludes to the capitalist mechanisms of control and growth that determine the configuration of all cities, whether they are African, European, global, modern, or contemporary. Mbembe and Nuttall thus combat the ideological description of African and Third World cities as the product of spontaneous heterogeneity, endless diversity and ultimate chaos, and as a model opposed to the orderly European metropolises and their corresponding centers at colonial cities. This description of the Third World city, they seem to imply, is in fact another form of culturalist othering, albeit presented as anti-colonialism and anti-Eurocentrism.

15 Statistical information from Koolhaas et al., *Mutations*, 2–3. For the United Nations' statistics on world population prospects, see <http://esa.un.org/unpp>.

16 See Jameson's *Postmodernism*, 38–45, and *The Cultural Turn*, 11–16.

17 Bohigas, Oriol. Personal interview. 23 December 2004.

18 Muñoz, Francesc M. Personal conversation. 8 April 2010.

19 For a summary of the Downtown Strategic Plan for Los Angeles, see Steele 466–69. See also Larice and Macdonald for the 1996 "Charter of the New Urbanism" as well as bibliography on the New Urbanism movement (308–11). In this Charter, we can read:

WE ADVOCATE the restructuring of public policy and development practices to support the following principles: neighborhoods should be diverse in use and population; communities should be designed for the pedestrian and transit as well as the car; cities and towns should be shaped by physically defined and universally accessible public spaces and community institutions; urban places should be framed by architecture and landscape design that celebrate local history, climate, ecology, and building practice. (309)

20 Office for Metropolitan Architecture's website: <http://www.oma.nl>. One is tempted to ask Koolhaas how this production of identity in Seoul would relate to his own dismissal of "the straitjacket of identity" (*Small* 1250) regarding the reconstruction of cities. But here we encounter a basic contradiction of today's architectural and also theoretical and political practices. While on the one hand we realize that identity is a category that has collapsed into the capitalist production of differential traits for goods, cities, or communities, on the other hand one cannot base transformative tactics or strategies

on non-identitarian (or non-ideological) premises. The contradiction between Koolhaas' radical theoretical texts and the necessary acquiescence to certain logics of the market in his own practice is not the product of an inadmissible hypocrisy; on the contrary, it is the perfect demonstration that there is always an uncontainable tension between theory and practice. Without this tension, one's ideas would simply be vacuous and one's actions would be conformist and automated.

21 OMA's website: <http://www.oma.nl>.

22 See Jameson, *The Seeds of Time* 205.

23 For analyses of these translations, see especially "On the Essence of Truth" (136–54), "The Origin of the Work of Art" (6), and "Anaximander's Saying" (280).

24 For Heidegger, this imperial logic ultimately culminates in the modern conception of technology as standing-reserve (*Bestand*) and as Enframing (*das Ge-stell*). On the one hand, the process of standing-reserve results from the technological challenging that "puts to nature the unreasonable demand that it supply energy that can be extracted and stored as such" ("Technology" 14); and, on the other hand, Enframing is part of the same challenging, but here set upon human beings so as to reveal reality as standing-reserve. As Heidegger writes, "[e]nframing means the gathering together of that setting-upon which sets upon man, i.e., challenges him forth, to reveal the real, in the mode of ordering, as standing-reserve" ("Technology" 20). Thus, this technological mode of being posits the modern world as a resource and as a supply of energy stored up for human use.

  Against this technological foreclosure of the world, Heidegger proposes to think through the most original experiences of Being, time, language, and place. For instance, while reading Anaximander's saying, Heidegger exposes how the most original experience of thought is found not in the conception of what is present as something that stands over against a subject, but rather in "the open region [*Gegend*] of unconcealment into and within which that which has arrived lingers [*verweilt*]" ("Anaximander" 261). This open region is the place in which what presences and sets up boundaries at the same time presences "without bounds." (278). For this reason, the most essential question for thinking is this unfolding of Being outside the foreclosure of the imperial logic and the representational and metaphysical concepts that have resulted from it. Thinking must preserve the essence of Being by remaining the "place-holder for the Nothing" (262), by erring in this open region of presencing ungraspable by conceptual language.

25 We must observe too that the permanent equivocality of this rural symbology vis-à-vis his thinking carefully avoids the "mistake" that Heidegger had made earlier in the famous paragraph 74 of *Being and Time* (350–54), where his philosophical project meshed with German nationalist ideology. In this paragraph, he irrevocably defined the being-in-the-world of Dasein as the common destiny of the community [*Gemeinschaft*: that is, the premodern, organic community opposed to *Gesellschaft* or association of interests] and of the people or nation [*Volk*]. But, especially after the so-called *Kehre* of the late 1930s, Heidegger draws from the symbology of German nationalism in a much more cautious way, leaving undetermined whether his examples and historical references are illustrations of his thinking, or whether they are a fundamental part of it.

26 In "Faith and Knowledge," Derrida also talks about *khōra* as "the name for place, a place name, and a rather singular one at that, for that spacing" which resists all anthropological, historical, theological, and ontological instances and appropriations of itself. (58–9)

27 For exciting analyses of these new urban struggles, see Juris, especially 61–121; Unió Temporal d'Escribes; Heeren; Degen; Marrero Guillamón; Assemblea de Resistències al Fòrum 2004; Espai en blanc.

28 For studies on Barcelona's modern social movements, see Kaplan; Balfour, *Dictatorship*; Smith.

Conclusion

One question traverses this study: Can we find in the conjuncture of Olympic Barcelona any directives for some type of urban and historical change? Are the immaterial production of new ideologies and the material reconstruction of the city exhausted in their own realization, or do they offer us guidance for future transformative politics?

The ideologies of postmodern Barcelona have provided a singular occasion to articulate a critical encounter between Marxism and deconstruction that has, perhaps, resulted in three main propositions. First, the question of spectrality. In Barcelona, the simulacrum of the Olympic spectacle turned every political figure and every social agent into specters (or, to quote Derrida, into the "fantastic, ghostly, 'synthetic,' 'prosthetic,' virtual happenings" [*Specters* 63] of our contemporary media society). On the one hand, this spectralization cancelled the access to the past, and even the access to any sense of history; a phenomenon constitutive of postmodernity but particularly detectable in a post-Franco Spain that was striving to forget the dictatorship years. But, on the other hand, it opened up the possibility of historicizing the politics of the Olympic spectacle by bringing to light their inherent spectrality. Marxism understands this spectrality as a consequence of the full commodification of the social, and deconstruction conceives it as a "hauntology" (*Specters* 51) that replaces the very possibility of an ontology of the present. Our task alternates between these two critiques: the critique of capitalism and the critique of ontology.

Secondly, Barcelona's urban cosmopolitanism. The city's industrial production of cosmopolitan ideologies must be read as a clever marketing strategy to attract global capital in the form of multinational companies, tourists, conventions, cruises, study abroad programs, and other specialized services of the economy of knowledge. However, the content of these ideologies can be radicalized toward the redefinition, or even the full implosion, of the nation-state. Two conditions of possibility of cosmopolitanism are also its conditions of impossibility: its enclosure within state law (as seen in Kant's foundational definition of cosmopolitanism as "rights") and its intrinsic connection with the logic of the capitalist market (Marx and Engels' "cosmopolitan character" of the world market). These two limits – the restrictions of state law and the unbounded logic of the market – remain contradictory to each other and make true cosmopolitanism ultimately impossible. The figure of the undocumented immigrant painfully embodies this contradiction. Thus, Barcelona's attempt to redefine cosmopolitanism as an urban matter (in which citizenship is not defined by nationality) can only be meaningful if it produces a politics that works to transform current capitalist labor conditions; and, in particular, labor conditions in connection with immigration and state control. Cosmopolitanism is a product of the state and the market, but true cosmopolitanism can only emerge beyond these two formations.

Finally, the restructuring of the urban through the master plan and public space. The transformation of Barcelona, master planned by municipal architect Oriol Bohigas, aimed to "return the city to the people" by enhancing urban compactness, easy readability, and mixture of uses, and especially by providing new public squares, parks, streets, and multiple open facilities. After the Olympic Games, the tourist industry quickly exploited the remodeled city, and the new spaces were soon occupied by large masses of visitors. But touristification was not an unfortunate consequence of the urban transformation; on the contrary, the touristification of post-Olympic Barcelona revealed what had been the goal of the renewal since the beginning, namely to equip the city with a good variety of tourist attractions and photogenic assets.

However, despite this turn of events, two key components of Bohigas' urban politics can be fruitfully endorsed and radicalized. On the one hand, the master plan, this absent element of today's megalopolises, constitutes the only tool that can control suburban growth propelled by capitalist expansion. The magnitude and totalizing aims of the master plan challenge urban (under)development. The limits that it imposes can be used against the production of urban discontinuity, which embodies and simultaneously generates social inequality. But, on the other hand, the politics of master planning must be complemented with the systematic creation of public space. Public space embodies and generates the realm of commonality for multiple collective endeavors. In post-Olympic Barcelona, the new public spaces of the city have experienced massive touristification, but they have also accommodated countless political events: anticorporate globalization parades, *okupes* protests, antiwar demonstrations, student sit-ins against the privatization of the university, and Catalanist groups rising up against the Spanish state. But public spaces entail a paradox: while they must always be defended against all (economic, political, communitarian, individual) appropriations, they cannot not be appropriated every time that a collective or an individual uses them for specific purposes. This paradox should compel us to define the essence of public space as the spatial assistance for the taking place of particular events, but also as the vindication of the same publicness of the place. The nature of this publicness opposes all proprietorial belongings and the constitution of powers based on this very publicness. Public space commands the imperative to be critical of the attempts to appropriate, by means of ideological foreclosures, economic interests, or political agendas, the places that must remain open to all.

In this combination of master planning and public space we find again the articulation of Marxism and deconstruction: while the master plan must be understood as the urban expression of a comprehensive strategy against the capitalist system, the paradoxes of public space point at the questioning of all forms of foreclosure of the constitutive and always hopeful openness of the city. The future city must be the product of an unstable balance between master plans that restrict their growth, and public spaces that welcome everybody.

These three heterogeneous points – the historical openings within the spectral nature of the postmodern simulacrum, an urban cosmopolitanism that points to the implosion of the state and the market, and control of capitalist expansion through master planning as well as the permanent enactment of the essence of public space – are critical possibilities that can be devised from the ideological analysis of postmodern Barcelona. Let us hope that they can contribute to the conception of future urban transformations.

Works Cited

Althusser, Louis. *For Marx*. Trans. Ben Brewster. London: Verso, 2005. Print.

Althusser, Louis, and Étienne Balibar. *Reading Capital*. Trans. Ben Brewster. London: Verso, 2006. Print.

Anderson, Perry. *A Zone of Engagement*. London; New York: Verso, 1992. Print.

A/parte. Publicación contrainformativa 1–5, 1992–3. Print.

Arrighi, Giovanni. "Fascism to Democratic Socialism: Logic and Limits of a Transition." *Semiperipheral Development: The Politics of Southern Europe in the Twentieth Century*. Ed. Giovanni Arrighi. Beverly Hills: Sage, 1985. 243–79. Print.

Ascher, François. *Métapolis ou l'avenir des villes*. Paris: Odile Jacob, 1995. Print.

Assemblea de Resistències al Fòrum 2004, et al. *La otra cara del "Fòrum de les Cultures, S.A."* Barcelona: Edicions Bellaterra, 2004. 23 August 2010 <http://www.ed-bellaterra.com/uploads/pdfs/FOTUT%202004X.pdf>.

Aub, Max. *La gallina ciega: Diario español*. Barcelona: Alba, 1995. Print.

Balfour, Sebastian. *Deadly Embrace: Morocco and the Road to the Spanish Civil War*. Oxford: Oxford UP, 2002. Print.

—. *Dictatorship, Workers, and the City: Labour in Greater Barcelona since 1939*. Oxford: Clarendon, 1989. Print.

Balibrea, Mari Paz. "Barcelona: del modelo a la marca." *Desacuerdos. Sobre arte, políticas y esfera pública en el Estado español*. Arteleku-Diputación Foral de Gipuzkoa, MACBA & U Internacional de Andalucía, 2004. 29 July 2008 <http://www.arteleku.net/desacuerdos/index.jsp>.

—. "Descobrint Mediterranis: la resignificació del mar a la Barcelona postindustrial" *Tour-ismes: La derrota de la dissensió. Itineraris crítics*. Barcelona: Fundació Antoni Tàpies, 2004. 34–52. Print.

—. "Urbanism, Culture and the Post-Industrial City: Challenging the 'Barcelona Model'." *Journal of Spanish Cultural Studies* 2.2 (2001): 187–210. Print.

Bambach, Charles. *Heidegger's Roots: Nietzsche, National Socialism, and the Greeks*. Ithaca: Cornell UP, 2003. Print.

Barral i Altet, Xavier, ed. *Josep Puig i Cadafalch: Escrits d'arquitectura, art i política*. Barcelona: Institut d'Estudis Catalans, 2003. Print.

Bassa, David. *L'operació Garzón: Un balanç de Barcelona '92*. Barcelona: Llibres de l'Índex, 1997. Print.

—. *Quan els malsons esdevenen realitat*. Lleida: el Jonc, 1999. Print.

Bell, Daniel. *The Coming of the Post-Industrial Society: A Venture in Social Forecasting*. New York: Basic Books, 1976. Print.

Benet, Josep. *Catalunya sota el règim franquista*. Barcelona: Blume, 1978. Print.—. *L'intent franquista de genocidi cultural contra Catalunya*. Barcelona: Publicacions de l'Abadia de Montserrat, 1995. Print.

Benjamin, Walter. *The Arcades Project*. Trans. Howard Eiland and Kevin McLaughin. Cambridge: Harvard UP, 1999. Print.

Bilbeny, Norbert. *Eugeni d'Ors i la ideologia del Noucentisme*. Barcelona: La Magrana, 1988. Print.

—. *Política noucentista: De Maragall a d'Ors*. Barcelona: Afers, 1999. Print.

Blinkhorn, Martin. "The 'Spanish Problem' and the Imperial Myth." *Journal of Contemporary History* 15.1 (1980): 5–25. Print.

Bohigas, Oriol. *Barcelona entre el Pla Cerdà i el barraquisme*. Barcelona: Edicions 62, 1963. Print.

—. *Combat d'incerteses: Dietari de records*. Barcelona: Edicions 62, 1989. Print.

—. *Contra la incontinència urbana: Reconsideració moral de l'arquitectura i la ciutat*. Barcelona: Diputació de Barcelona, 2004. Print.

—. *Dit o fet: Dietari de records II*. Barcelona: Edicions 62, 1992. Print.

—. *El present des del futur: Epistolari públic (1994–1995)*. Barcelona: Edicions 62, 1996. Print.

—. *Reconstrucció de Barcelona*. Barcelona: Edicions 62, 1985. Print.

Boix Angelats, Jaume, and Arcadi Espada. *El deporte del poder: Vida y milagros de Juan Antonio Samaranch*. Madrid: Temas de Hoy, 1991. Print.

Borges, Jorge Luis. *Ficciones*. Madrid: Alianza, 1995. Print.

Borja, Jordi. *Llums i ombres de l'urbanisme a Barcelona*. Barcelona: Empúries, 2010. Print.

Bouman, Ole, and Roemer van Toorn, eds. *The Invisible in Architecture*. New York: Saint Martin's Press, 1994. Print.

Brown, Jules. *The Rough Guide to Barcelona*. New York: Rough Guides, 2006. Print.

Burnham, James. *The Managerial Revolution*. Bloomington: Indiana UP, 1960. Print.

Busquets, Joan. *Barcelona: The Urban Evolution of a Compact City*. Rovereto, Italy: Nicolodi; Harvard University Graduate School of Design, 2005. Print.

Cabana, Francesc. *25 anys de llibertat, autonomia i centralisme (1976–2000): Una visió econòmica*. Barcelona: Pòrtic, 2002. Print.

—. *Les multinacionals a Catalunya*. Barcelona: Magrana, 1984. Print.

Cabré, Rosa, Montserrat Jufresa, and Jordi Malé, eds. *Polis i nació: Política i literatura (1900–1939)*. Barcelona: Societat Catalana d'Estudis Clàssics, 2003. Print.

Calavita, Kitty. "Immigration, Law, and Marginalization in a Global Economy: Notes from Spain." *Law & Society Review* 32.3 (1998): 529–66. Print.

Calavita, Nico, and Amador Ferrer. "Behind Barcelona's Success Story. Citizen Movements and Planners' Power." *Journal of Urban History* 26.6 (2000): 793–807. Print.

Capel, Horacio. *El modelo Barcelona: Un examen crítico*. Barcelona: Serbal, 2005. Print.

Cardús, Salvador. *Política de paper: Premsa i poder a Catalunya (1981–1992)*. Barcelona: La Campana, 1995. Print.

—. "Politics and the Invention of Memory. For a Sociology of the Transition to Democracy in Spain." *Disremembering the Dictatorship: The Politics of Memory in the Spanish Transition to Democracy*. Ed. Joan Ramon Resina. Amsterdam: Rodopi, 2000. 17–28. Print.

Carr, Raymond. *Spain, 1808–1939*. Oxford: Clarendon Press, 1975. Print.

Casavella, Francisco. *El triunfo*. Barcelona: Anagrama, 1997. Print.

Castells, Manuel. *The Informational City: A New Framework for Social Change*. Toronto: U of Toronto, 1991. Print.

—. *The Power of Identity*. Malden, MA: Blackwell, 1997. Print.

—. *The Rise of the Network Society*. Cambridge: Blackwell, 1996. Print.

Castells, Manuel, and Jordi Borja. *Local and Global: The Management of Cities in the Information Age*. London: Earthscan, 1997. Print.

Castro Alcaide, Román, ed. *Jocs Olímpics, comunicació i intercanvis culturals: L'experiència dels últims quatre Jocs Olímpics d'estiu*. Bellaterra: Centre d'Estudis Olímpics i de l'Esport, 1992. Print.

Cerdà, Ildefons. *Teoría general de la urbanización y aplicación de sus principios y doctrinas a la reforma y ensanche de Barcelona*. Barcelona: Instituto de Estudios Fiscales, 1988. Print.

Certeau, Michel de. *The Practice of Everyday Life*. Trans. Steven Rendall. Berkeley: U of California P, 1984. Print.

Choay, Françoise. *The Rule and the Model: On the Theory of Architecture and Urbanism*. Ed. Denise Bratton. Cambridge: MIT, 1997. Print.

Chung, Chuihua Judy, et al., eds. *Great Leap Forward: Harvard Design School Project on the City*. Köln: Taschen, 2001. Print.

—. *Harvard Design School Guide to Shopping*. Köln: Taschen, 2001. Print.

Colectivo Ioé (Walter Actis, et al.). *Marroquins a Catalunya*. Barcelona: Enciclopèdia Catalana, 1994. Print.

Collinson, Sarah. *Shore to Shore: The Politics of Migration in Euro–Maghreb Relations*. London: Royal Institute of International Affairs, 1996. Print.

Colomines i Companys, Agustí. *El catalanisme i l'estat: La lluita parlamentària per l'autonomia (1898–1917)*. Barcelona: Publicacions de l'Abadia de Montserrat, 1933. Print.

Company, Eduard, and Josep Maria Pascual. *Hola, Espanya! Guia per desemmascarar el nacionalisme espanyol de Pasqual Maragall*. Barcelona: El Llamp, 1993. Print.

Corporación Metropolitana de Barcelona. *Plan general metropolitano de ordenación urbana de la entidad municipal metropolitana de Barcelona: Programa de actuación*. Feb. 1976. Print.

Coubertin, Pierre de. *Olympism: Selected Writings*. Ed. Norbert Müller. Lausanne: International Olympic Committee, 2000. Print.

Crexell, Joan. *Nacionalisme i Jocs Olímpics del 1992*. Barcelona: Columna, 1994. Print.

Crumbaugh, Justin. *Destination Dictatorship: The Spectacle of Spain's Tourist Boom and the Reinvention of Difference*. Albany: SUNY, 2009. Print.

Davidson, Robert A. *Jazz Age Barcelona*. Toronto: U of Toronto P, 2009. Print.

Davis, Diane E. *Urban Leviathan: Mexico City in the Twentieth Century*. Philadelphia: Temple UP, 1994. Print.

Davis, Mike. *City of Quartz: Excavating the Future in Los Angeles*. London: Verso, 1990. Print.

Degen, Mónica Montserrat. *Sensing Cities: Regenerating Public Life in Barcelona and Manchester*. London: Routledge, 2008. Print.

Degen, Mónica Montserrat, and Marisol García, eds. *La metaciudad: Barcelona: Transformación de una metrópolis*. Barcelona: Anthropos, 2008. Print.

Delgado, Manuel. *La ciudad mentirosa: Fraude y miseria del "modelo Barcelona."* Barcelona: Catarata, 2007. Print.

de Riquer i Permanyer, Borja. "Social and Economic Change in a Climate of Political Immobilism." *Spanish Cultural Studies: An Introduction.* Ed. Helen Graham and Jo Labany. Oxford: Oxford UP, 1995. 259–71. Print.

Derrida, Jacques. "Faith and Knowledge: The Two Sources of 'Religion' at the Limits of Reason Alone." Trans. Samuel Weber. *Acts of Religion.* Ed. Gil Anidjar. New York: Routledge, 2002. 40–101. Print.

—. *Margins of Philosophy*. Trans. Alan Bass. Chicago: U of Chicago P, 1982. Print.

—. "Marx & Sons." *Ghostly Demarcations: A Symposium on Jacques Derrida's* Specters of Marx. Ed. Michael Sprinker. London: Verso, 1999. 213–69. Print.

—. *On Cosmopolitanism and Forgiveness*. Trans. Mark Dooley and Michael Hughes. London: Routledge, 2001. Print.

—. *On the Name*. Ed. Thomas Dutoit. Trans. David Wood, John P. Leavey, Jr., and Ian McLeod. Stanford: Stanford UP, 1995. Print.

—. *Specters of Marx: The State of the Debt, the Work of Mourning, and the New International.* Trans. Peggy Kamuf. London: Routledge, 1994. Print.

"Display Ad 6—No Title." *New York Times (192–Current file)* 17 Jul 1992, ProQuest Historical Newspapers The New York Times (1851–2006), ProQuest. 5 Mar. 2010.

Dissidència: Butlletí antiolímpic. Mar. 1988. Print.

Domènech i Montaner, Lluís. *Escrits polítics i culturals, 1875–1922.* Ed. Maria Lluïsa Borràs. Barcelona: La Magrana, 1991. Print.

Domingo i Clota, Miquel, and Maria Rosa Bonet i Casas. *Barcelona i els moviments socials urbans.* Barcelona: Mediterrània, 1998. Print.

D'Ors, Eugeni. *Glosari (Selecció)*. Ed. Josep Murgades. Barcelona: Edicions 62, 1990. Print.

Ealham, Chris. *Class, Culture and Conflict in Barcelona 1898–1937.* New York: Routledge, 2005. Print.

Els Pets. "Terra-Billy." *Els Pets*. Discmedi, 1989. CD.

Epps, Brad. "Els llocs d'enlloc: Aspiracions utòpiques i limitacions materials del Pla Cerdà." *Treballs de la Societat Catalana de Geografia* 63 (2007): 105–20. Print.

—. "Modern Spaces: Building Barcelona." *Iberian cities.* Ed. Joan Ramon Resina. New York: Routledge, 2001. 148–97. Print.

Espai en blanc. 6 June 2010 <http://www.espaienblanc.net>.

Etxezarreta, Miren, ed. *La reestructuración del capitalismo en España, 1970–1990.* Barcelona: Icaria, 1991. Print.

Etxezarreta, Miren, Albert Recio, and Lourdes Viladomiu. "Barcelona, an Extraverted City." *La ciutat de la gent.* Manuel J. Borja-Villel, Jean-François Chevrier, and Craigie Horsfield. Barcelona: Fundació Antoni Tàpies, 1997. 221–55. Print.

Falcones, Ildefonso. *La catedral del mar.* Barcelona: Grijalbo, 2006. Print.

Falola, Toyin, and Steven J. Salm, eds. *Globalization and Urbanization in Africa.* Trenton, NJ: Africa World Press, 2004. Print.

Works Cited 227

Federació d'Associacions de Veïns de Barcelona (FAVB). *La veu del carrer* 1, Oct. 1991. Print.

Fernàndez, Josep-Anton. *El malestar en la cultura catalana: La cultura de la normalització 1976-1999.* Barcelona: Empúries, 2008. Print.

—. "My Tragedy is Bigger Than Yours: Masculinity in Trouble and the Crisis of Male Authorship in Quim Monzó's Novels." *Forum for Modern Language Studies* 34.3 (1998): 262-73. Print.

Ferrater Mora, Josep. *Les formes de la vida catalana i altres assaigs.* Barcelona: Edicions 62, 1980. Print.

Fishman, Robert. *Bourgeois Utopias: The Rise and Fall of Suburbia.* New York: Basic Books, 1987. Print.

Frampton, Kenneth. "1977-1996. Excerpts from a Golden Age." *Arquitectura a Catalunya: L'era democràtica, 1977-1996.* Barcelona: Generalitat de Catalunya, 1996. 26-31. Print.

—. *Labour, Work and Architecture: Collected Essays on Architecture and Design.* London: Phaidon, 2002. Print.

—. *Martorell, Bohigas, Mackay: 30 años de arquitectura 1954-1984.* Ed. Adolf Martínez. Barcelona: Xarait, 1985. Print.

—. *Modern Architecture: A Critical History.* London: Thames and Hudson, 1985. Print.

Fukuyama, Francis. *The End of History and the Last Man.* New York: Free Press, 1992. Print.

Fundació Joan Miró. *Barcelona: Spaces and Sculptures (1982-1986).* Barcelona: Fundació Joan Miró, 1987. Print.

Gebrewold, Belachew, ed. *Africa and Fortress Europe: Threats and Opportunities.* Burlington, VT: Ashgate, 2007. Print.

Geddes, Andrew, and Adrian Favell, eds. *The Politics of Belonging: Migrants and Minorities in Contemporary Europe.* Brookfield, VT: Ashgate, 1999. Print.

Genovès, Dolors. *Les Barcelones de Porcioles: Un abecedari.* Barcelona: Proa, 2005. Print.

Giddens, Anthony. *The Third Way: The Renewal of Social Democracy.* Malden, MA: Blackwell, 1998. Print.

Gil de Biedma, Jaime. *Las personas del verbo.* Barcelona: Seix Barral, 1982. Print.

Giménez Micó, María José. *Eduardo Mendoza y las novelas españolas de la transición.* Madrid: Pliegos, 2000. Print.

Gottmann, Jean. *Since Megalopolis: The Urban Writings of Jean Gottmann.* Ed. Robert A. Harper. Baltimore: Johns Hopkins UP, 1990. Print.

Goytisolo, Juan. *El furgón de cola.* Barcelona: Seix Barral, 2001. Print.

Gramsci, Antonio. *Selections from the Prison Notebooks.* Ed. and trans. Quintin Hoare and Geoffrey Nowell Smith. New York: International Publishers, 1971. Print.

Gruen, Victor. *The Heart of Our Cities: The Urban Crisis, Diagnosis and Cure.* New York: Simon and Schuster, 1964. Print.

Gruen, Victor, and Larry Smith. *Shopping Towns USA: The Planning of Shopping Centers.* New York: Reinhold, 1960. Print.

Güell, Casilda. *Lluís Companys, inèdit: El símbol més enllà de l'home.* Barcelona: L'esfera dels Llibres, 2006. Print.

Guillamet, Jaume. *Els escriptors de l'Empordà.* Barcelona: L'Avenç, 2009. Print.

Guillamon, Julià. *La ciutat interrompuda: De la contracultura a la Barcelona postolímpica.* Barcelona: La Magrana, 2001. Print.

Hadid, Zaha. *Planetary Architecture Two.* London: Architectural Association, 1983. Print.

Hall, Tim, and Phil Hubbard, eds. *The Entrepreneurial City: Geographies of Politics, Regime and Representation.* Chichester: Wiley, 1998. Print.

Hardt, Michael, and Antonio Negri. *Labor of Dionysus: A Critique of the State-Form.* Minneapolis: U of Minnesota P, 1994. Print.

Hardwick, M. Jeffrey. *Mall Maker: Victor Gruen, Architect of an American Dream.* Philadelphia: U of Pennsylvania P, 2004. Print.

Hargreaves, John. *Freedom for Catalonia? Catalan Nationalism, Spanish Identity, and the Barcelona Olympic Games.* Cambridge: Cambridge UP, 2000. Print.

Harvey, David. *The Condition of Postmodernity.* Oxford: Blackwell, 1992. Print.

—. *The Limits to Capital.* London: Verso, 2006. Print.

Heeren, Stefanie von. *La remodelación de Ciutat Vella: Un análisis crítico del modelo Barcelona.* Barcelona: Veïns en defensa de la Barcelona Vella, 2002. Print.

Hegel, G. W. F. *Elements of the Philosophy of Right.* Ed. Allen W. Wood. Trans. H. B. Nisbet. Cambridge: Cambridge UP, 2006. Print.

Heidegger, Martin. "Anaximander's Saying." *Off the Beaten Track.* Ed. and trans. Julian Young and Kenneth Haynes. Cambridge: Cambridge UP, 2002. 242–81. Print.

—. *Being and Time: A Translation of* Sein und Zeit. Trans. Joan Stambaugh. Albany: SUNY P, 1996. Print.

—. "Building Dwelling Thinking." *Basic Writings.* Ed. David Farrell Krell. Trans. Albert Hofstadter. New York: HarperCollins, 1993. 343–63. Print.

—. "On the Essence of Truth." *Pathmarks.* Ed. William McNeill. Trans. John Sallis. Cambridge: Cambridge UP, 1998. 136–54. Print.

—. *Parmenides.* Trans. André Schuwer and Richard Rojcewicz. Bloomington: Indiana UP, 1992. Print.

—. "The Origin of the Work of Art." *Off the Beaten Track.* Ed. and trans. Julian Young and Kenneth Haynes. Cambridge: Cambridge UP, 2002. 1–56. Print.

—. "The Question Concerning Technology." *The Question Concerning Technology and Other Essays.* Trans. William Lovitt. New York: Harper Torchbooks, 1977. 3–35. Print.

—. "Why do I stay in the provinces?" *Heidegger: The Man and the Thinker.* Ed. and trans. Thomas Sheehan. Chicago: Precedent Publishing, 1981. 27–30. Print.

Herráez, Miguel. *La estrategia de la postmodernidad en Eduardo Mendoza.* Barcelona: Ronsel, 1998. Print.

Hillgarth, J. N. *The Problem of a Catalan Mediterranean Empire 1229–1327.* London: Longman, 1975. Print.

Horta, Gerard. *L'espai clos: Fòrum 2004: notes d'una travessia pel no-res.* Barcelona: Edicions de 1984, 2004. Print.

Howard, Ebenezer. *To-morrow: A Peaceful Path to Real Reform.* Ed. Peter Hall, Dennis Hardy, and Colin Ward. London: Routledge, 2003. Print.

Howard, Marc Morjé. *The Politics of Citizenship in Europe.* New York: Cambridge UP, 2009. Print.

Huertas Claveria, Josep Maria, and Marc Andreu. *Barcelona en lluita: El moviment urbà 1965–1996*. Barcelona: Federació d'Associacions de Veïns, 1996. Print.

Hughes, Robert. *Barcelona*. New York: Vintage Books, 1993. Print.

Institut d'Estudis Metropolitans. *Análisis de un conflicto urbano: El caso de Sant Adrià del Besòs*. Barcelona: Institut d'Estudis Metropolitans, 1991. Print.

Ireland, Patrick. *Becoming Europe: Immigration, Integration, and the Welfare State*. Pittsburgh: U of Pittsburgh P, 2004. Print.

Jacobs, Jane. *The Death and Life of Great American Cities*. New York: Modern Library, 1993. Print.

Jameson, Fredric. *Archaeologies of the Future: The Desire Called Utopia and Other Science Fictions*. London: Verso, 2005. Print.

—. *Jameson on Jameson: Conversations on Cultural Marxism*. Ed. Ian Buchanan. Durham: Duke UP, 2007. Print.

—. "Marx's Purloined Letter." *Ghostly Demarcations: A Symposium on Jacques Derrida's Specters of Marx*. Ed. Michael Sprinker. London: Verso, 1999. 26–67. Print.

—. *Postmodernism, or, The Cultural Logic of Late Capitalism*. Durham: Duke UP, 1991. Print.

—. *The Cultural Turn: Selected Writings on the Postmodern, 1983–1998*. London: Verso, 1998. Print.

—. "The End of Temporality." *Critical Inquiry* 29.4 (2003): 695–718. Print.

—. *The Seeds of Time*. New York: Columbia UP, 1994. Print.

Juris, Jeffrey S. *Networking Futures: The Movements Against Corporate Globalization*. Durham: Duke UP, 2008. Print.

Kamen, Henry. *Empire: How Spain Became a World Power, 1492–1763*. New York: HarperCollins, 2003. Print.

Kant, Immanuel. *Political Writings*. Ed. Hans Reiss. Trans. H. B. Nisbet. Cambridge: Cambridge UP, 1991. Print.

Kaplan, Temma. *Red City, Blue Period: Social Movements in Picasso's Barcelona*. Berkeley: U of California P, 1992. Print.

King, Russell, and Isabel Rodríguez-Melguizo. "Recent Immigration to Spain: The Case of Moroccans in Catalonia." *Into the Margins: Migration and Exclusion in Southern Europe*. Ed. Floya Anthias and Gabriella Lazaridis. Aldershot, UK: Ashgate, 1999. 55–82. Print.

Knutson, David. *Las novelas de Eduardo Mendoza: La parodia de los márgenes*. Madrid: Pliegos, 1999. Print.

Koolhaas, Rem. "Junkspace." *Harvard Design School Guide to Shopping*. Ed. Chuihua Judy Chung et al. Köln: Taschen, 2001. 408–21. Print.

—. "Miestakes." *Back from Utopia: The Challenge of the Modern Movement*. Ed. Hubert-Jan Henket and Hilde Heynen. Rotterdam: 010, 2002. 238–51. Print.

—. *Small, Medium, Large, Extra-Large: Office for Metropolitan Architecture, Rem Koolhaas, and Bruce Mau*. Ed. Jennifer Sigler. Photography Hans Werlemann. New York: Monacelli, 1995. Print.

Koolhaas, Rem, et al. *Mutations*. Barcelona: Actar, 2001. Print.

Krüger, Arnd, and William J. Murray, eds. *The Nazi Olympics: Sport, Politics and Appeasement in the 1930s*. Urbana: U of Illinois P, 2003. Print.

Labanyi, Jo, ed. *Constructing Identity in Twentieth-Century Spain: Theoretical Debates and Cultural Practice.* Oxford: Oxford UP, 2002. Print.

Lacoue-Labarthe, Philippe, and Jean-Luc Nancy. "The Nazi Myth." Trans. Brian Holmes. *Critical Inquiry* 16.2 (1990): 291–312. Print.

Lahuerta, Juan José. *Antoni Gaudí 1852–1926: Architecture, Ideology and Politics.* Milan: Electa-architectura, 2003. Print.

Landry, Charles. *The Art of City-Making.* London: Earthscan, 2006. Print.

Larice, Michael, and Elizabeth Macdonald, eds. *The Urban Design Reader.* New York: Routledge, 2007. Print.

La cerimònia d'inauguració dels Jocs Olímpics de Barcelona. Dir. Manuel Huerga. TV3, Barcelona, 25 Jul. 1992. Television.

La cerimònia d'inauguració dels Jocs Olímpics de Barcelona: Llibre de premsa. Barcelona: COOB'92, 1992. Print.

La cerimònia de clausura dels Jocs Olímpics de Barcelona: Llibre de premsa. Barcelona: COOB'92, 1992. Print.

Le Corbusier. *The City of Tomorrow and Its Planning.* New York: Dover, 1987. Print.

Le Galès, Patrick. *European Cities: Social Conflicts and Governance.* Oxford: Oxford UP, 2002. Print.

LeGates, Richard T., and Frederic Stout, eds. *The City Reader.* New York: Routledge, 2000. Print.

Lenin, Vladimir Ilyich. "Imperialism, the Highest Stage of Capitalism." *Essential Works of Lenin.* Ed. and introd. Henry M. Christman. New York: Dover, 1987. 177–270. Print.

Llanas, Manuel. "Notes sobre la recepció de Paul Valéry en les lletres catalanes." *Professor Joaquim Molas: Memòria, escriptura, història.* Barcelona: Publicacions de la Universitat de Barcelona, 2003. 589–99. Print.

Lloyd Wright, Frank. "Broadacre City: A New Community Plan." *The City Reader.* Ed. Richard T. LeGates and Frederic Stout. New York: Routledge, 2000. 344–9. Print.

López, Pere. "1992, objectiu de tots? Ciutat-empresa i dualitat social a la Barcelona olímpica." *Revista Catalana de Geografia* 15.6 (1991): 91–9. Print.

Lynch, Kevin. *A Theory of Good City Form.* Cambridge: MIT, 1981. Print.

McDonough, Gary. "Discourses of the City: Policy and Response in Post-Transitional Barcelona." *Theorizing the City: The New Urban Anthropology Reader.* Ed. Setha M. Low. New Brunswick: Rutgers UP, 1999. 342–76. Print.

Mackenzie, Michael. "From Athens to Berlin: the 1936 Olympics and Leni Riefenstahl's *Olympia.*" *Critical Inquiry* 29.2 (2003): 302–35. Print.

McMorrough, John. "Good Intentions." *Harvard Design School Guide to Shopping.* Ed. Chuihua Judy Chung et al. Köln: Taschen, 2001. 370–9. Print.

McNeill, Donald. *Urban Change and the European Left: Tales from the New Barcelona.* London: Routledge, 1999. Print.

—. "Writing the New Barcelona." *The Entrepreneurial City: Geographies of Politics, Regime and Representation.* Ed. Tim Hall and Phil Hubbard. Chichester: Wiley, 1998. 241–52. Print.

Mandel, Ernst. *Late Capitalism.* Trans. Joris De Bres. London: Verso, 1978. Print.

Mandell, Richard. *The Nazi Olympics.* New York: Macmillan, 1971. Print.

Manent, Albert. *La literatura catalana a l'exili*. Barcelona: Curial, 1976. Print.

Maragall, Joan. *Obres completes*. Vol. 1. Barcelona: Selecta, 1970. Print.

Maragall, Pasqual. *Per una Barcelona olímpica i metropolitana*. Barcelona: Ajuntament de Barcelona, 1982. Print.

—. *Refent Barcelona*. Barcelona: Planeta, 1986. Print.

Maragall, Pasqual, and Josep Maria Espinàs. *El tema és Barcelona: Converses*. Barcelona: La Campana, 1995. Print.

Maragall, Pasqual, and Jaume Guillamet. *Barcelona, la ciutat retrobada*. Barcelona: Edicions 62, 1991. Print.

Marazzi, Christian. *Capital and Language: From the New Economy to the War Economy*. Trans. Gregory Conti. Introd. Michael Hardt. Los Angeles: Semiotext(e), 2008. Print.

Marcuse, Peter. "Depoliticizing Globalization: From Neo-Marxism to the Network Society of Manuel Castells." *Understanding the City: Contemporary and Future Perspectives*. Ed. John Eade and Christopher Mele. Malden, MA: Blackwell, 2002. 131–58. Print.

Marfany, Josep Lluís. *La cultura del catalanisme: El nacionalisme català en els seus inicis*. Barcelona: Empúries, 1995. Print.

Marín, Martí. *Porcioles: Catalanisme, clientelisme i franquisme*. Barcelona: Base, 2005. Print.

Marrero Guillamón, Isaac. "La fábrica del conflicto. Terciarización, lucha social y patrimonio en Can Ricart, Barcelona." Diss. Universitat de Barcelona, 2008. 29 August 2010 <http://www.tesisenxarxa.net/TDX-0430109-110459/>.

Marsé, Juan. *El amante bilingüe*. Barcelona: Planeta, 2000. Print.

—. *Si te dicen que caí*. Barcelona: Seix Barral, 1993. Print.

—. *Últimas tardes con Teresa*. Barcelona: Seix Barral, 2005. Print.

Marshall, Tim, ed. *Transforming Barcelona: The Renewal of a European Metropolis*. London: Routledge, 2004. Print.

Martí-Olivella, Jaume, and Eugenia Afinoguenova, eds. *Spain is (Still) Different: Tourism and Discourse in Spanish Identity*. Lexington: Rowman and Littlefield, 2008. Print.

Martín, Esteban, and Andreu Carranza. *La clave Gaudí*. Barcelona: Plaza & Janés, 2007. Print.

Martínez Veiga, Ubaldo. "Immigrants in the Spanish Labour Market." *Immigrants and the Informal Economy in Southern Europe*. Ed. Martin Baldwin-Edwards and Joaquin Arango. London: Frank Cass, 1999. 105–28. Print.

Marx, Karl. *Capital: A Critique of Political Economy*. Trans. Ben Fowkes. London: Penguin, 1976. Print.

—. *Grundrisse*. Trans. and fwd. Martin Nicolaus. New York: Penguin, 1993. Print.

Marx, Karl, and Frederick Engels. *The Communist Manifesto*. Ed. Frederic L. Bender. New York: Norton, 1988. Print.

Maspero, François. *Roissy Express: A Journey Through the Paris Suburbs*. London: Verso, 1994. Print.

Mbembe, Achille, and Sarah Nuttall. "Writing the World from an African Metropolis." *Public Culture* 16.3 (2004): 347–72. Print.

Mendoza, Cristóbal. "Foreign Labour Immigration in High-Unemployment Spain: The Role of African-Born Workers in the Girona Labour Market." *Southern Europe and the*

New Immigrations. Ed. Russell King and Richard Black. Brighton: Sussex Academic P, 1997. 51–74. Print.

Mendoza, Eduardo. *La ciudad de los prodigios*. Barcelona: Seix Barral, 1991. Print.

—. *La verdad sobre el caso Savolta*. Barcelona: Seix Barral, 1985. Print.

Moix, Llàtzer. *La ciudad de los arquitectos*. Barcelona: Anagrama, 1994. Print.

Moldoveanu, Mihail, Jaume Capó, and Aleix Casasús. *Barcelona: Open-Air Sculptures*. Barcelona: Polígrafa, 2001. Print.

Molinero, Carme, and Pere Ysàs, eds. *Construint la ciutat democràtica: El moviment veïnal durant el tardofranquisme i la transició*. Barcelona: Icaria, 2010. Print.

Molloy, Bernard, trans. *The City of Marvels*. By Eduardo Mendoza. San Diego: Harcourt Brace Jovanovich, 1988. Print.

Monclús, Francisco-Javier. "The Barcelona Model: an Original Formula? From 'Reconstruction' to Strategic Urban Projects (1979–2004)." *Planning Perspectives* 18.4 (2003): 399–421. Print.

Montaner, Josep Maria. *Repensar Barcelona*. Barcelona: UPC, 2003. Print.

Monzó, Quim. *Catorze ciutats comptant-hi Brooklyn*. Barcelona: Quaderns Crema, 2004. Print.

—. *El perquè de tot plegat*. Barcelona: Quaderns Crema, 1993. Print.

—. *Guadalajara*. Barcelona: Quaderns Crema, 1996. Print.

—. *La magnitud de la tragèdia*. Barcelona: Quaderns Crema, 1989. Print.

—. *L'illa de Maians*. Barcelona: Quaderns Crema, 1985. Print.

Moragas, Miquel de, et al. *Television in the Olympics*. Luton: John Libbey Media, 1995. Print.

Moreiras, Alberto. *The Exhaustion of Difference: The Politics of Latin American Cultural Studies*. Durham: Duke UP, 2001. Print.

Moreiras-Menor, Cristina. *Cultura herida: Literatura y cine en la España democrática*. Madrid: Ediciones Libertarias, 2002. Print.

—. "¿La agonía de Franco? Políticas culturales de la memoria en la democracia." *Intransiciones: Crítica de la cultura española*. Ed. Eduardo Subirats. Madrid: Biblioteca Nueva, 2002. 99–131. Print.

Morén-Alegret, Ricard. "Tuning the Channels: Local Government Policies and Immigrants' Participation in Barcelona." *Multicultural Policies and Modes of Citizenship in European Cities*. Ed. Alisdair Rogers and Jean Tillie. Burlington, VT: Ashgate, 2001. 61–84. Print.

Moriel, Enrique. *La ciudad sin tiempo*. Barcelona: Destino, 2007. Print.

Muniesa, Bernat. *Dictadura y transición: La España lampedusiana*. Barcelona: Publicacions i Edicions, Universitat de Barcelona, 2005. Print.

Muñoz, Francesc M. "Deconstrucció de Barcelona. Projecte urbà i realitat metropolitana, 1980–1995." *Expansió urbana i planejament a Barcelona*. Ed. Joan Roca i Albert. Barcelona: Institut Municipal d'Història de Barcelona and Proa, 1997. 249–68. Print.

—. "La *ciutat multiplicada*: polítiques urbanes i condicions de centralitat a la metròpoli postindustrial." *Revista Catalana de Sociologia* 14 (2001): 77–85. Print.

—. *UrBANALización: Paisajes comunes, lugares globales*. Barcelona: Gustavo Gili, 2008. Print.

Murgades, Josep. "Assaig de revisió del noucentisme." *Els Marges* 7 (1976): 35–53. Print.

—. "Ús ideològic del concepte de 'classicisme' durant el Noucentisme." *Polis i nació*.

Política i literatura (1900–1939). Ed. Rosa Cabré, Montserrat Jufresa and Jordi Malé. Barcelona: Societat Catalana d'Estudis Clàssics, 2003. 9–32. Print.

Nadal, Jordi. "Spain, 1830–1914." *The Emergence of Industrial Societies Part 2*. Ed. Carlo M. Cipolla. Sussex: Harvester, 1976. 532–627. Print.

Negri, Antonio. *The Politics of Subversion: A Manifesto for the Twenty-First Century*. Trans. James Newell. New York: Polity, 1989. Print.

Nolan, James, trans. *Longing: Selected Poems*. By Jaime Gil de Biedma. San Francisco: City Lights, 1993. Print.

O'Connor, Anthony. *The African City*. New York: Africana Publishing, 1983. Print.

Olympia. Dir. Leni Riefenstahl. Aikman Archive, 2004. Film.

Pack, Sasha D. *Tourism and Dictatorship: Europe's Peaceful Invasion of Franco's Spain*. New York: Palgrave Macmillan, 2006. Print.

Pàmies, Sergi. *La gran novel·la sobre Barcelona*. Barcelona: Quaderns Crema, 1997. Print.

Panyella, Vinyet. *Cronologia del noucentisme (Una eina)*. Barcelona: Publicacions de l'Abadia de Montserrat, 1996. Print.

Papadakis, Alexandra, and Andreas Papadakis, eds. *Zaha Hadid: Testing the Boundaries*. London: New Architecture, 2005. Print.

Payne, Stanley G. *Fascism in Spain, 1923–1977*. Madison: U of Wisconsin P, 1999. Print.

—. *The Franco Regime 1936–1975*. Madison: U of Wisconsin P, 1987. Print.

Penninx, Rinus, et al., eds. *Citizenship in European Cities: Immigrants, Local Politics and Integration Policies*. Burlington, VT: Ashgate, 2004. Print.

Peran, Martí, Alícia Suàrez, and Mercè Vidal, eds. *Noucentisme i ciutat*. Barcelona: Centre de Cultura Contemporània de Barcelona, 1994. Print.

Pericay, Xavier, and Ferran Toutain. *El malentès del noucentisme: Tradició i plagi a la prosa catalana moderna*. Barcelona: Proa, 1996. Print.

Petras, James. "Spanish Socialism: The Politics of Neoliberalism." *Mediterranean Paradoxes: Politics and Social Structures in Southern Europe*. Ed. James Kurth and James Petras. Oxford: Berg, 1993. 95–127. Print.

Piñón, Helio. *Nacionalisme i modernitat en l'arquitectura catalana contemporània*. Trans. Joan Costa i Costa. Barcelona: Edicions 62, 1980. Print.

Pla, Josep. *El meu país: Obra completa*. Vol. VII. Barcelona: Destino, 1968. Print.

—. *Escrits empordanesos: Obra completa*. Vol. XXXVIII. Barcelona: Destino, 1980. Print.

—. *Les escales de Llevant: Obra completa*. Vol. XIII. Barcelona: Destino, 1969. Print.

Pla, Xavier. *Josep Pla: Ficció autobiogràfica i veritat literària*. Barcelona: Quaderns Crema, 1997. Print.

Powell, Charles T. *España en democracia, 1975–2000*. Barcelona: Plaza & Janés, 2001. Print.

Prat de la Riba, Enric. *La Nacionalitat Catalana*. Barcelona: Edicions 62, 1986. Print.

Preston, Paul. *Franco: A Biography*. New York: Basic Books, 1994. Print.

—. *The Triumph of Democracy in Spain*. London; New York: Methuen, 1988. Print.

Prego, Victoria. *Así se hizo la transición*. Barcelona: Plaza & Janés, 1995. Print.

Prystupa, John, trans. *Poesies-Poems*. By Joan Maragall. Chapel Hill: U of North Carolina at Chapel Hill, 1983. Print.

Puig, Valentí. *L'os de Cuvier: Cap a on va la cultura catalana*. Barcelona: Destino, 2004. Print.

Pujadas, Xavier, and Carles Santacana. *L'altra Olimpíada, Barcelona '36: Esport, societat i política a Catalunya*. Barcelona: Llibres de l'Index, 1990. Print.

Pujadó, Miquel. *Diccionari de la cançó: Dels Setze Jutges al rock català*. Barcelona: Enciclopèdia Catalana, 2000. Print.

Pujol, Jordi. *Antologia política de Jordi Pujol*. Ed. Albert Alay. Barcelona: Pòrtic and Enciclopèdia Catalana, 2003. Print.

—. *Entre l'acció i l'esperança/1: Des dels turons a l'altra banda del riu*. Barcelona: Pòrtic, 1978. Print.

—. *Entre l'acció i l'esperança/2: Construir Catalunya*. Barcelona: Pòrtic, 1979. Print.

—. *La immigració, problema i esperança de Catalunya*. Barcelona: Nova Terra, 1976. Print.

Rancière, Jacques. *Disagreement: Philosophy and Politics*. Trans. Julie Rose. Chicago: U of Chicago P, 1999. Print.

Rasch, William. *Sovereignty and its Discontents: On the Primacy of Conflict and the Structure of the Political*. London: Birkbeck Law P, 2004. Print.

Recio, Albert, and Jordi Roca. "The Spanish Socialists in Power: Thirteen Years of Economic Policy." *Oxford Review of Economic Policy* 14.1 (1998): 139–58. Print.

Resina, Joan Ramon. *Barcelona's Vocation of Modernity: Rise and Decline of an Urban Image*. Stanford: Stanford UP, 2008. Print.

—. "Money, Desire, and History in Eduardo Mendoza's *City of Marvels*." PMLA 109.5 (1994): 951–68. Print.

—, ed. *Disremembering the Dictatorship: The Politics of Memory in the Spanish Transition to Democracy*. Amsterdam: Rodopi, 2000. 17–28. Print.

—, ed. *Iberian Cities*. New York: Routledge, 2001. Print.

Rius Sant, Xavier. *El libro de la inmigración en España*. Córdoba: Almuzara, 2007. Print.

Roca i Albert, Joan. "Recomposició capitalista i periferització social." *El futur de les perifèries urbanes*. Barcelona: Institut de Batxillerat "Barri Besòs" and Generalitat de Catalunya, 1994. 509–788. Print.

—, ed. *Expansió urbana i planejament a Barcelona*. Barcelona: Institut Municipal d'Història de Barcelona and Proa, 1997. Print.

—, ed. *La formació del cinturó industrial de Barcelona*. Barcelona: Institut Municipal d'Història de Barcelona and Proa, 1997. Print.

Roche, Maurice. *Mega-Events and Modernity: Olympics and Expos in the Growth of Global Culture*. London: Routledge, 2000. Print.

Rogers, Alisdair, and Jean Tillie, eds. *Multicultural Policies and Modes of Citizenship in European Cities*. Burlington, VT: Ashgate, 2001. Print.

Rossi, Aldo. *L'Architettura della città*. Macerata: Quodlibet, 2011. Print. [English trans.: *The Architecture of the City*. Trans. Diane Ghirardo and Joan Ockman. Cambridge: MIT, 1982. Print.]

Rubert de Ventós, Xavier. *Arribada de la torxa olímpica a Empúries, 13 de juny de 1992*. Unpublished script. Print.

—. *Catalunya: De la identitat a la independència*. Barcelona: Empúries, 1999. Print.

Ruiz Zafón, Carlos. *El juego del ángel*. Barcelona: Planeta, 2008. Print.

—. *La sombra del viento*. Barcelona: Planeta, 2001. Print.

Samsó, J. *La cultura catalana: Entre la clandestinitat i la represa pública (1939-1951)*. Barcelona: Publicacions de l'Abadia de Montserrat, 1994. Print.

Sánchez, Antonio. *Postmodern Spain: A Cultural Analysis of 1980s-1990s Spanish Culture*. Oxford: Peter Lang, 2007. Print.

Sassen, Saskia. *The Global City: New York, London, Tokyo*. Princeton: Princeton UP, 1991. Print.

—. *Globalization and its Discontents: Essays on the New Mobility of People and Money*. New York: New Press, 1998. Print.

Saval, José V. *La ciudad de los prodigios, de Eduardo Mendoza*. Madrid: Síntesis, 2003. Print.

Schmitt, Carl. *The Concept of the Political*. Trans. and introd. George Schwab. Chicago: U of Chicago P, 1996. Print.

Scott, Allen J., and Edward W. Soja. *The City: Los Angeles and Urban Theory at the End of the Twentieth Century*. Berkeley: U of California P, 1996. Print.

Shakespeare, William. *Coriolanus*. Ed. Lee Bliss. Cambridge: Cambridge UP, 2000. Print.

—. *Hamlet, Prince of Denmark*. Ed. Philip Edwards. Cambridge: Cambridge UP, 2003. Print.

Shelton, Barrie. *Learning from the Japanese City: West Meets East in Urban Design*. London: E & FN Spon, 1999. Print.

Sieverts, Thomas. *Cities Without Cities: An Interpretation of the* Zwischenstadt. London: Spon, 2003. Print.

Simone, AbdouMaliq. *For the City Yet to Come: Changing African Life in Four Cities*. Durham: Duke UP, 2004. Print.

Simonis, Damien. *Lonely Planet Barcelona*. London: Lonely Planet, 2006. Print.

Simson, Vyv, and Andrew Jennings. *The Lords of the Rings: Power, Money and Drugs in the Modern Olympics*. London: Simon & Schuster, 1992. Print.

Smith, Angel, ed. *Red Barcelona: Social Protest and Labour Mobilization in the Twentieth Century*. London: Routledge, 2002. Print.

Soja, Edward W. *Postmodern Geographies: The Reassertion of Space in Critical Social Theory*. London: Verso, 1989. Print.

—. "Six Discourses on the Postmetropolis." *The Blackwell City Reader*. Ed. Gary Bridge and Sophie Watson. Malden, MA: Blackwell, 2002. 188-96. Print.

Soldevila, Ferran. *Història de Catalunya*. Barcelona: Alpha, 1962. Print.

—. *Jaume I, Pere el Gran: Els grans reis del segle XIII*. Barcelona: Teide, 1955. Print.

Solé i Sabaté, Josep M. *Consell de guerra i condemna a mort de Lluís Companys*. Barcelona: Generalitat de Catalunya, 1999. Print.

Solé Tura, Jordi. *Catalanisme i revolució burgesa: La síntesi de Prat de la Riba*. Barcelona: Edicions 62, 1967. Print.

Steele, James. *Architecture Today*. London: Phaidon, 1997. Print.

Subirós, Pep. "Barcelona. Cultural Strategies and Urban Renewal, 1979-1997." *Composing Urban History and the Constitution of Civic Identities*. Ed. John J. Czaplicka and Blair A. Ruble. Baltimore: Johns Hopkins UP, 2003. 291-320. Print.

—. *El vol de la fletxa: Barcelona 92: Crònica de la reinvenció de la ciutat.* Barcelona: CCCB/Electra, 1993. Print.

Sweet, Dennis. *Heraclitus: Translation and Analysis.* Lanham, MD: UP of America, 1995. Print.

Termes, Josep. *Les arrels populars del catalanisme.* Barcelona: Empúries, 1999. Print.

Termes, Josep, and Agustí Colomines i Companys. *Patriotes i resistents: Història del primer catalanisme.* Barcelona: Base, 2003. Print.

The AA KeyGuide to Barcelona. Besingstoke, Australia: AA Publishing, 2006. Print.

Time Out. London: Time Out, 2006. Print.

Tour-ismes: La derrota de la dissensió: Itineraris crítics. Barcelona: Fundació Antoni Tàpies, 2004. Print.

Triadú, Joan. *La novel·la catalana de postguerra.* Barcelona: Edicions 62, 1982. Print.

Tusell, Javier, ed. *La transición a la democracia y el reinado de Juan Carlos I.* Madrid: Espasa Calpe, 2003. Print.

Ucelay-Da Cal, Enric. *El imperialismo catalán: Prat de la Riba, Cambó, D'Ors y la conquista moral de España.* Barcelona: Edhasa, 2003. Print.

Unió Temporal d'Escribes. *Barcelona, marca registrada: Un model per desarmar.* Barcelona: Virus, 2004. Print.

Urban Task Force. *Towards an Urban Renaissance.* London: Taylor & Francis, 1999. Print.

Varela Ortega, José, et al. *El poder de la influencia: Geografía del caciquismo en España, 1875–1923.* Madrid: Centro de Estudios Políticos y Constitucionales, 2001. Print.

Vázquez Montalbán, Manuel. *Barcelonas.* Trans. Andy Robinson. London: Verso, 1992. Print.

—. *El laberinto griego.* Barcelona: Planeta, 1991. Print.

—. *El pianista.* Barcelona: Grijalbo Mondadori, 1996. Print.

—. *Sabotaje olímpico.* Barcelona: Planeta, 1993. Print.

Vázquez Montalbán, Manuel, and Eduard Moreno. *Barcelona, cap a on vas? Diàlegs per a una altra Barcelona.* Barcelona: Llibres de l'Index, 1992. Print.

Venturi, Robert, Denise Scott Brown, and Steven Izenour. *Learning from Las Vegas: The Forgotten Symbolism of Architectural Form.* Cambridge: MIT, 1977. Print.

Verdaguer, Jacint. *Obres completes.* Barcelona: Selecta, 1974. Print.

Vicens i Vives, Jaume. *Notícia de Catalunya.* Barcelona: Destino, 1962. Print.

Vicky Cristina Barcelona. Dir. Woody Allen. Mediapro, 2008. Film.

Vila, Enric. *Lluís Companys: La veritat no necessita màrtirs: Crònica d'un drama personal i polític.* Barcelona: L'esfera dels llibres, 2006. Print.

Vilar, Pierre. *La Catalogne dans l'Espagne moderne: Recherches sur les fondements économiques des structures nationales.* Vol. I, II and III. Paris: Sevpen, 1962. Print.

Vilaregut, Ricard. *Terra Lliure: La temptació armada a Catalunya.* Barcelona: Columna, 2004. Print.

Vilarós, Teresa M. *El mono del desencanto: Una crítica cultural de la transición española (1973–1993).* Madrid: Siglo Veintiuno, 1998. Print.

—. "The Lightness of Terror: Palomares, 1966." *Journal of Spanish Cultural Studies* 5.2 (2004): 165–86. Print.

—. "The Passing of the *Xarnego*-Immigrant: Post-Nationalism and the Ideologies of Assimilation in Catalonia." *Arizona Journal of Hispanic Cultural Studies* 7 (2003): 229–46. Print.

Vincent, Mary. *Spain 1833–2002: People and State*. Oxford: Oxford UP, 2007. Print.

Wall, Alex. *Victor Gruen: From Urban Shop to the New City*. Barcelona: Actar, 2005. Print.

Wallerstein, Immanuel. "The Relevance of the Concept of Semiperiphery to Southern Europe." *Semiperipheral Development: The Politics of Southern Europe in the Twentieth Century*. Ed. Giovanni Arrighi. Beverly Hills: Sage, 1985. 31–9. Print.

Wells, Caragh. "Re-presenting the City in Quim Monzó's *L'illa de Maians*." *Bulletin of Hispanic Studies* 81.1 (2004): 81–94. Print.

Woolard, Kathryn A. *Double Talk: Bilingualism and the Politics of Ethnicity in Catalonia*. Stanford: Stanford UP, 1989. Print.

Wright, Patrick. *A Journey Through Ruins: A Keyhole portrait of British Postwar Life and Culture*. London: Flamingo, 1993. Print.

Yates, Alan. *Una generació sense novel·la? La novel·la catalana entre 1900 i 1925*. Barcelona: Edicions 62, 1984. Print.

Index

MARX — Hegel — "History" (3)
Althusser